PEASANT WARS
of the
TWENTIETH
CENTURY

PEASANT WARS
of the
TWENTIETH
CENTURY

ERIC R. WOLF

FABER AND FABER
3 Queen Square
London

First published in England in 1971
by Faber and Faber Limited
3 Queen Square London WC1
Printed in Great Britain by
John Dickens & Co Ltd Northampton
All rights reserved

ISBN 0 571 09611 5

Excerpts quoted from "Reminiscences of the Cuban Revolutionary War" by Che Guevara are reprinted with the permission of Monthly Review Press, New York & London, 1968.

Excerpts taken from "Enquete sur Leniveau de vie des Populations Rurales" by Andre Nouschi were translated and are included by permission of Presses Universitaires de France, Paris, 1961.

Maps by Willow Roberts

CONTENTS

ACKNOWLEDGMENTS

In the preparation of this manuscript the author has incurred both intellectual and personal debts. Over the last three years he has presented parts of the argument to many different groups; an outstanding role in this continuing exchange of views has been played by a discussion group that has met regularly over the years at the University of Michigan which includes among its core members Frithjof Bergmann, David Gutmann, John Higham, Ingo Seidler, and Frederick Wyatt. Angel Palerm, Roy Rappaport, Jane Schneider, and Peter Schneider read the entire manuscript and provided excellent detailed criticism. Marshall Sahlins and James Meisel read the manuscript and made general comments. A number of friends and colleagues gave me much needed advice on particular chapters: Friedrich Katz and Frederick Wyatt on Mexico; Arthur Mendel on Russia; Norma Diamond, Albert Feuerwerker, and Frederick Wyatt on China; Aram Yengoyan on Viet Nam; Jeanne Favret, Richard Mitchell, and William Schorger on Algeria; Friedrich Katz and Julie Nichamin on Cuba. Friedrich Katz also read the conclusions. They all saved me from egregious errors, but contributed even more to my thinking through disagreement with particular formulations and explanations. Their help is acknowledged with gratitude; their sustained efforts on my behalf clear them of any guilt through association with particular statements and arguments which the author has stubbornly refused to delete. I am also grateful to Michael Maccoby for a particularly valuable reference on Mexico.

Finally, the author would like to give thanks to the U.S. Public Health Service, which has supported his work on "Social Strategies of Peasant Groups" with a Research Scientist Development Award (5 Ko2 MH25434-05) from the National Institutes of Health.

PREFACE TO THE ENGLISH EDITION

It was not very long ago that the exchanges of gunfire between colonizers and natives were heard only at a vast distance from the centers of the industrializing world, but for some time now the sound of shots has been drawing closer. Frontier and center are rapidly becoming one, and battles once fought in distant lands are now fought increasingly in our own streets and in our own consciousness. And as our awareness of the world undergoes a massive change, so we also experience a change in the character of our running dialogue with that world. This is true of economics and political science, of sociology and history; it is also true of anthropology. Once conceived as the study of the Primitive, of that radically Other beyond the pale of civilization, this comparative science of savages and barbarians is now experiencing a major change in its subject matter: the far and distant populations "out there" have become participants in a drama set upon our own stage. They are no longer exotic, and hence capable of being admired or despised at a safe distance; they wear our own robes, address us in our own idiom, affect in tangible and immediate ways the outcome of a play we so willingly began with a sense of our own enduring superiority. As the object of study changes, therefore, anthropology must also change.

How is this change to come about? The Study of Man has long lost the pristine unity it once enjoyed when political economy still held sway; it is now fragmented into the separate study of men as economic beings and as political actors. Sociologists and anthropologists between them divide in increasingly arbitrary ways the study of men as members of social groups and categories. What we need, perhaps, is a return, after this experience of separation and specialization, to the realization of a common human endeavor, and to accomplish this, I believe, we need above all a return to history. "Anthropology," Maitland once wrote, "will be history or it will be nothing." He meant, of course, a different history and a different anthropology, for each epoch will rewrite history as the result of its different experience. Yet the dictum stands; we do need a new kind of history as an account of our growing existential involvement with one another. There is need for a history which will draw upon the several specialized disciplines, and yet transcend them, a history capable of telling us how the modern world was made in the systematic interaction of Bush and Sown, of city dweller and peasant, of metropolis and satellite, of colonizer and colonized.

What can anthropology contribute to such a new and more unified accounting of ourselves? It does offer, first of all, a history of populations long thought to be people without a past, but whose past is now very much a part of our present. It offers, secondly, a holistic perspective which strives to study a people's way of life in its many-stranded interconnectedness, without falling prey to the tendency to apportion human reality among several sets of rival specialists. It possesses, thirdly, a lively sense of the importance of life as lived in small groups and ordered in narrow social networks, and a recognition that life in such social microcosms persists in a powerful dialectic with the engulfing social macrocosm. In this recognition it not only draws attention to the many-layered character of complex society, but also emphasizes its sense that these layers and segments affect each other in a continuous process of the "interpenetration of opposites." This sense is certainly strong when we focus our attention on the peasantries of the world, each with its very specific social gravity, and yet each engaged in complex and often antagonistic relationships with other social actors, with other contending groups.

This book is dedicated to a better understanding of these relationships, through the examination of six cases of peasant involvement in the revolutions of our time. It hopes to specify, in each case, cause and effect of such involvement. The cases utilized all deal with revolutions which, from one point of view or another, present a "successful" outcome; yet our focus is not upon the strategy and tactics of successful revolution as such. The outlines of the stories presented here will be familiar to many more expert than the author in analysis and understanding of the larger social processes described. If this book has any merit, however, it should be sought in its focus upon the microscopic processes in peasant life which contributed, cumulatively and ultimately, to macroscopic upheaval. We do have accounts of the view from the windows of the palace; we hope to explore that same view from the edge of the peasant village.

PREFACE

With the embers of destruction barely cooling after the conclusion of World War II, the United States became involved in Viet Nam—through a series of commissions and omissions—in what may well become one of the economically and morally costliest wars in history. First through military aid to the embattled French, then through its military missions, and finally—since 1962—by the ever expanding commitment of its own troops, the United States sought military and political victory in a war fought for control over the hearts and minds of a peasant people. During these years, "the raggedy little bastards in black pajamas"—as United States military officers referred to their new enemies—have not only fought to a standstill the mightiest military machine in history, but caused many an American to wonder, silently or aloud, why "our" Vietnamese do not fight like "their" Vietnamese, why ever new recruits replenish the ranks of an army destroyed many times over in our dispatches and news communiqués. Specially insulated from other continents and their tribulations by virtue of her geographic position and by her extraordinary prosperity, America finds herself ill prepared in the twentieth century to understand the upheavals which are now shaking the poor nations of the world. Yet ignorance courts disaster. Viet Nam has become a graveyard because Americans did not know enough or care enough about a little-known part of Southeast Asia. The roads to the Mekong delta, to Tay Ninh, to Khe San are strewn with the wreckage of false premises, perceptions, and evaluations. Therefore it is important to America that she bend all her available knowledge—and her considerable power of passion and compassion—to the task of comprehending the world in which she has become such a stranger. Four years ago, on March 17 and 18, some of us at the University of Michigan initiated the "teach-in" movement on the Viet Nam war; from here the great debate spread to more than a hundred campuses and into the national capitol at Washington. But that was only a beginning, and a small beginning at that. Viet Nam constitutes the overriding issue of the moment, but there have already been other "Viet Nams" in Cuba, Guatemala, and the Dominican Republic, and there will be other "Viet Nams" in the future, unless America reverses her present course. If we must know more in order to live in a changed world, if we must know more so we can act with clear reason rather than with prejudice, with humanity rather than with inhumanity, with wisdom rather than with folly, all of us must undertake the task of understanding in order to learn and of learning in order to understand. This is no longer an undertaking only for the academic specialist, if indeed it has ever been; it is an obligation of citizenship. This book is the outcome of this conviction. I have been, by profession, an anthropologist interested in peasant studies, and in this book I have attempted to review—as an anthropologist—the evidence of six cases of rebellion and revolution in our time in which peasants have been the principal actors.

Why should an anthropologist undertake to write on this subject? What can he contribute, as an anthropologist, to an understanding of a topic already familiar to economists, sociologists, and political scientists? Obviously they have skills which they bring to bear on the topic which an anthropologist cannot duplicate. There is, for example, the intriguing question of how inflation and deflation affect social cohesion in the village, a question to which economists could appropriately address themselves. There are serious questions to be asked about the psychology of deprivation or authority which are better answered by social psychologists or sociologists. Similarly, the political scientist is better fitted than the anthropologist to analyze the interplay of power groups on the level of the nation or in the relationships between nations. Yet the anthropologist reading the accounts of his peers misses dimensions which he has been taught to consider decisive. It is to an understanding of these dimensions that he may properly address himself.

He will interest himself, for example, in trying to spell out, as precisely as possible, just what kinds of peasants we refer to when we speak of peasant involvement in political upheaval. To the layman and even to many specialists the distinctions between different kinds of peasants are unimportant; they are content to speak of an all-encompassing "peasantry" without further qualification. But the anthropologist, with field experience in small-scale communities, knows that there are differences in behavior and outlook between tenants and proprietors, between poor and rich peasants, between cultivators who are also craftsmen and those who only plow and harvest, between men who are responsible for all agricultural operations on a holding they rent or own and wage laborers who do their work under supervision of others in return for money. He also knows that one must distinguish between peasants who live close to towns and are involved in town markets and urban affairs and those living in more remote villages; between peasants who are beginning to send their sons and daughters to the factories and those who continue to labor within the boundaries of their parochial little worlds. Distinctions of property and involvement in property, in relation to markets, in relation to systems of communication, all seem important to him when he observes real populations "on the ground." Therefore he will look for such distinctions and differential involvements in accounts of peasant involvement in revolution, because he suspects that such differentials have an important bearing on the genesis and course of a revolutionary movement.

Secondly, he brings to the problem a concern with microsociology, born of an understanding gained in the field that the transcendental ideological issues appear only in very prosaic guise in the villages. For example, peasants may join in a national movement in order to settle scores which are age-old in their village or region. Here too he will be aware of the importance of regional differences between peasants. He will stress the concatenation of particular circumstances in particular regions in shaping peasant dissatisfaction or satisfaction, in the knowledge that mobilization of the peasant "vanguard" is less an outcome of nationwide circumstances than of particular local features. In this respect, then, as in trying to break down the category "peasant" into finer categories, he seeks to approach the problem of peasant involvement with a more finely grained understanding of the variety of peasantry in their variable local and regional ecologies.

Thirdly—and this is perhaps one of the main burdens of the accounts to be presented here—the anthropologist is greatly aware of the importance of groups which mediate between the peasant and the larger society of which he forms a part. The landlord, the merchant, the political boss, the priest stand at the junctures in social, economic, and political relations which connect the village to wider-ranging elites in markets or political networks. In his study of peasant villages he has learned to recognize their crucial role in peasant life, and he is persuaded that they must play a significant role in peasant involvement in political upheaval. To describe such groups, and to locate them in the social field in which they must maneuver, it is useful to speak of them as "classes." Classes are for me quite real clusters of people whose development or decline is predicated on particular historical circumstances, and who act together or against each other in pursuit of particular interests prompted by these circumstances. In this perspective, we may ask—in quite concrete terms—how members of such classes make contact with the peasantry. In our accounts, therefore, we must transcend the usual anthropological account of peasants, and seek information also about the larger society and its constituent class groupings, for the peasant acts in an arena which also contains allies as well as enemies. This arena is characteristically a field of political battle. As an anthropologist the writer is perhaps less schooled in problems of political organization and competition than his reader might have reason to expect of him. This is due primarily to the fact that his master discipline, anthropology, has in the past paid only marginal attention to the realities of power. The writing of this book has thus itself proved to be a major learning experience. The writer hopes that, in focusing on peasant involvement in politics, he may contribute also to broadening the framework of peasant studies as these have been carried on in the past.

Who is it, then, that speaks to the peasant and what is it that they communicate which moves the peasant to violent political action? Peasants often harbor a deep sense of injustice, but this sense of injustice must be given shape and expression in organization before it can become active on the political scene; and it is obvious that not every callow agitator will find a welcome hearing in village circles traditionally suspicious of outsiders, especially when they come from the city. What circumstances and what sets of people will prove propitious to the establishment of such communication? The social scientist used to viewing the peasantry from the vantage of the national level may often be tempted to forget that social or economic or political mobilization of a peasantry involves contact with many small groups not always eager to receive guidance and leadership from the outside. How this resistance is overcome, if indeed it *is* overcome, is not always a foregone conclusion.

Finally, the anthropologist will have to ask how much the action of a peasantry in rebellion and revolution is prompted by traditional patterns and to what extent a peasant revolution produces not only an overturning of political power holders but an overturning in the patterns of the peasantry itself. Here the anthropologist may well have to guard against a professional bias. Studies of primitives and peasant populations have tended to give him an unusual respect for the strength of tradition. Yet the persistence of tradition needs explanation as much as change. It may be that people cleave to ancestral ways through general inertia, but it is more likely that there are good and sufficient reasons behind such persistence, much as there are good and sufficient reasons for change. Of these reasons people may or may not be conscious; but then it is the task of the anthropologist to inquire into what the causes for persistence or change may be.

In seeking a more sophisticated understanding of the political involvement of peasant groups it is perhaps not amiss to indicate quite specifically how the term *peasant* is utilized in this book. Definitions are of course no absolutes, but merely aids in analysis. It is my conviction that this purpose is best served by drawing the boundaries of definition quite narrowly, rather than broadly. It has become customary to distinguish peasants from primitives by opposing rural populations which are subject to the dictates of a superordinate state from rural dwellers who live outside the confines of such a political structure. The first are peasants, the second are not. But the category of rural people who are subject to control by a state can include not only cultivators, but also artisans, fishermen, or itinerant merchants who supply rural markets. The category may further cover people who own and operate their farms, tenants and sharecroppers, and landless laborers. It is important, it seems to me, not to presuppose that all these people are alike in their economic, social, and political relationships or in their outlook upon the world in which they live. Important differences, for example, may distinguish cultivator from fisherman, or landless worker from landed proprietor. I therefore define peasants as populations that are existentially involved in cultivation and make autonomous decisions regarding the processes of cultivation. The category is thus made to cover tenants and sharecroppers as well as owner-operators, as long as they are in a position to make the relevant decisions on how their crops are grown. It does not, however, include fishermen or landless laborers.

If we distinguish peasants from primitives, we must also differentiate them from "farmers." The major aim of the peasant is subsistence and social status gained within a narrow range of social relationships. Peasants are thus unlike cultivators, who participate fully in the market and who commit themselves to a status game set within a wide social network. To ensure continuity upon the land and sustenance for his household, the peasant most often keeps the market at arm's length, for unlimited involvement in the market threatens his hold on his source of livelihood. He thus cleaves to traditional arrangements which guarantee his access to land and to the labor of kin and neighbors. Moreover, he favors production for sale only within the context of an assured production for subsistence. Put in another way, it may be said that the peasant operates in a restricted factor and product market. The factors of production—land, labor, equipment—are rendered relatively immobile by prior liens and expectations; products are sold in the market to produce the extra margin of returns with which to buy goods one does not produce on the homestead. In contrast, the farmer enters the market fully, subjects his land and labor to open competition, explores alternative uses for the factors of production in the search for maximal returns, and favors the more profitable product over the one entailing the smaller risk. The change-over from peasant to farmer, however, is not merely a change in psychological orientation; it involves a major shift in the institutional context within which men make their choices. Perhaps it is precisely when the peasant can no longer rely on his accustomed institutional context to reduce his risks, but when alternative institutions are either too chaotic or too restrictive to guarantee a viable commitment to new ways, that the psychological, economic, social, and political tensions all mount toward peasant rebellion and involvement in revolution.

The case studies presented here are built up on the basis of secondary materials. In only the rarest of cases were the events recorded observed by an investigator with the anthropological eye, with an interest in the questions we have just outlined. This means that the anthropologist is necessarily handicapped by the nature of material he himself has done nothing to collect. The facts which are relevant for him must be winnowed from accounts written for other audiences, with other purposes in mind. Their presentation and analysis is thus an exercise in imagination in which we arrange the material so that it can speak to us for our purposes, and so we may find the occasional telltale fact that allows us the privilege of an anthropological diagnosis. This task is of necessity incomplete: there will be accounts we have not read and telltale facts we have not recorded. Certainly, our effort will be superseded the moment it achieves formulation in book form. This is how it should be. If we can raise questions in terms of new perspectives, we will have accomplished our task.

Our minimum expectation, then, is to present an integral account of peasant involvement in six cases of rebellion and revolution; but our maximal hope is that we will be able both to point to recurrent features and to account for the strategic differences which distinguish each case from its forerunner.

ONE

MEXICO

Compañeros del arado
y de toda herramienta
nomás nos queda un camino
¡ agarrar un treinta-treinta!

Brothers all, of plow
and working implements
there's only one way now:
the rifle in our hands!

"Song of the 30-30 Carbine"

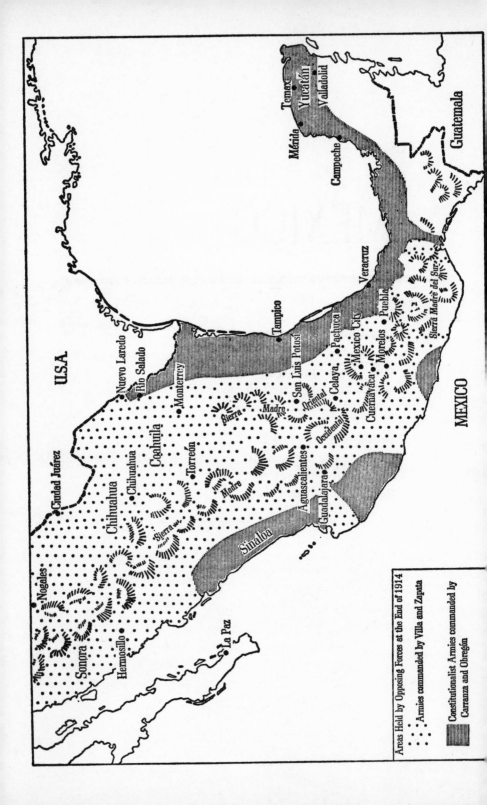

When the Mexican Revolution burst upon the world in 1910, it came as a surprise to most; "very few voices—all of them weak and muffled—had predicted it" (Paz, 1961, 136). For more than a quarter of a century the Mexican dictator Porfirio Díaz had ruled his country with an iron hand in the interests of Liberty, Order, and Progress. Progress had meant rapid industrial and commercial development; liberty was granted to the individual private entrepreneur; and order was enforced through a judicious policy of alternating economic rewards with repression—Díaz's celebrated tactic of *pan y palo* (bread and club). In the course of a few months rebellion was raising its head everywhere, under the stimulus of Francisco Madero's uprising against the aging dictator. In May 1911, Díaz departed for exile in France. The revolution had begun in earnest. "Madero," he said, "has unleashed a tiger, let us see if he can control him."

With the privilege of hindsight we can now see that many of the causes of the revolution had their origins not in the period of the Díaz dictatorship, but in an earlier period, when Mexico was still New Spain and a colony of the Spanish mother country. When Mexico had declared her independence in 1821, she had also inherited a set of characteristic problems, which Spain had been unable and unwilling to solve and which were bequeathed integrally to the new republic.

All these problems derived ultimately from the original encounter of an Indian population with a band of conquerors who had taken possession of Middle America in the name of the Spanish crown. To make use of Indian labor, the Spaniards introduced a system of large estates, *haciendas*.

These large estates or haciendas came to be worked by Indians drawn chiefly from two sources: a supply of resident laborers, tied to the hacienda through debt servitude; and nonresident Indians who continued to live in Indian communities that ringed the haciendas, but who increasingly gained their livelihood on the estates. The aim of the hacienda was commercial, to produce for profit agricultural produce or livestock products which could be sold to neighboring mining compounds and towns; at the same time the haciendas soon became separate social worlds underwriting the social standing and aspirations of their owners. Laborers were often paid in kind, either in tokens which could be traded in at the hacienda store or through the use of plots which they were permitted to farm for their own subsistence. Both means tied the laborers ever more securely to the Big House, from which the hacienda owner ruled his large domain. In 1810, shortly before the Spaniards took their departure, there were some five thousand such large estates, a quarter of which raised livestock. These cattle estates were most characteristic of the arid north where light rainfall and scant vegetation had also inhibited the growth of a sizable Indian population in pre-Spanish times. At any rate, cattle keeping required relatively few hands. The agricultural haciendas, however, were generally located in the central heartland of the country, the area where the Indian population had always been numerous and dense. Yet this meant, too, that the haciendas were forced to share the landscape with communities of Indians. Under Spanish rule, these had received the special protection of the state. They had been granted the legal status of corporations, and each community was allowed to retain a stipulated amount of land under its own communal management, as well as its own autonomous communal administration. In actuality, many communities lost their land to haciendas, and many a local communal authority was overturned by power holders exercising their domain in the vicinity. Yet there were still more than forty-five hundred autonomous landholding Indian communities in 1810 (McBride, 1923, 131), and even a restricted measure of autonomy had permitted them to maintain many traditional cultural patterns. These were highly variable from community to community; there was no uniform Indian culture, just as there existed no one Indian language. Each community retained its own custom and language, and ringed itself about with a wall of distrust and hostility against outsiders. A set of such communities might be subservient to a hacienda down-valley from them, but they also retained a strong sense of their cultural and social separateness from the hacienda population. Thus Mexico emerged into its period of independence with its rural landscape polarized between large estates on the one hand and Indian communities on the other—units, moreover, which might be linked economically, but which remained set off against each other socially and politically. Seen from the perspective of the larger social order, each hacienda constituted a state within a state; each Indian community represented a small "republic of Indians" among other "republics of Indians."

Within the landscape of haciendas and republics of Indians there stood the cities, the seats of the merchants who supplied both haciendas and mines, of officials who regulated privileges and restrictions, of the priests who managed the economy of salvation. From their stores, offices, and churches extended the commercial networks which supplied the mines and drew off their ores; the bureaucratic network which regulated life in the hinterland; and the ecclesiastic network which connected parish priests with the hierarchy at the center. In the shadow of palace and cathedral, moreover, there labored the artisans who supplied the affluent with the amenities and luxuries of a baroque colonial world, the army of servants, and the enormous multitude of the urban poor.

It was a society organized around an armature of special privileges. This was to be one of the gravest problems bequeathed by the colony to the independent republic. In 1837, the liberal José M. L. Mora was to write that one of the greatest sources of difficulties

> resides in the habits formed by the old constitution of the country. Among these figured and still figures as one of the major ones the corporate spirit found among all social classes, and which strongly weakens and destroys the national spirit. Whether by deliberate design or as the unforeseen result of unknown causes which are now at work, in the civil state of old Spain there existed a marked tendency to create corporations, to heap upon them privileges and exemptions from the common law; to enrich them by donations from the living or through testamentary disposition; to grant them

everything, in the end, which could lead to the formation of a body that is perfect in its ideology, complete in its organization, and independent in its privileged legal status and in the means of subsistence which have been assigned to it and placed at its disposition. . . . Not only did the clergy and the militia possess general legal codes, which were subdivided into those of friars and nuns in the first case, and into those of the artillery, engineers and navy in the second; the Inquisition, the University, the Mint, the possessions of the Marqués del Valle, the estates guaranteed through primogeniture, the sodalities, and even the gilds had their privileges and their goods, in one word their separate existence. If independence had come forty years ago, a man born or living in the country would not have esteemed in any way the title of Mexican, and would have considered himself to be alone and isolated in the world, if that was the only one he had . . . to discuss national interests with him would have been to speak in Hebrew; he did not know and could not know others than those of the corporation or the corporations to which he belonged and he would have labored to keep them separate from the remainder of society (1837, Vol. 1, pp. xcvi–xcviii).

In this context, Mora should also have mentioned the Indian communities, legally corporations similar to the other bodies enumerated. Each set of privileges, be they in the hands of high-placed merchants or lowly Indians, granted a monopoly over resources. Like all monopolies, they could be exercised against competitors drawn from the same interest-group or class; but like all monopolies, too, they could be exercised also against claimants "from below," against all those who wished to participate in the social and economic process, but were barred from it by virtue of the various barriers of special privilege. This structure of special privilege was rendered even more complex in New Spain through discriminations, recognized by law, against all portions of the population unable to trace their descent either from Spaniards or from Indians. These, the so-called *castas*, recruited from unions between Indians, Negroes, and Spaniards, soon came to make up a sizable part of the total population and to be responsible for filling many of the economic, political, and religious occupations on which the structure of privilege depended. The overt structure of privilege thus came to be supplemented by a covert social underworld of the disprivileged.

There was little correspondence between law and reality in the utopian order of New Spain. The crown wished to deny the colonist his own supply of labor; the colonist obtained it illegally by attaching peons to his person and his land. Royal prescript supported the trade monopoly over goods flowing in and out of the colony; but along the edges of the law moved smugglers, cattle-rustlers, bandits, the buyers and sellers of clandestine produce. To blind the eyes of the law, there arose a multitude of scribes, lawyers, go-betweens, influence peddlers, and undercover agents. . . . In such a society, even the transactions of everyday life could smack of illegality; yet such illegality was the stuff of which this social order was made. Illicit transactions demanded their agents; the army of the disinherited, deprived of alternative sources of employment, provided these agents. Thus a tide of illegality and disorder seemed ever ready to swallow up the precariously defended islands of legality and privilege (Wolf, 1959, 237).

Yet, at the same time, and paradoxically, society could not do without them. Thus

as society abdicated to them its informal and unacknowledged business, they became brokers and carriers of the multiple transactions that caused the blood to flow through the veins of the social organism. Beneath the formal veneer of Spanish colonial government and economic organization, their fingers wove the network of social relations and communication through which alone men could bridge the gaps between formal institutions (1959, 243).

The colonial society thus incubated a stratum of the socially disinherited who yet filled certain strategic positions within its social system. These positions would serve as leverage when they began to make demands on the social order in which they found themselves; resentment would be the social and psychological fuel behind their demands.

The movement for independence had three related yet often contradictory aspects. It was, in part, an assertion of the periphery against the bureaucratic center. It began in the commercial-industrial-agricultural region of the Bajío northwest of Mexico City and in the provinces to the south of the capital. Socially and militarily it aimed at control over the bureaucratic pivot in Mexico City, and its lifeline to the port of Veracruz which connected it with Spain. It was also, in part, a movement of militarists against the grip of a centralized officialdom, regardless of whether they fought for or against the insurgents. New Spain had relied for internal control and external defense on a combination of Spanish troops with troops recruited in the country. The domestic soldiery, raised largely by merchants and landowners, joined primarily in order to gain the protection of the special juridical privileges accorded to the military and as a means of augmenting social status through military titles and uniforms. The war of independence, however, gave many a part-time soldier his first taste of military power and of the personal benefits to be derived from its exercise, thus laying the basis for the emergence of a stratum of military entrepreneurs which was to plague Mexican society for more than a century.

The movement for independence was also, in the third place, a movement for social reform. This element became evident as leadership of the insurrection was assumed by the village curate José María Morelos y Pavón. On November 17, 1810, he proclaimed an end to the discriminatory system of *castas*: henceforth all Mexicans—whether Indians, *castas*, or American-born Creoles of Spanish parents—were to be known simply as "Americans." There was to be an end to slavery and to special Indian tribute. Land taken from Indian communities was to be restored to them. Property owned by Spaniards and Hispanophile Creoles was to be taken from them:

> All the wealthy, nobles and officials of the first rank are to be treated as enemies, and as soon as a settlement is occupied, their property is to be taken from them and divided in equal parts between the poor citizens and the Military treasury. . . . Neither furniture, nor jewelry and treasure of the churches are to be exempt from this measure. . . . All customs houses, royal guard-houses and buildings, are to be torn down, all archives are to be burned, with the exception of parish records, as well as foreign goods, not exempting luxury objects or tobacco. The offices of rich hacienda owners, mines and sugar mills are to be destroyed, preserving only seed and basic foodstuffs. . . . Haciendas larger than two leagues are to be destroyed in order to promote small-scale

agriculture and property distribution, as the positive benefit of agriculture lies in having many work on their own a small piece of land in which they may apply their labor and industry, than in having one man own large unproductive holdings, keeping thousands of people in slavery so that as day laborers or slaves they can cultivate them under duress when they can do so as owners of a limited amount of land in liberty and for the benefit of society (quoted in Cué, 1947, 44).

The insurrection was thus not only a reaction against control by the metropolis and an unfolding of military power, it was also "an agrarian revolt in gestation" (Paz, 1961, 123).

It was also this third aspect which proved decisive in shaping the course of the revolt. As soon as it became evident that the revolt was also a war of the poor against entrenched privilege, the army, the Church, and the great landowners came to the support of the Spanish crown and crushed the rebellion. Morelos himself was executed in 1815. Yet a few years later Spain herself adopted a liberalizing constitution aimed primarily at disestablishing the Church, and the Creole elite was forced to reverse its course and to rise in support of independence. Mexico became an independent state in 1821, firmly committed to the maintenance of property rights and special privilege for officialdom, Church, landed magnates, and army. The soldiers who cut the tie with Spain thus

established a firmly based military regime which had not existed in the country before 1810 and in addition the interests of the soldiery were linked to those of the ecclesiastical aristocracy and of the viceregal bureaucracy (Cué, 1947, 60).

The movement for independence which had begun with demands for social reform ended in the maintenance of elite power. This was true especially of the large estates. No matter what attempts at reform were carried through in the course of the nineteenth century, every one of them served to strengthen and extend rather than to weaken the grip of the latifundium over its subject population. Many different kinds of change occurred in nineteenth-century Mexico, but the latifundium proved victor over them all.

All the themes announced by the movement for independence

were to recur throughout the nineteenth century. With Mexico independent of Spanish control, the various military had free reign in military and political competition. Thereafter, the rule of the praetorians brought on what Francisco Bulnes called "the public auction of the imperial purple." The *coup d'état* was to be "the hammerblow that opened the auction of power under the praetorian system," accompanied by offers of "generalcies, coronelcies, quashing of criminal cases, contracts for clothing, arms, equipment, bank drafts, and if possible, a little cash" (1904, 205–206). Each palace coup would be followed by a division of spoils: and yet these never proved enough. From 1821 on the country found itself in increasingly desperate financial straits.

> Racked by internal dissension which became a constant in Mexican politics, robbed by a hungry horde of public officials whose capacity for graft far outweighed their ability to govern, pushed into a financial morass by long-term foreign loans at ruinous rates and short-term domestic loans at rates sometimes as high as 50 per cent for ninety days, the government stumbled from one financial crisis to the next. Normal revenues never met the needs, and every tactic known to desperate public financiers was resorted to: forced loans, special taxes, advances on taxes, confiscations, hypothecations, refundings, paper money, debasement. By 1850 the foreign debt had grown to over 56 million, and the domestic debt reached 61; by 1867, after thirteen years of intermittent war and revolution, of which the French Intervention and Maximilian empire was a part, the foreign debt had climbed to a staggering 375 million and the domestic to nearly 79. By that time almost 95 per cent of the customs revenues had been hypothecated to the payment of various debts (Cumberland, 1968, 147).

Under these conditions, "the government was no more than a bank of employees, guarded by armed employees who called themselves the army" (Sierra, 1950, 139). Commerce "dragged out a precarious existence between the ravenous exaction of the fiscal agent and contraband organized as a national institution" (1950, 143).

> The merchant, the landowner, fought fiercely against the government, robbed their extortioners of whatever they could, defrauded the law with profound devotion, and slowly abandoning their enterprises to foreigners (to the Spaniard who had already returned, hacienda, ranch, food stores; to the Frenchman, clothing

and jewelry stores; to the Englishman, the mining enterprise), they gradually took refuge, in mass, in public office, that magnificent school of sloth and misuse in which the middle class of our country has educated itself (1950, 158).

Moreover, while armed struggle atomized society overtly and financial distress undermined its foundations covertly, two additional issues set Mexicans against Mexicans. The war between periphery and center which had marked the movement for independence recurred over and over again in the political and ideological battles between federalists who hoped for a measure of regional autonomy and the centralists who wanted to maintain a unified grip on the country. Another conflict rallied liberals who wanted to disestablish the Church against conservatives who hoped to maintain ecclesiastical power. While in general the federalists were also against the Church and the centralists favored continuation of Church privileges, individual leaders often compounded chaos by entering into individual alliances or schisms, in accordance with personal or local interests.

These continuing conflicts between liberal and anticlerical federalists and conservative and proclerical centralists, fought out with unmatched ferocity, in turn invited outside powers to fish in troubled Mexican waters. From the beginning of the republic, British interests had allied themselves with the centralists, American interests with the federalists, further raising the level of conflict between them. In 1835 Texas revolted against Mexican rule, and in 1847 the United States moved to annex the state, prompted partly by Southern slaving interests who hoped to add still another slave state to the proslavery roster, partly by hopes of access to California and the Pacific Ocean. In the wake of Mexican defeat in 1848, the struggling republic lost—with Texas, New Mexico, and California—more than half of its national territory. It was weakened further by Indian rebellions along the northern frontier, and by the ferocious Maya uprising in Yucatán of 1847, spurred on by the expansion of sugar production in the peninsula. In 1861, a joint British, French, and Spanish expeditionary force landed in Mexico to collect debts owing to them, and while the British and Spaniards withdrew, France proceeded between 1862 and 1867 to turn Mexico into a French client state under the satellite emperorship of an Austrian Habsburg. Contrary to expectation, the Mexican forces under the leadership of Benito Juárez successfully forced the evacuation of the French, leaving the hapless Emperor Maximilian to face a Mexican firing squad in 1867.

Paradoxically, both the American and the French intervention worked to strengthen the hand of the liberals and to weaken the conservatives. The war against the United States had been mismanaged by the conservative leadership, and in the wake of defeat they had lost both power and prestige. As a result, the liberals had been able to push through, in 1855, a corpus of legislation, the laws of the Reforma, aimed at making Mexico a secular and progressive state. The privileged special courts of the military and of the church were abolished. Landed corporations, including church holdings and Indian communities, were to be dissolved; church lands were to be sold and Indian lands to be assigned as individual properties to their current tenants. The Law of Expropriation (*Ley de desamortización*) of June 25, 1856, held that

> no civil or ecclesiastical corporation could acquire or administer any property other than the buildings devoted exclusively to the purpose for which that body existed. It provided that properties then owned by such corporations must be sold to the tenants or usufructuaries occupying them and that properties not rented or leased would be sold at public auction (Whetten, 1948, 85).

When the Church resisted the decrees and the conservatives took to arms once again, Juárez went further, confiscating all real property held by the Church, suppressing all monastic orders, instituting civil marriage, and making cemeteries public property. When the conservatives proved unable to dislodge the liberal government which maintained control of Veracruz and access to the sea they invited French assistance. In turn, they supported Maximilian and the French army throughout the six-year war. Yet in the end Juárez won, both against the French and against their Mexican allies. The hold of privileged corporations had been broken, and a new era was to begin. The protagonists of the Reform laws projected the founding of a new society. That is to say, the historical project of the liberals was to replace the colonial tradition, based on Catholic doctrine, with an affirmation equally universal: the freedom of the individual (Paz, 1961, 126).

Yet the gods that watch over Mexico's destiny appear to take pleasure in reversing the signs. The war of independence had begun in social protest and with demands for social equity. Independence had been won for Mexico not by Hidalgo and Morelos, but by their pro-Spanish enemies. Similarly, the laws of the Reform were to free the individual from traditional fetters, but they succeeded only in creating a new form of servitude. Freedom for the landowner would mean added freedom to acquire more land to add to his already engorged holdings; freedom for the Indian—no longer subject to his community and now lord of his own property —would mean the ability to sell his land, and to join the throng of landless in search of employment. In the course of another thirty-five years, Mexico would discover that it had abandoned the fetters of tradition only to invite social anarchy. The revolution was to be the ultimate result.

In 1876, Benito Juárez yielded power to one of his most brilliant generals in the war against the French, Porfirio Díaz. Under his autocracy economic development went on apace, while beneath the surface the unsolved problems of Mexico continued to fester unsolved and unattended.

Under the dictatorship of Díaz Mexico underwent profound change. During this period, foreign capital investment in Mexico greatly outpaced Mexican investment. Concentrating first on the construction of railroads and the mining of precious ores, it began to flow increasingly, after 1900, into the production of raw materials: oil, copper, tin, lead, rubber, coffee, and sisal. The economy came to be dominated by a small group of businessmen and financiers whose decisions affected the welfare of the entire country. Thus, in 1908, out of sixty-six corporations involved in finance and industry, thirty-six had common directorates drawn from a group of thirteen men; nineteen of the corporations had more than one of the thirteen. During the final decade of the nineteenth century, the

c

leaders of this new controlling group formed a clique which soon came to be known as the *Científicos*. Claiming to be scientific positivists, they saw the future of Mexico in the reduction and obliteration of the Indian element, which they regarded as inferior and hence incapable of development, and in the furtherance of "white" control, national or international. This was to be accomplished through tying Mexico more strongly to the "developed" industrial nations, principally France, Germany, the United States, and Britain. Development, in their eyes, would thus derive from abroad, either in the form of foreign settlers or in the form of foreign capital. Many of them became the representatives of foreign firms operating in Mexico. Some did so directly, as Olegario Molina who controlled the Yucatecan sisal market on behalf of International Harvester Corporation; others did so indirectly, as lawyers acting for foreign firms seeking concessions from the government. During the last years of the regime, some of them became outright business partners of foreign firms. At the same time, however, they combined their interests in business with an interest in acquiring land. Where some of them had begun their careers as landowners and others as lawyers, at the end of the period they were all owners of large tracts of land.

Díaz carefully preserved the forms of the constitutional process as laid down in the Mexican constitution of 1856, but adjusted the content to suit the purposes of his nationwide political machine. There were frequent elections, but they were carefully rigged. Representatives and senators of the Mexican parliament were nominated by the ruling clique and then confirmed through the organized electoral process. The judiciary was appointed by the government and made to serve its purposes. Freedom of the press was restricted severely, and opposition journalists were jailed or exiled. Strikes were prohibited. Rural rebellions, such as the Yaqui Indian insurrections of 1885 and 1898, were put down with a great display of ferocity. A special police force, the *rurales,* recruited from among criminals and bandits, patrolled the rural areas. Opponents of the regime who were apprehended by the *rurales* were frequently killed, and their murder excused under the *ley fuga,* a law permitting the shooting of prisoners trying to escape.

Within the guarantees provided through such organized violence, Díaz played a masterful game of rewarding the faithful, while punishing the resistant, in the dialectic of *pan y palos,* bread and cudgels. Power seekers who followed Díaz received positions or concessions; opponents were rendered harmless. Political loyalty was purchased through distributions from the public treasury. On the village level, this of course meant a reliance on local strong men who often used their power to their own advantage (e.g., Lewis, 1951, 230–231). It is estimated that by 1910 close to three-quarters of the middle class had found employment within the state apparatus, at an annual cost of seventy million pesos (Bulnes, 1920, 42–43). A nationwide system of patronage underwrote the political machine which concentrated power at the top, in the hands of the dictator. Masterfully, Díaz set various aspirants for power against each other, as he also created a measure of independence for his regime by playing off against each other American, French, German, and English investors, together with their respective governments. At the same time, all of these governments saw in Díaz the guarantor of their investments and the pivot of stability.

The Reform laws of 1856–1857 had initiated a major change in the ownership of agricultural land, with the first thrust of these efforts directed at Church holdings. The total amount of land in Church hands is difficult to estimate; some writers hold that about $100,000,000 worth of ecclesiastical real estate was transferred from Church hands to private holders, and that forty thousand properties changed hands (Simpson, 1937, 24). While the announced purpose of this measure was to create a viable rural middle class in Mexico, "in the main the Church estates passed in large, unbroken tracts into the hands of the followers of Juárez, and although in this fashion a new landed aristocracy was created, it was nonetheless an aristocracy" (Ibid.).

The same was true of communal lands possessed by Indian communities. As we have seen, communal lands were declared illegal and forced to divide into individual holdings. Land was thus turned into a marketable commodity, capable of being sold or mortgaged in payment of debts. Many Indians quickly forfeited their land to third parties, often to finance socially required ceremonial expenses. Practically all such land went into the hands of haciendas and land companies. It is estimated that more than two million acres of communal land were alienated in the Díaz period (Phipps, 1925, 115).

Under new legislation, moreover, the government obtained the right to sell public lands to development companies, or to enter into contracts with companies that would survey and divide the land in return for a third of the land surface measured. By 1889, 32 million hectares had been surveyed. Twenty-nine companies had obtained possession of over 27.5 million hectares, or 14 percent of the total land area of the republic. Between 1889 and 1894 an additional 6 percent of the total land area was alienated. Thus roughly one-fifth of the Republic of Mexico was given away in this form. At the same time, cultivators who could not show clear title to their lands were treated as illegal squatters and dispossessed. What had begun as a campaign to create a viable rural middle class composed of small farmers ended in a triumphant victory of a landed oligarchy.

McBride has estimated that at the end of the Díaz period there were 8,245 haciendas. Three hundred of them contained at least 10,000 hectares; 116, around 250,000; 51 possessed approximately 30,000 hectares each; 11 measured no less than 100,000. Unfortunately McBride did not take into account in his enumeration that one hacienda owner might own more than one hacienda; the degree of concentration on landholding probably was even greater than suggested by McBride's figures. Southworth (1910) lists for 1910, 168 proprietors with two holdings each, 52 with three holdings each, 15 with four, 4 with six, 3 with seven, 5 with eight, and 1 with nine. Luis Terrazas, archetype of the Porfirian hacienda owner, had fifteen holdings, comprising close to two million hectares. People joked that Chihuahua had less claim to him—as its native son—than he had claim to Chihuahua. He owned about 500,000 head of cattle and 250,000 sheep, exporting between

40,000 and 65,000 head of cattle annually to the United States. Yet not all haciendas were large; taking McBride's figures at face value, 7,767, or more than 90 percent, were below 10,000 hectares. The average hacienda was probably closer to 3,000 hectares.

The application of the law, putting an end to landholding by corporations—ecclesiastical or communal—hastened the demise of the Indian landholding *pueblo* which had endured throughout the period of Spanish colonial rule and through the first half-century of independence. The Spaniards had reinforced the cohesion of the Indian communities by granting them a measure of land and demanding that they make themselves responsible collectively for payments of dues and for the maintenance of social order. The communities had responded by developing, within the framework of such corporate organization, their own internal system of political organization, strongly tied to religious worship. Nearly everywhere, sponsorship of a sequence of religious festivities qualified a man to become one of the decision makers for the community as a whole. A man who sought power, therefore, had to do it largely by meeting criteria laid down by the community; when qualified he had to do so through participating on a committee of elders like himself who acted and spoke for the community. Power was thus less individual than communal. With the coming of new land laws, however, the very basis of this system was undermined. Not only did the haciendas seize much Indian land, but Indians themselves began to pawn land, to which they were now entitled individually, in order to meet the ordinary expenses of living and the extraordinary expenses of religious sponsorship. The very mechanism which at one time had guaranteed the continued solidarity of the community now turned into a means for destroying it. Thus Indian communities of the old type survived, but only in the more inaccessible regions of the center and south, while the vast mass of Indians faced the prospect of relating themselves individually to the power holders of the outside world, be they credit merchants attaching the crops and belongings of small farmers, or hacienda owners or industrialists seeking labor for their plantations and plants.

Tannenbaum has sought to supply a measure for the size of the population which became dependent upon the hacienda, as compared to the population which remained "free." Thus he showed that in six states (Guanajuato, Michoacán, Zacatecas, Nayarit, Sinaloa) more than 90 percent of all inhabited places were located on estates; in eight more states (Querétaro, San Luis Potosí, Coahuila, Aguascalientes, Baja California, Tabasco, Nuevo León) more than 80 percent were so situated. In ten states, between 50 and 70 percent of the rural population lived in estate communities; five states had between 70 and 90 percent of their population on estates. According to Tannenbaum,

> the number of villages and the proportion of the total that were located upon plantations in any state indicates the extent to which the plantation had absorbed not merely the land but the self-directing life of the communities, and had succeeded in destroying their *mores*. It was essentially a difference between slavery and freedom. The village that survived, even with its lands gone, was essentially free when compared to the villages that had lost both lands and village organization (1937, 193).

In this light it is notable that in the eight states surrounding the core region of the valley of Mexico, the independent settlement cluster continued to predominate. In three states more than 90 percent of the rural population continued to live in independent clusters; in another five, such clusters housed more than 70 percent of the rural population. It was against these persisting independent villages that the Porfirian regime unleashed its power. Hard-pressed, these villages, however, countered with a revolutionary response: "These villages ultimately made the social revolution in self-defense, rather than become reduced to the same condition as the Indians in other parts of Mexico" (Ibid.).

Despite the fact that the haciendas obviously dominated the rural scene, other data suggest that the Porfirian period also witnessed an increase in the number of individually owned family-worked farms or *ranchos*. The number of ranchos should not be taken as absolute, since the term *rancho* does not possess a standardized meaning; in the north it may refer to enormous estates, in the center to holdings up to 1,000 hectares. Nevertheless, we may say with certainty that there was a measurable increase in the number of small holdings. McBride estimates that at the time of the outbreak of the Revolution there were 47,939 ranchos, as compared with 8,245 haciendas. Some 29,000 of these had been created since 1854 through the breakup of communal lands (19,906), allotment of public lands (8,010), and land grants to colonists (1,189). The area occupied by these ranchos was insignificant when compared to that held by the haciendas; but the social relevance of this increase in small farms should not be neglected. More than one-third of these holdings had been established at the expense of communal tenures, thus undermining the solidarity of the Indian villages; but two-thirds, however, continued a trend toward the growth of a rural middle class, already in evidence during the preceding century. François Chevalier (1959) has shown that throughout the eighteenth century and on into the nineteenth, there had been a slow "comeback" of small farmers, especially among the non-Indian populations of the north.

Yet, despite the growth of the latifundium, agricultural production as a whole did not grow steadily and consistently. From 1877 to 1894, in fact, agricultural production declined at an annual rate of 0.81 percent. From 1894 to 1907 it rose once more, but only at a slow annual rate of 2.59 percent. The upward trend was due in major part to the growth of industrial crops for consumption within the country and even more to the growth of export crops. The production of cotton and sugar cane increased, with cotton grown for the Mexican textile industry, and coffee, chick-peas, vanilla, sisal, and cattle were grown in ever larger quantities for the international market. But food crops declined steadily. This was especially true of the production of maize, the staple food of the population. Per capita production of maize declined from 282 kilograms in 1877 to 154 in 1894, to 144 in 1907. Similar declines are noted for beans and chile, similarly vital food crops.

Not only did the amount of maize produced per capita decline, but corn prices rose, while wages remained stationary. All indications are that the average daily wage had not increased between the beginning of the nineteenth century and 1908. The middle class, accustomed to higher expenditures for clothing, housing, and servant help, also felt the impact of rising food prices (González Navarro, 1957, 390).

Industrial development went on apace during the Díaz regime. Mining output rose 239 percent between 1891 and 1910 (Nava Otero, 1965, 179). Industrial production rose at the annual rate of 3.6 percent between 1878 and 1911 (p. 325). Between 1876 and 1910, moreover, railroad tracks laid increased from 666 to 19,280 kilometers. Yet the industrial work force increased at a slower rate. Between 1895 and 1910, for instance, the number of industrial workers increased at a rate of only 0.6 percent of the economically active population to a total of 606,000, in contrast to the agricultural labor force which rose by an annual rate of 1.3 percent during the same period. This was due in part to the fact that the new industry was mechanized and hence required relatively few workers to produce more output, in part to the haciendas which monopolized the labor supply on the farms through various forms of debt peonage.

Yet by 1907 there were close to 100,000 miners, many of them working in large mines such as those of the Greene Consolidated Copper Company of Cananea, which employed 5,000 workers. Employment in the textile industry rose from 19,000 to 32,000 between 1895 and 1910. Most of the textile workers were employed in large mills, such as that at Río Blanco, Veracruz, with 34,000 spindles and 1,000 looms, manned by 2,350 workers, or close to half of all the workers employed by eleven large plants in Veracruz. The plant was owned by a company of French merchants. Finally, there were several tens of thousands employed on the growing railroads, where workers received for the first time a "real salary." Molina Enríquez, discussing the spread of railroads in Mexico during the Porfiriato, says that

> the construction of railways . . . involved the employment of laborers who . . . for the first time received real [i.e. cash] wages, wages which radically improved their economic condition. Along the whole length of the railway lines which traversed the

country gathered laborers, peons who had escaped the yoke of our great haciendas. . . . The temporary bonanza, produced by the millions invested in our railways, constituted for a few years the true secret of the Porfirian peace, at the same time that the profound changes which they brought on in the conditions of production within the country, already laid the bases of the future Revolution (1932, 292).

"The dynamite of the railways charged the mine which later the Revolution was to set off" (1932, 291).

This new industrial work force recruited its members among former peasants displaced from the land by the predatory expansion of the latifundia; among the numerous artisans unable to withstand the onslaught of mechanized competition; and among escaped peons who had fled from debt bondage into the relative freedom of industrial wage labor. They were largely unskilled and lacked a skilled elite of their own; most skilled positions were held by foreigners. Though many of them had come into industrial employment only recently, they tended to be concentrated in large plants and in large settlements, such as those of Cananea or Orizaba. They were markedly antiforeign in sentiment, due to the fact that most often foremen and employers were actually foreigners. They lacked organizational experience, because union activity was forbidden, but they had made acquaintance with anarcho-syndicalist ideas, largely through the contacts of migratory workers in the United States with members of the International Workers of the World (I.W.W.). As time went on, they began increasingly to assert themselves in strikes. Some 250 strikes occurred during the Porfiriato, their number increasing after 1880. Strikes were common on the railroads, in textiles, in mining, and in tobacco factories. Two strikes stand out as precursors of revolutionary activity: the strike of Cananea in 1906, put down by American volunteers and *rurales,* and the strike in Río Blanco of 1907, quelled by army, police, and *rurales,* at a cost of 200 dead and 400 imprisoned.

Development, however, had a differential impact on the northern and southern peripheries of the republic (Katz, 1964). In the south, the growing market for tropical crops and foodstuffs for industrial centers led to an expansion of estate agriculture, coupled with an intensified exploitation of Indian labor. To supplement the labor furnished by the local population, rebellious Indians and criminals were transported to work on plantations as forced laborers. This intensified pressure on the Indian population also produced an entire segment of overseers, labor contractors, and moneylenders interested in getting Indians into debt and converting them into estate workers. While each local hacienda had its own apparatus of coercion, its own police and whipping post, the entire structure of coercion depended ultimately on the apparatus of coercion maintained by the government. Thus the southern hacienda owners tended to support Díaz for internal reasons, just as their dependence on foreign markets and firms led them to support the symbiosis of the regime with foreign interests.

Opposition to the regime, however, was pronounced in the north where conditions differed markedly from the rest of the country. Here labor had always been scarce and hence obtainable only at a higher premium than in the center or south. Work in the mines and in the growing number of cotton mills, or migration to the nearby United States, offered opportunities which weakened the structure of debt peonage and increased the mobility of the labor force. Sharecropping arrangements were taking the place of indebted labor, especially on estates growing cotton. In the north, also, islands of smallholders had maintained themselves here and there; during the period under discussion their number grew. Owners of large estates not only were able to sell cereals and meat in the growing cities of the north, like Torreón, Nogales, Ciudad Juárez, Nuevo Laredo, and across the border in the United States, but had begun to invest in local industry producing mainly for a domestic market. Such increased mobility and opportunity in turn furthered the growth of independent merchants, quite different from the middlemen of the south whose main source of employment was to recruit Indian labor or to lend money at interest. At the same time, the northerners found themselves at a disadvantage in competition with foreign business firms, mainly American, whose operations received the protection of the Científicos and of Díaz. Foreign competition was especially strong in the field of mining where most Mexican firms were forced to sell their ores to the American Smelting and Refining Company. Only the Madero family had been able to maintain an independent smelter at Monterrey, fed with ores from their own mines. The northerners also came to realize increasingly that foreign control of raw materials and processing curtailed their ability to enter heavy industry, while light industry was limited in its expansion by the narrow scale of the Mexican domestic demand, held down by the autarchic structure of the hacienda. All their interests thus lay in opposing the foreign influence and the decision makers in the capital who abetted it. During the Díaz period, the motives for rebellion which had once impelled the Bajío region to revolt against the Spaniards in 1810, had thus spread to the entire northern Mexican periphery.

Just as industrial labor was shaken by increasing strikes and rural labor rebelled spasmodically against the wholesale encroachment of the latifundia on their lives, so both middle and upper classes grew restive as Díaz approached a new term of office in 1910. We have already spoken of the dissatisfaction of the northern landowners and industrialists whose interests began to conflict with those of the dictatorship. The middle classes also began to strain against the limitations imposed by the Díaz machine. Iturriaga (1951, 28) has estimated the members of the middle class in 1895 at 989,783, or 7.78 percent of the population. 776,439, or 6.12 percent, were urban; 213,344, or 1.66 percent, were rural. Following the sociologist Gino Germani, he divided the middle class into two groups: the economically "autonomous" middle class of artisans, small and middle merchants, commercial agents, members of the free professions, and small and middling *rentiers;* and the "dependent" middle class whose skills are at the service of a larger organization which employs them. The dependent middle class in the countryside—made up of hacienda administrators and employees, government employees—was only 8.97 percent of the rural middle class; the remainder were "autonomous." In the city, however, the dependent middle classes composed 39.07 percent of the total. Most of these were probably in the employ of the government. Some of them had benefited greatly by appointment to positions that gave them access to foreign concessions or sources of graft; most lived off exceedingly meager salaries, discovering—in Justo Sierra's phrase—that while the state held all wealth, the state itself was poor. Still others, proud of their diplomas and education, could find no employment at all; all berths had been pre-empted, and often by officials grown old and senile in office. Hence the Revolution—when it came—proved as much of a conflict between successive generations of claimants for power as an attempt to right injustice and to create new social and political conditions. In the nineteenth century federalist liberals had fought conservative centralists for greater regional autonomy, as well as for the new positions which such autonomy might open up. In 1910, this old struggle was to be repeated in a new form, as the diploma elite of the provinces rose against a regime composed of "political cadavers."

This new educated class did not possess an elaborate ideology of its own, but in the first years of the new century a number of them had begun to respond to new and more radical themes. Between 1901 and 1910 more than fifty so-called Liberal clubs had been organized, mostly in the north and on the Gulf Coast (Barrera Fuentes, 1955, 39); among the delegates to the Liberal Congress of 1901 figured engineers, law students, lawyers, merchants, and even one "burgués acomodado." Their demands were aimed mainly at free elections and municipal liberty, but they also hoped to put an end to peonage and the inhuman conditions of life on the haciendas of the tropical zone. With growing repression, however, many of these liberals began to move "left"; by 1903 they were reading Kropotkin, Bakunin, and Marx, and from 1906 on they increasingly urged armed rebellion against the government. This shift was reinforced by political events in Spain. A growing movement against Spanish military intervention in Morocco, industrial exploitation, clericalism, and lack of political freedom ended in suppression; and a number of Spanish socialists and anarchists found refuge in Mexico. Rebellions and armed incursions from the sanctuary of the United States took place in 1906 (five in number) and 1908 (two). At the same time, increasing numbers of Mexican migratory workers in the United States became acquainted with anarcho-syndicalism through their contact with the "wobblies," the members of the International Workers of the World. "The positive points of this anarchist ideology," says Paul Friedrich, who studied its impact on one community of the Tarascan area of Michoacán (1966, 206),

> were material improvements, especially land reform, and a socioeconomic organization, based on the voluntary association of village communities, labor unions, and other small groups. On the negative side was an extreme hostility toward institutionalized large-scale authority, especially the state and the church.

The two currents, middle class and proletarian, met in the figure of Ricardo Flores Magón, one of the prime movers of the liberals, and later, from 1905 on, an important anarchist organizer and ideologue. His newspaper *Regeneración,* published in the United States after his exile from Mexico, traveled from hand to hand within the republic; even Zapata is said to have been influenced by it (Pinchon, 1941, 41–44). Flores Magón himself, "the ideological precursor of the Mexican Revolution" (Barrera Fuentes, 1955, 302–303), in and out of U.S. jails after 1911, died in 1922 at Leavenworth. The anarchist theme of a society organized into small communities, however, survived, underwriting the restoration of Indian communities in the land reforms which were to follow the Revolution. It thus provided a link between the experience of the past and the future in terms which could make that experience intelligible to a people caught up in the throes of a revolutionary apocalypse.

In 1910 the Revolution broke out. The starting signal was given by Francisco Madero, liberal landowner from Coahuila, who—in his Declaration of San Luis Potosí—assumed the provisional presidency of Mexico and designated November 20, 1910, as the date when Mexicans were to rise up in arms against the hated dictator. It seems paradoxical that this call for more orderly electoral procedures unleashed a storm of disorder and violence that was to sweep through Mexico for the period of an entire decade. In contrast to other revolutionary movements of the twentieth century, the Mexican Revolution was not to be led by any one group organized around a central program. In no other revolutionary movement did the participants in the drama prove so unaware of their roles and their lines. The movement resembles a great avalanche, essentially

> anonymous. No organized party presided at its birth. No great intellectuals prescribed its program, formulated its doctrine, outlined its objectives (Tannenbaum, 1937, 115–116).

Its military leaders

> were children of the upheaval. . . . The Revolution made them, gave them means and support. They were the instruments of a movement; they did not make it, and have barely been able to guide it. (Ibid)

It moved by fits and starts, and in numerous directions at once; it carried with it the bastions of power and the straw-covered huts of the peasantry alike. When it was finished, it had profoundly altered the characteristics of Mexican society. More than any other revolution of the twentieth century, therefore, it grants us insight into the conditions of imbalance which underlie a revolutionary epoch.

Almost immediately two areas of rural participation delineated themselves, a southern area centered upon Morelos, and a northern area centered upon Chihuahua. The southerners came to be led by Emiliano Zapata, the northerners by Doroteo Arango, better known under his adopted name of Pancho Villa.

To understand these movements we need to know more about their respective areas of origin. Located in the temperate zone, Morelos with its well-irrigated agriculture supported, in 1910, a relatively high population density of sixty people per square mile. The concentration of population, in turn, had been instrumental in maintaining Indian customs and the use of Nahuatl among the Indians. Settlements of Spaniards in the area had been scarce. Its valleys favored the commercial exploitation of sugar cane on plantations first manned largely by imported Negro slave labor and owned by powerful landowners and religious orders located in nearby Mexico City. Indian communities survived in the surrounding hills. With the reform law depriving corporations of their landholdings, however, the private haciendas began to encroach on church lands and Indian lands alike. Their purpose was not only to obtain additional good land for their productive purposes, but—even more—to deny the indigenous population sufficient land, thus forcing them into dependence on the sugar estates. Initially unwilling to modernize techniques and plants at the beginning of the Díaz regime, the sugar growers of Morelos were forced—through competition—to improve their plants. In 1880

> the first machinery using the centrifuge method was set up in the haciendas, with Santa Clara being the first to employ this modern procedure. This event would come to change radically the life of the State. To increase sugar production the hacienda owners naturally attempted to increase the area under cultivation and this had to take place necessarily at the expense of village lands; irrigation works spread and the very Public Administration had to modify its taxes and its method of using them. In one word, it can be said that the establishment of modern machinery brought on a complete change, the landowners prospered, their cane yielded greater profit, the Government raised its taxes, only the villages were forced to yield up their lands and water supply. Gradually they began to shrink, a few disappeared altogether, and there grew in intensity the social disequilibrium which was to be broken by the Revolution of 1910 (Diez, 1967, 130).

At the turn of the century, Morelos was by far the largest aggregate producer of sugar among the various Mexican states (Figueroa Domenech, 1899, I, 373–381).

While the haciendas took over Indian land wherever possible, they had not, however, brought under control most of the surrounding Indian villages themselves. This was probably due to the fact that sugar production requires large supplies of labor, but on a seasonal basis; the greatest number of workers are required for the relatively short harvest period of between two and three months a year. Thus they were quite willing to use the Indian villages as labor reserves, tapping their labor—when needed—through such mechanisms as debt advances. They thus, however, also left intact cohesive social units, which possessed the advantage of a social solidarity built up over long periods of time, as compared with the looser organization of hacienda workers, often drawn from numerous unrelated villages.

These communities were also very much aware of their freedom and special interests, interests which consisted in resolute resistance to the encroachment of the hacienda owners. San Miguel Anenecuilco, for instance, had, over the centuries, waged numerous and generally successful legal battles against the superior power of the *hacendados*. This battle had been under the guidance of the community's council of elders. In 1909, an assembly of all members of the community, under the leadership of the council, elected a committee of defense. The head of the committee was a local ranchero by the name of Emiliano Zapata. All members of the community contributed to a joint treasury, and Zapata was entrusted with the care of the community's legal documents, dating back to the early seventeenth century. When—at the beginning of the rainy season of 1910—the neighboring hacienda began to occupy community land already readied for corn planting, Zapata organized a group of eighty men to carry through the planting operation in defiance of the hacienda. Shortly after, Villa de Ayala and Noyotepec—two other communities—began to contribute to Zapata's defense fund. Thereupon Zapata proceeded to take over communal lands occupied by the haciendas, destroy the fences erected by them, and distribute land to villagers (Sotelo Inclán, 1943).

Historically, the Zapata revolt presents interesting analogies with the earlier revolt—in much the same general area—led by José María Morelos from 1810 to 1815. It is probably not accidental that a number of forebears of Zapata had taken part in that movement. Like Zapata, Morelos proved to be a first-class guerrilla leader. Like Zapata, too, his zone of operations remained largely confined to the southern tier of the central mesa.

> Morelos had no effect on the main agricultural and mining area of the plateau; he fought in the hot region of the Pacific; he staged his advances from small settlements, and his most important triumphs: Tixtla, Taxco, Izucar, Tenancingo, though they threatened the cities of Toluca and Puebla, never really called into question the fate of the colony (Zavala, 1940–41, 46).

Like Zapata after him, Morelos also called for the breakup of haciendas and the restitution of land to the Indian communities. Like the Zapatistas, finally, the insurgents of 1810 made use of the symbol of the dark-faced Virgin of Guadalupe as their supernatural protagonist. Writers have spoken of Morelos' "thaumaturgic" devotion to the Virgin of Guadalupe. Said to have appeared to an Indian shortly after the Spanish Conquest, the Virgin of Guadalupe had come over the centuries to represent Mexican hopes for a supernatural deliverance from Spain and for a return to a golden age (Wolf, 1958). In contrast, the pro-Spanish party adopted for their supernatural *Capitana General* the white Virgin of the Remedies. The Zapatistas both carried the image of the Virgin of Guadalupe in their battle flags and on their broad-brimmed hats, thus validating their demands for a return to an old agrarian order with symbols which also promised a return to a more pristine supernatural state.

While the Zapatista struggle had its origin in the local problems of a locally oriented peasantry, it did not develop wholly in isolation from the larger movements which began to shake the foundations of the social order. Zapata himself did not depend on the communal lands of the villages: his father was the owner of a small farm—the Zapatas were rancheros. The family was identified with past struggles against the conservative party in Mexico and against the French. A granduncle had fought with Morelos in the wars of independence; the wife of a Morelian hero of the wars, Francisco Ayala, may have been a relative. His grandfather and father, as well as his paternal uncles, had served with Díaz against the French. The family also had a record of defending the area against the incursions of bandits. Moreover, Emiliano Zapata was used to horses and horse-riding; he was—as Octavio Paz has said—a *"charro* of *charros,"* a cowboy among cowboys, familiar with the horse, the dominant symbol of mastery introduced in the country by the Spaniards, while its use remained denied to the Indians. He always dressed, not in the style of the villagers, but as a *charro,* with tight trousers, big spurs, short vest, and big gold-braided hat. All the Zapatista generals were to copy his style of dress. Furthermore, friends and kin on whom he relied at the beginning of the rebellion

D

were horsemen like himself. His two brothers-in-law were, one, a muleteer, the other, a horseman; his brother Eufemio was a fruit merchant. One friend, Jesus Sánchez, was a ranchero; another friend, Gabriel Tepepa, a veteran of the wars against the French, had become a foreman on a nearby hacienda. It is also incorrect that Zapata could not read and write; he attended school for two years at Anenecuilco, apparently long enough to be able to read newspapers. He participated in the unsuccessful political campaign in Morelos of 1909 in favor of General Leyva against the Porfirian candidate and had made the acquaintance of Otilio Montaño, the radical schoolteacher of Ayala. Another friend was the village letter writer and amateur lawyer, Pablo Torres Burgos, commonly called the "Little Inkpot." Moreover, during a brief stay in Mexico City he had met a number of intellectuals, among them Díaz Soto y Gama, who was to become the ideologue of the Zapatista rebellion, Dolores Jiménez y Muro, a schoolteacher, and the three Magaña brothers, one of whom, Gildardo, was to play an important military and intellectual role in the Revolution. Montaño's ideological role is illuminated by a letter written in 1909 to Francisco Bulnes and paraphrased by the recipient (1920, 406):

> I do not believe that the French Revolution has been prepared with more audacity and materials for destruction than the Mexican which is in preparation. I am horrified! The speakers for Leiva, without hesitation and shame, have raised the holy banner of the war of the poor against the rich; everything now belongs to the poor; the haciendas, with all their land and waters, cattle and brush pasture; the women, the honor and the life of those who are not Indians. Crime is being preached like a new Gospel, the landowners are to be killed like vipers, smashing their heads with a stone. Their wives and children belong to the people, in revenge for the wantonness of untrammelled hacienda owners, violators of the virgins of the people. Charity and compassion are considered cowardice: already who cannot avenge himself is not a man, and only the one who would give quarter not even to his father is capable of avenging himself. The haciendas belong to the poor because they were stolen from them by the Spaniards. When a just accounting is made of the daily wages which belong to the people and which they have received from their exploiters, the

hacienda owners turn out to be in debt, even after they have paid with their haciendas. These were the themes of Leivista oratory, taught by the professor of Villa de Ayala, don Otilio Montaño, who teaches normal school, to the tribunes of the people, so they can teach them to the illiterate, darkskinned (*zambos*) and crooked peasants, called together in 1908 for the redeeming revolution of the oppressed, choosing—as Montaño wanted it and achieved it—Tlaltizapan as the "proletarian capital of Mexico."

We thus see in the making of the Zapatista revolution two ingredients of signal importance: one, the participation from the first of disaffected intellectuals with urban ties; and second, the importance of a peasant group endowed with sufficient independent resources of its own to embark on the road to independent political action. The anarcho-syndicalist idiom served as the bond between them. From Ricardo Flores Magón came the slogan *"tierra y Libertad,"* first pronounced by the anarchist leader in *Regeneración* on November 19, 1910, and a sweet sound to the ears of the Indians who had risen to defend and regain their lands. Having begun land redistributions as head of the defense committee of Anenecuilco, Zapata made this the main purpose of his movement. With the assistance of Díaz Soto y Gama, he pronounced in November 1911 his *Plan de Ayala:*

> be it known: that the lands, woods and waters which have been usurped by hacendados, Científicos, or caciques, through tyranny and venal justice, will be restored immediately to the pueblos or citizens who have the corresponding titles to such properties, of which they were despoiled through the bad faith of our oppressors. They shall maintain such possession at all costs through force of arms.

Important as these ideological ingredients of the Zapatista movement were, however, the movement itself was primarily based on the peasantry, and fought for peasant ends. This was both its advantage and its limitation. The base of the Zapatistas was in the villages, to which they would return after combat. They fought in units of thirty to three hundred, clad in their broad-brimmed hats, sandals, and white cotton twill shirts and trousers. Among their leaders were women as well as men, *coronelas* as well as coronels.

Their arms were rudimentary; they made use of homemade grenades and dynamite; modern firearms and cannon they obtained from the enemy. They had no organized system of supplies. Their proximity to Mexico City enabled them to seize supplies destined for the capital, or they lived off the land, especially off the haciendas they had seized. When they made their victorious entry into Mexico City, members of the army—armed to the teeth— humbly knocked on the doors of private houses and asked for something to eat. The army fought best on its own territory, but the peasant soldiers did not want to fight in areas unfamiliar to them. Their military capacity was defensive rather than offensive; despite this they scored some notable successes against the armies of the government and held them at bay for years. Seventy thousand strong in 1915, the Zapatista army declined to 30,000 in 1916. By 1919 there were only 10,000 left (Chevalier, 1961).

Essentially the army wanted land; once they obtained land, all other issues seemed paltry in comparison. This narrow focus of aims, together with the unwillingness of the Zapatistas to extend their military operations beyond the vicinity of Morelos, limited their appeal to other Mexicans not determined by the same background and not caught up in the same circumstances. Zapata, for example, had no comprehension of the needs and interests of the industrial workers and never knew how to attract their support. Similarly, the agrarian struggle in Morelos had been fought in the main against Mexican landowners, not against foreigners. The Zapatistas therefore had little understanding for the struggle of Mexican nationalists to assert Mexico's national integrity in the face of foreign influence and investment (Katz, 1964, 236). When Zapata attained that insight, in 1917, it came too late to prevent defeat at the hands of men of wider horizons and greater capability in building viable political coalitions.

The second hearth of rural rebellion was located in Chihuahua, and found its captain in Pancho Villa. Chihuahua resembled much of the north, with its greater mobility of labor on estates, mines, and railroads; its landed upper class doubling to some extent as an industrial and commercial elite; its urban-centered middle groups of small merchants, professionals, and ranchers. Tendencies to concentration of landed property, however, had been fierce in this region. By 1910 seventeen persons owned two-fifths of the state; the Terrazas family had come into ownership of five million hectares; 95.5 percent of all heads of families held no individual property in land (Lister and Lister, 1966, 176; McBride, 1923, 154). Much cattle was sold to the United States; silver mining was in full swing; railroad construction had laid the basis for a network that connected the area both with the center and with the United States. Towns had grown apace. In spite of the near complete monopolization of land, there had grown up a lively urban-centered middle class. "In sharp contrast to the remainder of Mexico," says Michael C. Meyer,

> in the first decade of the twentieth century, Chihuahua possessed a relatively large middle class of merchants, artisans, coachmen, railroad men, and clerks. There is some evidence to suggest that these middle groups maintained a limited contact with their social counterparts in the United States and, in emulation of the better-defined middle sector north of the Rio Grande, desired to better their lot. As a result, the middle groups within the state were especially susceptible to the endless stream of revolutionary propaganda that saturated Chihuahua during the last few years of the Díaz dictatorship (1967, 9).

Two other categories of people could be counted upon to furnish support for the Revolution. One was the cowboy population, laboring on the large cattle ranches. Paradoxically, while cattle population had shown a steady increase, sales had not kept pace with the increase in stock, and some areas even suffered a temporary decline. This may well have had economic repercussions among the cowhands, always highly mobile, and mounted on horseback, easily mobilizable in opposition to the large landowners. At the same time, however, they also looked down upon the settled cultivators and showed no interest in becoming sedentary peasants: throughout the revolutionary period one of their outstanding characteristics would be their disinterest in problems of land reform. Linked to the cowboy segment there also existed clusters of illegal operators whose involvement in smuggling, banditry, and cattle rustling benefited as much from the proximity of the United States as from the asylum for their bands provided by mountains and desert.

A report, written in Zacatecas some fifty years earlier, gives us a glimpse into the life style of these groups (quoted in Pimentel, 1866, 120–123):

> there are other classes of men on the ranches whom one cannot properly call agriculturalists and whose character, occupations, customs and style of life differ greatly from the character and customs of the cultivators.

They consist of various social clusters. Some

> are artisans or craftsmen, usually very backward in techniques, or merchants with little capital who settle on the haciendas with or without permission of the owner. They live in continuous opposition and enmity with that same owner, tend to be involved in retail trade, and since it is not to the interest of the owner to permit this, they always carry it on fraudulently, subjugating all the country people with their most sordid and usurious contracts. Most of them also buy and sell contraband tobacco; are in touch with all the smugglers; supply the rural settlements with playing cards and intoxicating drink; buy from cowboys and shepherds the animals they steal from the hacienda owner; keep taverns and gambling dens in their houses; offer hospitality to vagabonds and bandits, and—finally—act as receivers of stolen property, especially in connection with cattle rustling. The so-called renters [*arrendatarios*] raise numerous animals, primarily mules and horses, an occupation which requires little work; they generally renege on the rent they ought to pay for the pasturing of their animals; they refuse to cultivate, and spend most of their days like Arabs, mounted on very good horses, roaming through the deserted countryside, or promoting arguments and fights in the hamlets. The rest of their time, and especially the feast days, they spend dancing and getting drunk, in games of chance and in cockfights for which they show an irresistible and strong attraction. The shepherds . . . are almost nomadic, and in the solitude of the countryside surrender themselves to all kinds of vices and excess. They appropriate for themselves and their families the best animals they have under their care, and also steal them in order to sell them. The cowboys also lead a lonely life, like the shepherds; always mounted on excellent horses, they ride through the coun-

tryside engaged in drilling them. Since their wages are very low, they get into large debts with the hacienda owners; steal many animals entrusted to them, and generally sell them to highwaymen and smugglers, or go to the big towns to live as horse-handlers or servants. There they establish contact with the thieves and professional outlaws who inhabit the lower class part of town, and since they are skilled in managing horses, finally enlist in a band of thieves.

The military conditions of the Revolution in the north were thus apt to be quite different from those which obtained in Morelos. Zapata was anchored in a peasantry able and willing to fight in the mountains, but unwilling to leave their mountain redoubt. In contrast, the northern rebellion could count on large troops of cavalry drawn from cowboys and bandits, and hence capable from the beginning of a wide range of operations. The Zapatistas were limited in their ability to obtain weapons and to supply their home base and the surrounding area. The northerners could confiscate cattle and cotton and sell it in the United States in return for smuggled armaments.

Pancho Villa, the leader of this military revolt, fitted completely into these circumstances. He had been a peon on a hacienda, and was involved in the murder of a hacienda owner supposedly killed in revenge for the ravishment of a sister. Taking to the hills, he had become a part-time muleteer, able to construct a wide network of social relations, and a bandit. Stealing from big haciendas, he had become a legendary figure among the peons, a Robin Hood who took from the rich to give to the poor. When the Revolution broke out he was quickly won to its cause and became one of its important leaders. Jailed by General Huerta who relied on the Díaz machine to restore a Díaz-type dictatorship, he met in jail Gildardo Magaña, the Zapatista intellectual who taught him the rudiments of reading and writing, and acquainted him with Zapata's agrarian program. After a successful escape from jail, he rallied a force of three thousand men, which became the nucleus of his *División del Norte*. By the end of 1914 he was in control of an army of forty thousand troops (Quirk, 1960, 82). Friedrich Katz has said of this redoubtable force that it was less an army than a "folk migration":

women and children accompanied the soldiers and were fed by them. Nothing is more characteristic of the Mexican revolutionary armies than the *soldaderas,* the soldiers' women, who travelled with the army by the thousands (1964, 243).

The heartland of Villa's rebellion was Chihuahua where he attracted his first following among cowboys, ranchers, and miners. When Villa began to seize the properties of Spanish landowners and of *Científicos,* however, these were not divided among peasants, as in the south, but handed over to the "state" with the provision that income derived from them would feed widows and orphans after the war. Although he himself was sympathetic to the demands of the Plan of Ayala, pronounced by the Zapatistas, he never carried on any wider land reform in the areas under his control. Katz (1964, 237–238, 325–326) ascribes this to a number of factors: the realization that cattle estates could not be subdivided into economically viable small parcels; that cattle were needed in large numbers to furnish the commodity with which the Villistas could obtain supplies and weapons in the United States; and the scant interest which cowboys had in a specifically agrarian reform. The decisive factor, however, may well have been the development of a new "bourgeoisie" within the army of the north itself. Numerous seized estates quickly passed into the hands of Villa's generals who used them to underwrite an upper-class way of life for themselves, thus becoming a landed group with interests of their own. They, of course, were directly opposed to land reform. A few of the more enterprising of these new military landowners even entered into regular alliances with enterprises in the United States, and began to benefit from trade and smuggling with the United States. In addition to northern cattle, they also came to control the cotton-growing country of the Laguna. Thus Villa's movement never undertook a viable land reform, in marked contrast to the Zapatistas. By March 27, 1915, the Villa delegates to the Revolutionary Convention of Aguascalientes even defended "the traditional nineteenth-century rights of private property and the individual" (Quirk, 1960, 213) against the radical Zapatistas. They had come full-cycle.

Thus, while Villa's armies and Zapata's forces were instrumental in destroying the power of the Díaz regime and its epigonous successor Victoriano Huerta, they were themselves unable to take the decisive steps to institute a new order in Mexico. Zapata, because he was unable to transcend the demands of his revolutionary peasantry, concentrated upon a narrow area of Mexico, and Villa gloried in warfare, but had no understanding for social and political exigencies. Symbolic of this tragic ineptitude of both parties is their historic meeting in Mexico City at the end of 1914 when they celebrated their fraternal union but could not create a political machine that could govern the country. "Both Pancho Villa and Emilio Zapata," says Pinchon in his biography of Zapata (1941, 306),

—typical regionalists without experience in the sphere of national affairs—not only refused office of any kind but felt themselves unequipped to do more than provide temporary protection for the formation of a revolutionary government. But no man of the right caliber for president appeared. Over the Palacio Nacional hung a wistful sign: "Wanted—an honest man."

Thus a third force did break the deadlock, the Constitutionalist army of only twenty-six thousand men. It consisted of a coalition between two wings, a liberal wing oriented toward political reform, and a radical wing intent upon social reform. The liberal wing was led by Venustiano Carranza, the radical wing by Alvaro Obregón. Each represented in his person the social orientation impressed upon them by their different origins. Carranza, like Madero, was a landowner. Under Díaz he had occupied a number of minor positions, including that of senator. He joined the Madero movement in order to secure the re-establishment of constitutional guarantees and federal liberty. His following was made up of

the same middle-class liberals, the Madero-style legislators, and their aim was also the same: to insure that the political control of Mexico remained in the hands of the middle class of the states. The Carranza men were federalists . . . troglodytes in the midst of the 20th century: they imagined that the problems of Mexico could be solved by a series of measures which had failed in the past century (Quirk, 1953, 509–510).

Unlike Madero, Carranza had realized that the re-establishment of formal constitutional guarantees would remain a hollow measure, as long as the Díaz machine—civil and military—remained in a position of power. He had warned Madero that his exclusive concentration on formal liberties would mean the death of the Revolution. He thus shared Madero's vision of political reform, but of a political reform equipped with teeth. This led him to take up the struggle against the Díaz machine, now captained by Victoriano Huerta. Yet he hoped to fashion a state which would neither return to the despotic centralism of Díaz, nor go forward to the unsettling social reforms proposed by the radicals.

> Anarchy and centralism were, for the liberals, the major enemies of the Carrancista revolution. Anarchy was incarnated in the radical agrarians who hoped to transform the political revolution into a social movement of violent character. And centralismo was incarnated in the old regime and the followers of Huerta. The liberals opted for a middle term: they wanted to create a federal and democratic republic, in which the middle class would play the leading role (1953, 511).

The radicals, however, had a different orientation and obeyed different impulses. Many of them had come from Sonora and Sinaloa, the Mexican northwest; Sonora and Sinaloa shared some of the characteristics of the arid north-central provinces like Chihuahua, but with an important difference. In Sonora and Sinaloa, too, there had been a growth of large landed estates. In 1910 there were 265 holdings larger than 1,000 hectares in Sinaloa, 35 of them larger than 10,000 hectares; 94.7 percent of all heads of households were landless. In Sonora, 77 holdings were composed of more than 1,000 hectares each; seven were larger than 10,000 hectares each. The percentage of landless heads of households amounted to 95.8 (McBride, 1923, 154). With the advent of the railroads, however, much of this land had come under the control of United States' firms; "the lines actually served better as a pipeline from the Mexican interior to United States' markets than they did as a stimulus to interior marketing and economic development" (Cumberland, 1968, 217). By 1902 U.S. firms held more than a million hectares in Sonora; in Sinaloa they owned 50 percent of the productive deltaic plain and 75 percent of all irrigable land, where sugar, cotton, and fresh vegetables were raised for the market (Pfeifer, 1939, 384). Increasing commercialization, at the same time, had also evoked a small middle group, at once stimulated by contact with the United States and increasingly antagonistic to its influence. It also lived in lively competition with Chinese traders who came to control much local commerce. One of the first acts of the Revolution would be to expel the Chinese from the state (Cumberland, 1960). Yet this was also a middle group very much more rural in character than its counterpart in Chihuahua.

Obregón well represented its rural orientation. His father had been an independent rancher who had lost his holding to floods and Indian raiders. The son became successively a mechanic, a traveling salesman for a shoe manufacturer, a mechanic in a sugar mill, a rancher growing chick-peas on rented land, and the inventor of a mechanical chick-pea planter that was soon adopted throughout the area of the Mayo River. He taught himself to speak both Mayo and Yaqui. A reader of Flores Magón's newspaper *Regeneración* since 1905, he favored Madero's revolution, and in 1912 gathered some three hundred well-to-do ranchers like himself into a fighting force that came to be known as the Rich Man's Battalion (Dillon, 1956, 262). He was by no means a socialist, but favored nationalist legislation and agrarian and labor reforms which would at one and the same time curtail United States encroachment, break the power of the great landed families, and widen opportunities in the market for both labor and his kind of middle class.

To express their radical demands for land and labor reform, the Zapatistas and Villistas had called a convention which was dominated by anarchist and socialist rhetoric. It called in no uncertain terms for the liquidation of the latifundia system, the return of lands to the Indian communities, the nationalization of lands held by enemies of the Revolution and foreigners, a program of land reform; voices were heard calling for legislation limiting work hours, protecting working women and children, industrial accident insurance, the establishment of cooperatives and mutual-aid societies, secular education, the formation of unions, and the right to strike. While the speakers were mostly radical intellectuals like Díaz Soto y Gama, Miguel Mendoza López, and Pérez Taylor, the delegates were for the most part the revolutionary generals of the Villa and Zapata forces, captains of peasant and cowboy armies. Endowed with military titles by the Revolution, they were not primarily militarists, but almost always "leaders of peasant bands who stood for some kind of land reform" (Quirk, 1953, 505). The liberals within the Constitutional coalition listened to these pleas with horror. They

> refused to accept the sovereignty of the Convention when they realized that this organism was dominated by the Villistas and Zapatistas, or—rather—by the radicals, by the rabble of the Revolution. They thought that stability could never be attained if the reins of the government were placed in the hands of the radicals. The constitutionalists were controlled, on the other hand, by various lawyers and men experienced in the art of ruling. Carranza had been senator and governor. Palavicini, Macías, Cabrera and Rojas had been congressmen during Madero's administration. Here, those who labored to their liking were lawyers, not generals (Quirk, 1953, 506).

They opposed reforms:

> Since the middle class had already taken over the government—and the Carranza regime was wholly liberal and civilian in type—they thought that the social reforms of an advanced type, at that period, would end in destroying order and peaceful progress. If the flood of the Revolution was allowed to spread, the middle class elements would lose control of the government, allowing the disorderly radical leaders of the masses to break loose (1953, 518).

With the passage of events, however, it became clear that there would have to be reform. There were radicals not only in the armies of the Convention, but also within the Constitutionalist forces themselves. From the first, Obregón and his followers had understood that they could only break the hold of Villa and Zapata by promising viable social reforms. Their arguments began to gain power, as the Constitutionalist regime was pushed to the wall by the continued success of Villa and Zapata's advances in 1914 and

1915. By the beginning of 1915 Carranza began to make vague pronouncements in favor of social reform from Veracruz. Already in August 1914 Obregón had reopened the *Casa del Obrero Mundial* in Mexico, and in mid-February 1915, this socialist organization signed a pact with Carranza in which it promised to furnish "red" battalions against Villa and Zapata. In 1915 the Constitutionalist general Salvador Alvarado entered Yucatán and abolished debt peonage in the state. Such accommodations enormously aided the Constitutionalist cause and attracted numerous sympathizers.

Constitutionalist methods are well illustrated by the invasion of Yucatán. Since mid-nineteenth century, the peninsula had witnessed a steady expansion of sisal production, especially after 1878 when the introduction of the McCormick reaper provided a growing market for baling twine in the United States. By 1900 the Yucatecan industry was well on its road to mechanization, with steam-driven raspers installed on more than five hundred haciendas. The market was largely controlled by International Harvester through its Yucatecan representative to whom soon most Yucatecan planters owed considerable debts. Labor for the growing industry was obtained through a vast system of debt peonage which drew between half and a third of the Maya-speaking population of the peninsula into work on the haciendas. Maya labor was supplemented by the introduction of Chinese and Korean laborers, and by Yaqui deported from Sonora to Yucatán after their last rebellion. On June 8, 1910, there had been an uprising in the east coast town of Valladolid, vaguely in favor of Madero's political reforms; it was put down in cold blood (Berzunza Pinto, 1956). The year 1911 had witnessed marginal risings in the hinterland. Yet the Porfirian oligarchy remained firmly in control of the state. In February 1915, however, a Constitutionalist Army of the Southeast, led by General Salvador Alvarado, disembarked in Yucatán, and defeated a local armed force sent against it. Alvarado immediately proceeded to decree an end to peonage, to promulgate labor laws, to initiate secular education, and to further municipal self-government. He also promoted labor organization and set up a commission to supervise the sale of sisal. This product provided a lucrative source of revenues for the Constitutionalists, since the onset of World War I had put a premium on Yucatecan supplies. To maintain this flow of income, Alvarado did nothing to alter the pattern of ownership and control in the sisal industry. Inconvenient agrarian rebels like those who had raised the flag of rebellion at Temax were jailed (Berzunza Pinto, 1962, 295). Yet Alvarado's resolute reforms "from above" found a wide echo in many parts of Mexico where peons were ardently awaiting the hour of their liberation.

Thus other advantages accrued to the Constitutionalist armies. Holding only peripheral positions within the country, on the Gulf Coast and in the far northwest, they were nevertheless in control of resources which could be turned into dollars with which to purchase arms: Tampico provided ever increasing quantities of oil, Yucatán had sisal. Veracruz, an easy gate of entry from the sea, offered income through customs duties. It is interesting to note in this regard how much this victorious strategy resembled the successful strategy followed by Benito Juárez, both in his struggle against the conservatives and later against the French. Use of Veracruz, in effect, allowed him to prevent consolidation of his enemies on the central plateau. Furthermore, Carranza and Obregón knew how to steer a clever middle course between the demands of the United States and Germany, soon to clash in a major war. Where Zapata had little understanding of international affairs, and Villa was outspokenly pro-American, the Constitutionalists could play the nationalist game, assuming an independent position between two rival camps. Finally, Obregón's generalship proved superior to that of Villa. Villa's fate was sealed in 1915 in the battle of Celaya, in which Obregón's numerically inferior troops won the day by turning Villa's predilection for massed cavalry charges and infantry attack to their own advantage. The well-entrenched Constitutionalist infantry, equipped with machine guns, cut the Villista charges to shreds. Obregón "had learned from the European war what Villa seemingly had not—massed attacks could not succeed against trenches, machine guns, and barbed wire" (Quirk, 1960, 224). On his own admission, Villa lost six thousand men killed at Celaya. Dead bodies, said an American observer of the occasion, "were strewn on both sides of the track as far as the eye could reach" (J. R. Ambrosins, quoted in Quirk, 1960, 225). On October 19, 1915, the United States decided to recognize Carranza. The revolutionary war continued, but Villa never recovered from the blow suffered at Celaya, and Zapata found himself increasingly isolated in his mountain redoubt.

As the tide began to turn in favor of the Constitutionalists, however, the liberal wing within the coalition also began to renege on its promises for reform. On January 1916 Carranza once again dissolved the red battalions and expelled the *Casa del Obrero Mundial* from the quarters of the Mexico City Jockey Club (now Sanborn's) where they had installed themselves. By August 1916 he felt strong enough to threaten the death sentence for strikers in industries which affected the public welfare. Yet the Carrancistas were clearly fighting a rear-guard action within their own forces. On the one hand, they could no longer afford to antagonize the military leaders in their own armies who had gained strength in the continued successes of the Constitutionalist cause. The Carranza cabinet was entirely made up of civilians, and could not afford to jeopardize their alliance with the more radical Obregón. On the other hand they fell victim to their own principles. When they issued the call for a constitutional assembly in Querétaro at the end of 1916, they barred from attendance not only Huerta men and Catholics, but also followers of Villa and Zapata.

> Yet the liberals allowed regional politics to dominate the result of the elections. Thus local leaders were elected, simple chieftains many of them, men who—like the conventionists, were agrarian radicals, with the obvious result that, from the beginning, the dream of a liberal convention and constitution was sentenced to die (Quirk, 1953, 525).

The resulting constitution bore the imprint of the radicals. Secular education, separation of Church and state, liquidation of the latifundium and land reform, wide-ranging labor legislation, and an assertion of the eminent domain of the nation over resources within the country were all written into constitutional provisions that became the law of the land. By that time the fate of the Revolution was also decided. Zapata himself was treacherously ambushed and assassinated in 1919. Carranza lost power and was assassinated in 1920; Obregón followed him into the presidency and the leadership of a more stable post-revolutionary Mexico committed to change and reform. Pancho Villa made his peace with Obregón in 1920 and retired to a farm in Chihuahua, where he was assassinated in 1923. The Revolution may have cost as many as two million lives (Cumberland, 1968, 241, 245–246). Yet with all its horror, it had laid the basis for a new Mexico in which—paradoxically—once again the principles of the defeated were to become the guidelines of the victors. Thus, says Robert Quirk,

> the inarticulate, militarily ineffectual Zapata accomplished in death what he could not win in life. His spirit lived on, and in a strange, illogical, but totally Mexican twist of fate, he became the greatest hero of the Revolution. In the hagiography of the Revolution the *caudillo* of Morelos continues to ride his white charger . . . (1960, 292–293).

The reforms themselves were initiated, with various ups and downs, over a twenty-year period. Just as it had taken a long time for the Mexican Revolution to define its program, so it took a long time for the abstract program to become institutional reality. The abolition of peonage created the legal condition for free labor mobility, but there was no general redistribution of land. Indian communities which had regained their land from the estates by force of arms—as in Morelos—were allowed to retain them, and communities which had clear title to land were permitted to regain their holdings; but massive land reform had to await the advent of the Cárdenas regime in 1934. Labor legislation put a measure of political leverage into the hands of an enlarged trade-union movement, but it received a stronger political voice only in exchange for political support of the new government. At the same time, under both Obregón and his successor Calles, the government slowly consolidated itself in power, weathering a number of military challenges from army leaders as well as from rural rebels in west-central Mexico who rose to defend clerical privileges against anti-clerical legislation. In 1929 Calles organized the National Revolutionary party. At first no more than a coalition of generals and political leaders who understood that they would hang separately if they did not hang together, it was to become later a flexible political instrument which allowed a measure of representation to various groups of sufficient political strength to make their voices heard in government councils. Cautious reform and political consolidation, in turn, made the government more able and willing to challenge the predatory American and British oil companies who operated on Mexican soil, and through the challenge to the foreign-owned companies also call into question foreign influence in Mexico in general. Yet this first challenge did not prove strong enough and fell back before foreign counterpressure. Calles, who followed Obregón as the undisputed boss of the "revolutionary family" for a time (1928–1934), reversed the trend toward reform and nationalism. Land and labor reform came to a standstill, foreign capital was once again favored over Mexican capital, and Mexico moved toward closer cooperation with the United States.

Retreat, however, lent renewed strength to the thrust for reform. Concessions to foreign capital and to the United States generated a widespread nationalist reaction, reinforced by the effects of the world-wide depression of 1929. General Lazaro Cárdenas, who succeeded Calles in 1934, opened the sluice gates to initiate land reform and labor organization on a massive scale. Cárdenas did what no Mexican leader had attempted before him: he dismantled the political power of the hacienda owners, and distributed hacienda lands among the peasantry. Before Cárdenas about 17 million acres of land had been redistributed; during the six years of his tenure in office this total was raised to 41 million acres. Most of this land was granted to village communities under communal forms of tenure (*ejidos*). Labor organization went on apace. Mexican capital was once again favored over foreign capital; Mexican capitalists became enthusiastic supporters of the regime. The rich oil fields of Mexico's eastern coast were expropriated, and foreign shareholders were deprived of their influence in the management of the national railway system. The vast mobilization of peasants and industrial workers in agrarian and industrial unions

E

provided the government with an instrument of great political power in its internal confrontation with the hacienda owners and in its external dealings with foreign governments, especially with the United States. The government party gained in strength through the inclusion of new peasant and labor representatives in its decision-making.

The Cárdenas years (1934–1940) thus laid the basis for a vigorous advance of Mexico's business and industry, especially in the period following upon the conclusion of World War II. Yet the sharp advance in one sector has again called attention to the relative stagnation of other parts of the society. Accelerated industrialization has produced a strong industrial and commercial elite, with extensive government connections. Land reform has once again become the economic stepchild: private landownership is favored over communal arrangements, and surplus funds have gone into industry, trade, and commercial private agriculture rather than into financial support for the *ejido* program. While industrial and urban growth has gone on apace, the countryside has once more fallen behind, reinforcing once again the gap between the Mexico Which Has and the Mexico Which Has Not, to use the phrase coined by the sociologist Pablo González Casanova. Foreign capital is once again welcome in the country. The government party has become as much an instrument of control as an instrument of representation. Within it interest groups—organized into formal associations of agrarians, workers, entrepreneurs, military, bureaucrats, and professionals—are linked to territorial groups, based on the several federated Mexican states. This linkage makes for a powerful executive, able to play off interest groups against territorial units and interest groups against each other. The final product bears a strong resemblance to the corporate state structure of fascist Italy or Spain, albeit with the rhetoric of social justice and socialism, causing some Mexican intellectuals to speak of a new Porfiriato.

Thus the Mexican Revolution produced, in the course of time, a new and stable center of power, from the manifold contradictions and oppositions of the past. The reform laws of the mid-nineteenth century had fostered private property in land as a means of underwriting the growth of the family-farm; but the land so freed from its social encumbrances merely intensified the growth of the lati-fundium. Thus the land-hungry large estates pushed ever more strongly against the remaining Indian communities and the small farms. The large estate with its bound labor also stood in marked contrast to a growing industry and transportation services, manned by free labor which, however, had not yet received the protection of effective labor legislation. These oppositions had also made them-selves felt in tension between the southern periphery—with its strong component of Indians organized into corporate communities —and the northern periphery—increasingly oriented toward com-mercialization and strongly nationalist—both ranged against the center, controlled by an increasingly inflexible bureaucracy. This central power group had sponsored a policy of commercialization and industrialization, but these processes had benefited only a small elite, while the new aspirants for power and the new interest groups thrown up by the process were granted neither a hearing nor representation. In contrast to other revolutions which we shall consider—notably those of Russia, China, and Viet Nam—the Mexican Revolution was not led by a tightly organized revolution-ary party endowed with a vision of a new society. While some ideological themes had been sounded in the course of the war—whether connected with the appeals of anarchism or with the Virgin of Guadalupe—these had remained muted within the gen-eral orchestration of violence. Again, in contrast to other cases, the revolutionary upheaval was wholly internal. The last time a foreign power interfered massively and outright in Mexican affairs had been almost fifty years before the Revolution; a brief episode of United States intervention through a landing in Veracruz in 1914 proved only a minor irritant. Factions of contenders for power emerged in the course of the struggle, rather than being present from the beginning. Initial success went to the peasant guerrillas of Morelos and the cowboy armies of the north, but final victory rewarded an elite which had created a viable army, demonstrated bureaucratic competence, and consolidated its control over the vital export sector of the economy. This elite also proved flexible enough to initiate agrarian and labor reforms demanded by the revolutionary generals within a larger policy of national economic progress, congruent with the interests of an expanding middle class of entrepreneurs and professionals. The result has been the formation of a strong central executive which fosters capitalist development, but is in a position to balance the claims of peasants and industrial workers against those of the entrepreneurs and the middle-class groups. In developing a political system of functional associations which crosscut territorial units within one overarching official party, the Mexican political system finally reproduced, under different historical and political circumstances, some aspects of the "parallel hierarchies" which—as we shall see—were to play such an important role in the Chinese and Vietnamese revolutionary movements.

TWO

RUSSIA

The Russian commune, such
as it exists in ancient Mos-
covia, is in fact an easy means
of gaining possession of the
soil on behalf of the masses.

Leroy-Beaulieu, 1876

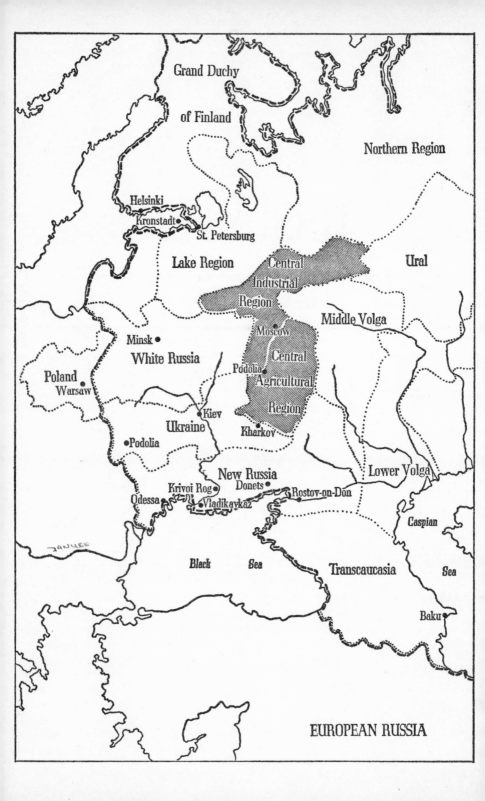

The development of Russian serfdom bears certain resemblances to the development of peonage in Mexico. There had been slaves in Russia, but by the sixteenth century, their number had become quite negligible. During the sixteenth century, however, there appeared in the area of the Moscow Rus a kind of peon bound by debt, an indentured worker on the land in the form of the *kabala kholop*, who worked the land either in return for a loan (*kabala*) or for some other form of assistance. As the plowland in the hands of lords expanded, lords began to exert more pressure to obtain a secure labor force, inducing more and more free or half-free peasants to accept debt bondage. This was usually done by lending out wasteland, together with loans of money and seed for fixed periods ranging from three to five years, to ten to twenty years, in return for obligatory labor on the lord's holding (*barshchina*), and for payments in kind or money (*obrok*). However, this system of increasing exploitation of the peasantry could not work as long as there remained an open frontier and as long as the peasant remained free to move away from his place of indenture. Nor could the system of migratory tillage be replaced by the more productive three-field system, as long as the peasant retained his mobility. Untrammeled movement from estate to estate or to the frontier was still common until the end of the sixteenth century; peasants were still able to repay their obligations and extinguish their debts. Often they were lured on by promises made by estate owners elsewhere, or even abducted. Continuous warfare and recurrent famines also further reinforced this migratory tendency of the Russian peasant. Sir John Maynard has written of the Russian peasant (*mujik*) that he has always been

> a peasant with a difference; a peasant in whom the nomad survived till yesterday, as much at home in Asia as in Europe. . . .
> There is something in him of the land-sailor, with a range from Minsk to Vladivostok, and with some of that flexibility of mind which a sailor acquires. The land led him on, as the inland sea led on the sailor, from headland to headland (1962, 31).

And he interprets the growth of serfdom as

> the story of the limitation of this "flitting," and of the organisation of the people for service, military and agricultural, under the control of a service squirearchy (1962, 32). . . .

> Lay the two aspects of Russian rural life side by side: the peasant who has the restlessness of the nomad in his blood, and the police-state which enforces upon him the static obligations of the serf status: the urge to be up and moving on the one hand, and the passport and the pursuing authority on the other: and you have the key to some of the contradictions of Russian history (1962, 33).

After passage of laws ever more restrictive of the peasant's right to free movement, the peasant was finally bound in full serfdom to a given estate in the legal code of 1649; and flight was made a criminal offense in 1658. There were numerous rebellions against this bondage, most often in conjunction with Cossack uprisings against the political center. Soviet historians have tended to equate peasant uprisings and the Cossack revolts of Bolotnikov (1606–1607), Razin (1667–1671), Bulavin (1707–1708), and Pugachev (1773–1775): but the prime movers in these movements were Cossacks reacting against the growing centralization of the state rather than the oppressed peasantry. None of the Cossack movements were directed against the institution of serfdom itself; rather, peasants in Cossack-dominated areas became Cosssacks, thus escaping from the peasantry rather than solving the problem of peasant oppression (see Yaresh, 1957). At the same time the Cossack uprisings benefited from peasant disturbances, and peasant disturbances in turn received an impetus from Cossack rebellion. Between the end of the Pugachev rebellion and the end of the eighteenth century, there were some 300 outbreaks in 32 provinces (Lyashchenko, 1949, 280), and there was never a time when the peasantry was completely quiescent. Between 1826 and 1861, there were 1,186 peasant uprisings, showing a steady increase with every five-year period (1949, 370). Nor did the Russian peasant forget his former condition of freedom. Before serfdom, St. George's Day on the twenty-sixth of November had been the traditional day for changing owners.

Even now, after three centuries of bondage, the *mujik* has not forgotten the feast day which once on a time restored him to freedom: the feast of St. George is incorporated in many proverbial expressions of disappointment (Leroy-Beaulieu, 1962, 11).

By mid-eighteenth century, the serfs composed a majority of the population: in 1762–1766, serfs composed 52.4 percent of a total rural population of 14.5 million in Great Russia and Siberia. By the end of the eighteenth century, the total male serf population stood at 10.9 million, a figure which remained nearly unchanged until emancipation from serfdom in 1861. At the time of Emancipation, serfs composed more than 55 percent of the rural population in the Central Agricultural Region, in Eastern White Russia, in the Western Ukraine, and in the Middle Volga Region; between 36 and 55 percent in Western White Russia, the Lake Region, the Central Industrial Region, the Eastern Ukraine, and the Lower Volga Region. Elsewhere percentages were lower (Lyashchenko, 1949, 311). Within the serf population there were two major categories: at the end of the eighteenth century, roughly half of the serfs belonged to individual squires, while somewhat less than half belonged to the state. The state serfs were somewhat better off than the private serfs: their payments were rendered in *obrok*, which was fixed at relatively moderate levels, and they were less exposed to the personal idiosyncrasies of individual squires. However, they constituted a labor reserve from which the rulers could make grants to private holders.

Nevertheless, Russian serf agriculture was not a great economic success. It depended entirely on the traditional and extensive agricultural technology of the peasantry; yields remained low and stationary throughout most of the nineteenth century. The ratio of yield to seed was 3.5 to 1 in 1801–1810, and 3.7 in 1861–1870 (Lyashchenko, 1949, 324). Any increase in income drawn from agriculture was thus won "through the quantitative expansion of its acreage and extensive grain raising by means of intensifying the exploitation of peasant labor, that is, by overburdening the peasant household still further" (1949, 323). There was no adequate cost accounting nor an economic adjustment to fluctuating markets. Political compulsions siphoned off whatever the peasant could produce.

As noted above, the two modes of using serf labor were *barshchina*, labor on the lord's fields with the peasant's own tools and livestock, and *obrok*, payment in kind. These often occurred in a variety of combinations; yet labor dues were most prevalent in the country of the black earth, while payment held sway in the non-black-soil provinces of the north. The black-earth country was fertile, and surpluses were derived in the main from agricultural operations. As grain exports grew, it was to the interests of the landlords in this region to maximize their landholdings and to increase the amount of peasant labor expended upon their lands. The amount of land allocated for peasant subsistence thus tended to be small; the plot allotted to each peasant "soul" seldom exceeded between 6.75 and 8.10 acres. The squires held more than 50 percent of the arable land. Throughout the nineteenth century, there was a tendency to raise the amount of peasant labor on squire land, from three days a week to four, five, or even six days. In addition, peasants had to work on construction projects and in brickmaking, while women produced linen and woolens. Peasants also had to supply carts and manpower to carry the squire's produce to market, an obligation which consumed 30 percent of their working time in winter, 8 percent in the summer months. On some farms, the squires were even successful in converting labor dues into outright wage labor, in which the worker did not have access to land, but received payment in food and clothing for work on the lord's domain.

In contrast to the system of labor dues, payment in kind or money prevailed in the non-black-soil provinces of the north where farming was both less productive and less profitable, but where peasant employment in home handicraft or town industries could yield payments in kind. Since land was less valuable than in the south, landowners retained only 20 to 25 percent of arable land and granted larger allotments per "soul," ranging on the average between 10.8 and 13.5 acres. This land enabled the peasant to feed himself and his family, while the dues in money or kind allowed the landlords to skim off the surplus produced by the peasant through a mechanism of social and political compulsion. Such payments also rose steadily during the period of serfdom. It was worth about 10 to 12.5 *rubls* on the average by the end of the eighteenth century; by the second decade of the nineteenth century their value had risen to 70 *rubls*.

In 1861 the serfs were freed in a major agrarian reform, stimulated by the fear voiced by Tsar Alexander II that "it is better to liberate the peasants from above" than to wait until they took their freedom by risings "from below." The pressures for emancipation were felt differently in the black-soil south and in the non-black-soil north. In the black-soil areas where cultivation was productive and profitable it was in the interests of the landowners to appropriate as much of the arable land as they could, and to leave the peasant as little as possible, thus forcing him to labor on the noble estates. In the north agriculture was poor and land of little value, but where the landlord's surplus had been derived from the payment of dues in kind or money, it was to the interest of the landlord to rid himself of unproductive land and to seek instead maximum compensation for the personal freedom of his serfs. Mediating between these divergent interests, Alexander II and his advisers—acting in the interest of the state as a whole—sought to avoid a situation in which the serfs would gain their personal liberty, but lose their land. With liberty instead of land,

> the peasant would have recovered his liberty only to fall into a condition often more miserable than that which he endured in his time of his bondage. He would have remained for years, maybe for centuries, totally debarred from the holding of land. All this host of freedom would have been turned into a nation of proletarians. . . . By giving land to the serfs, it was confidently hoped to avoid proletariate, and to avoid proletariate was to steer clear of the social and political commotions of the West (Leroy-Beaulieu, 1962, 27–28).

The upshot was a compromise in which the peasant was not deprived of all land, while at the same time being made to pay for the liberation of his person. To meet the differential exigencies of the landowners in north and south, the compromise was applied differently in the black-soil and non-black-soil belts. In the black-soil provinces the allotment of land per person granted was generally smaller than it had been before the reform; in sixteen black-soil provinces the average allotment before the reform was 9.18 acres; after it, it was 6.75 acres. In the non-black-soil industrial provinces, on the other hand, where *obrok* had dominated, the reverse was true. The landlords benefited by ridding themselves of unproductive land, transferring this to the peasants on the basis of excessive valuations. In eight such provinces, the average prereform allotment per person had been 10 acres; after the reform, it was 11.6 acres.

The full allotment was granted to the peasantry only with additional stipulations. The peasants, if they possessed sufficient funds, could buy their liberty outright. To aid in the process, the state advanced 80 percent of the necessary sum; the peasant had to furnish the remaining 20 percent. These advances by the state were to be repaid by the peasants in the course of forty-nine years at a rate of 6 percent annual interest. Unfortunately, this venture was not a success. Even where peasants were able to raise the required 20 percent, they met great difficulties in keeping up the necessary payments and fell increasingly into arrears. These increased from 22 percent of the total annual payments in 1875 to 119 percent by the end of the century (Robinson, 1949, 96). Still other peasants became "temporarily obligated" persons who had to continue to pay dues to the squires of twelve *rubls* per full allotment in *obrok* country or to furnish forty days of labor a year for males and thirty for females. By 1881 there remained, in thirty-seven provinces, more than three million peasants under such temporary obligations. Their social situation had thus changed little; a Russian journalist quipped that they would require still "another emancipation" (Leroy-Beaulieu, 1962, 43). Finally, there were many peasants who accepted a curtailed allotment in exchange for their complete freedom, thus buying their personal freedom at the cost of economic impoverishment.

The reform was thus a great disappointment to many.

When the manifesto of the 19th of February, 1861, was published, setting forth the conditions of the emancipation, the peasants could not conceal their disappointment. In the churches, where the imperial manifesto, announcing freedom, was read to them, they murmured aloud; more than one shook his head, exclaiming, "what sort of liberty is that?" (Leroy-Beaulieu, 1962, 29–30).

In many localities the peasants refused to believe that the manifesto was genuine. There were troubles, and troops had to be called in to disperse the angry crowds.

It was rumored in the villages that the manifesto read in the churches was a fabrication of the landlords, and that the genuine Emancipation Act would be forthcoming later on; there may even yet be peasants who are looking for it to appear. There assuredly are many who in the long winter evenings dream of a new emancipation with a redistribution of lands, gratuitous this time (1962, 30).

Still several years later, "certain prophets from the people . . . announced that, by the will of God, the land was soon to be made over to the peasants, with nothing to pay" (1962, 31). With notable insight, Leroy-Beaulieu noted that these agitations followed from premises which had "a semi-juridical character" (1962, 72).

It is evident that in the people, obscurely, but down to a great depth, a tradition has survived, a memory of a time when landed property was not yet, or not to any great extent, in the hands of the nobles, when nearly all the meadow lands and the forest lands in particular were used indiscriminately and in an undefined way by all. For one brief instant the peasant has had a vision of the return of this good old time, and even now he firmly cherishes the conviction that the government, if it had the right and power to suppress serfdom, has the no less incontestable right and power to change all other conditions of landed property, at least such as are galling to the peasant (1962, 73).

Thus, the attacks of radicals on the inadequate reform

are at one in this with the *mujik's* secret instincts, and strive with might and main to second them still more by demonstrating to him that another expropriation of the noble landholders and a redistribution of the land will be the natural sequel and clinching of the task left incomplete at the first installment (1962, 70).

While the Emancipation made the peasant legal owner of his own allotment, transferring the right to ownership from the landlord to the peasant, it did not, however, at the same time remove the manifold limitations placed on the use of peasant property by his fellow peasants. The new holding, severed from its vertical tie to the landlord, remained subject to the demands of the village Commune, the *mir*. If anything, the new legislation strengthened the commune as one of the bulwarks against the spread of social disorder.

The persistence of the *mir* in Russia—and of communal forms of organization among peasants elsewhere, as in Mexico—inspired a vast romantic literature extolling supposed peasant communalism, as if individual peasants never strove to maximize their individual advantages. Antiromanticists, on the other hand, pointed to the numerous symptoms of peasant self-centeredness to discredit this picture of group warmth and solidarity. In reality, communal forms of organization do not abolish individual striving; they merely strive to control them. Conversely, a rampant individualism could sometimes subjugate the communal organization to its own purposes, as when an oligarchy of powerful peasants seized control of a commune and used it to bend others to their purposes. We must not, therefore, think of peasant communalism and individualism as mutually exclusive. Rather, they are contingent upon each other; they often work against each other in mutual constraint within a common setting.

By throwing its support to the maintenance of the commune as the chief unit within the rural framework of organization, therefore, the state also turned each commune into a field of battle between mutually dependent and yet divergent social tendencies.

How was the *mir* organized, and what were its functions? It usually was formed by former serfs and their descendants settled in a single village, though on occasion a village comprised more than one commune or one commune might in turn comprise a number of villages. Within the framework of the commune, each household had a right to an allotment. Before the emancipation, each household within the commune was entitled to an allotment of commune land; in addition, each household held its house and kitchen garden in hereditary tenure. There was no collective cultivation; each household farmed its allotment on its own. Rights to pasture, and sometimes to meadows and forest, however, were held jointly by the commune. Finally, in Great Russia and Siberia the commune had the power to reallot land at intervals among its constituent households. Approximately three-fourths of the peasant households in the fifty provinces of European Russia—not counting Congress Poland and Finland—held more than four-fifths of the land in "repartitional" tenure. Hereditary tenure predominated in the Ukraine and the western provinces.

The principles governing repartition differed from region to region. While it was usual to reallot land every few years, a given commune could refrain from reallotment at any time, retaining its power to reallot in the future. According to Lazar Volin (1940, 125–127), population pressure was an important factor in bringing about reallotment. In the 1880's, 65 percent of 6,830 communes in sixty-six scattered districts of European Russia had not repartitioned their land; but during the period 1897–1902 only 12 percent failed to do so. Most of them (59 percent) repartitioned on the basis of males in the family, with a minority repartitioning on the basis of working adults (8 percent), on the total number of souls in the household (19 percent), while 2 percent repartitioned only partially. As long as the commune claimed the rights to reallot, it placed severe restrictions on the freedom of the peasant to use his land as his interest dictated. The peasant could not sell, mortgage, or inherit land without consent of the entire commune. Nor could the peasant refuse to accept a new allotment, less productive than the one held before. The commune also limited the right of the peasant to grow what crops he wanted by enforcing a rigid cropping system. Fields were divided into strips, in order to equalize opportunities with regard to soil, topography, or distance from village; any given peasant holding consisted of strips in various fields. The strips in any one field were planted with the same crop in three-field rotation; they were unenclosed by fences, and when cultivation was over, were opened to common pasture at the same time.

In its everyday operation, the commune enjoyed the most complete autonomy. Wallace has said that

> the higher authorities not only abstain from all interference in the allotment of the Communal lands, but remain in profound ignorance as to which system the Communes habitually adopt. . . . In spite of the systematic and persistent efforts of the centralized bureaucracy to regulate minutely all departments of the national life, the rural Communes, which contain about five-sixths of the population, remain in many respects entirely beyond its influence, and even beyond its sphere of vision (1908, 114–115).

It was governed by a council of all heads of households, called the *shkod,* from *shkodit',* to come together. At the head of the council stood the village elder or *starosta,* whose function it was to formulate the consensus of the village assembly and to represent it in dealings with outsiders.

Wallace has described for us how such a village council operated:

> The simple procedure, or rather the absence of all formal procedure, at the Assemblies, illustrates admirably the essentially practical character of the institution. The meetings are held in the open air, because in the village there is no building—except the church, which can be used only for religious purposes—large enough to contain all the members; and they almost always take place on Sundays or holidays, when the peasants have plenty of leisure. Any open space may serve as a Forum. The discussions are occasionally very animated, but there is rarely any attempt at speech-making. If any young member should show an inclination to indulge in oratory, he is sure to be unceremoniously interrupted by some of the older members, who have never any sympathy with fine talking. The assemblage has the appearance of a crowd of people who have accidentally come together and are discussing in little groups subjects of local interest. Gradually some one group, containing two or three peasants who have more moral influence than their fellows, attracts the others, and the discussion becomes general. Two or more peasants may speak at a time, and interrupt each other freely—using plain, unvarnished language, not at all parliamentary—and the discussion may become a confused, unintelligible din; but at the moment when the spectator imagines that the consultation is about to be transformed into a free fight,

the tumult spontaneously subsides, or perhaps a general roar of laughter announces that some one has been successfully hit by a strong *argumentum ad hominem*, or biting personal remark. In any case there is no danger of the disputants coming to blows. No class of men in the world are more good-natured and pacific than the Russian peasantry. . . . Theoretically speaking, the Village Parliament has a Speaker, in the person of the Village Elder. The word Speaker is etymologically less objectionable than the term President, for the personage in question never sits down, but mingles in the crowd like the ordinary members. Objection may be taken to the word on the ground that the Elder speaks much less than many other members, but this may likewise be said of the Speaker of the House of Commons. Whatever we may call him, the Elder is officially the principal personage in the crowd, and wears the insignia of office in the form of a small medal suspended from his neck by a thin brass chain. His duties, however, are extremely light. To call to order those who interrupt the discussion is no part of his functions. If he calls an honourable member "Durak" (blockhead), or interrupts an orator with a laconic "Moltchi!" (hold your tongue!), he does so in virtue of no special prerogative, but simply in accordance with a time-honored privilege, which is equally enjoyed by all present, and may be employed with impunity against himself. Indeed, it may be said in general that the phraseology and the procedure are not subjected to any strict rules. The Elder comes prominently forward only when it is necessary to take the sense of the meeting. On such occasions he may stand back a little from the crowd and say, "Well, Ladno! ladno!" that is to say, "Agreed! agreed!" (1908, 116–117).

This quote exhibits both the mood of egalitarianism of the commune and its mode of achieving consensus. The achievement of unanimity produced

a profound sense of satisfaction and of village solidarity, and the members of the village assembled at the *mir* disperse without a vote having been taken, with no committee formed and yet the feeling that each man knows what is expected of him (Gorer and Rickman, 1951, 233).

The commune also had functions in addition to those involved in regulating agriculture. It elected the elder, the tax collector of the community, the community watchman, and the herb boy.

F

Jointly responsible for taxes since 1722, it supervised the tax performance of its members. It voted to admit new members, and issued permits for those who wished to leave, after satisfying itself that the emigrants furnished security for fulfillment of liabilities, past and future. Men could be recalled if they failed to pay taxes: the commune could hire out a member of the defaulting household to work off the tax burden; or it could remove an ineffective head of household and appoint another to be head in his place. The commune prepared and signed all contracts between commune and outsiders, or between commune and any of its members. Finally, it exercised fierce social controls over the conduct of its members, ranging from corporal punishment in the case of nonpayment of taxes to public shaming. "The spirit of their community . . . gave the members strength when they were in accord with it, and they lived in misery and isolation when they broke, in thought or mood, with the opinion and sentiment of their neighbors" (Gorer and Rickman, 1951, 59).

But the *mir* was more than a form of social organization. Its role as a kind of collective superego imparted to it a truly religious aura. The term *mir* signifies both commune and universe, comparable to the Greek word *kosmos*. Sir John Maynard has suggested that it would not have been inappropriate to translate *mir* as "congregation," and says:

> The idea that a congregation of the faithful, not necessarily including ecclesiastics, is the repository of truth, enters deeply into Russian thought, is the origin of *sobornost*, perhaps the most characteristic and fundamental doctrine of Russian orthodoxy, and has passed by strange and unexpected ways into the mental equipment of the modern Communist (1962, 40).

Instead of the Western concept of truth as a series of approximations allowing of negotiations, the *mir* was seen as being in possession of absolute truth, represented by the practice of achieving unanimous decisions in the village assembly (Gorer and Rickman, 1951, 233).

Half-secular and half-religious, the commune ideally functioned as a machine for the equalization of opportunities among its members. It was, in Leroy-Beaulieu's words, an impregnable stronghold for small proprietors. Common property is inalienable and so constitutes a sort of entail, with this difference that, whereas family entail ensures the future of only the first-born of the family, communal inheritance provides for all the members of the community. In both cases unborn generations are protected against the thriftlessness of the living, the children against the father's wrongdoing or improvidence. There is a degree of destitution or disaster below which a father cannot drag down his descendants or himself. To the disinherited the *mir* offers a shelter. This is the light in which the peasants themselves regard the matter, and that is why those of them who have achieved competence and become individual landholders, hesitate to go out of the commune. If they cannot attend to their lot, they let it or give the use of it to others, looking on the communal lands as a safety plank for their children or for themselves, should their private fortunes ever be wrecked (1962, 173).

In addition to setting a minimum floor under a man's livelihood, the commune also equalized tax burdens, by laying down the

law to the rich, forcing on them supplementary lots and thus compelling them to pay more than their share of the dues. In the north, where the peasants frequently make their living chiefly by industry and trade, it is no rare thing for a commune to let in a particularly skilled artisan or a more than usually successful tradesman for two lots, i.e. for a double quota of taxes, which is but another way of taxing capital or income (1962, 137).

But twenty years after the Emancipation the equalizing operations of the village had not succeeded in stemming the process of differentiation. The well-off, composing 20 percent of all households, had clearly achieved a dominant position in concentrating land allotments, and in purchasing or renting additional land. Because these households were generally larger, comprising between 26 and 36 percent of the rural population, they also received larger allotments where allotments were given out on the basis of "souls." Moreover, they had bought land of their own, often from the nobility which between 1877 and 1905 lost through sales nearly one-third of their land (Robinson, 1949, 131). These 20 percent of peasant households thus held, by the end of the century, between 60 and 99 percent of purchased land in the various provinces. Again, they were the chief renters of land from their poor fellow villagers. In the different provinces, they came to control between 49 and 83 percent of the total rented land, while the village poor in turn accounted for between 63 to 98 percent of all the land let out for rent. Thus, by the end of the century, the rich peasants used between 35 and 50 percent of all land; the middle peasants who made up 30 percent of all peasant households used between 20 and 45 percent of land; the poor who constituted 50 percent of all households used only 20 to 30 percent of all land. The top 20 percent, finally, also accounted for one-half of all commercial-industrial establishments, and constituted between 48 and 78 percent of all households using hired laborers (Lyashchenko, 1949, 457–458).

Among these well-off peasants there were also many who became moneylenders to the poor. "There are in these Russian villages," says Leroy-Beaulieu,

> men who would be called in the West *exploiteurs*, vampires: enterprising, clever men, who fatten themselves at the cost of the community. The *mujik* has for them the frightfully expressive name of "*mir*-eaters" (*miro-yedy*). In many governments—those of Kaluga, Saratof, and others—most villages are pictured as being under the control of two or three wealthy peasants, who beguile the commune out of its best lands "for a song"—or for no compensation at all . . . it is usually through debt that the poor fall into the power of the rich. The vampire extends to the peasant reduced to want through improvidence, sickness, or accident, loans beyond his power of repayment. The frequent failures of crops in the southeast are a standing danger to the needy, a standing opportunity for the unscrupulous rich. The insolvent debtor is compelled to give up to his creditor, often for a nominal price, a lot which he has no longer the means of tilling. Liquor is the bait most freely used, and the keeper of the *kabak* (saloon-keeper) the habitual "*mir*-eaters." Usury is the ulcer that gnaws at the peasants' vitals, and collective tenure is not free from blame in this (1962, 137–138).

Since land could not be mortgaged or attached as security for loans, credit remained personal, granted at the rate of 10 percent per month, and often reaching 150 percent per annum (1962, 138).

Since the *mir*-eaters increasingly came to dominate the villages economically, they also came to dominate them socially and politically. They became truly "the masters of the village." The meetings of the commune gave formal recognition to all members on an equal basis, but the peasant well understood that the will of the powerful was more important than the will of the poor. This development of a village oligarchy dovetailed, furthermore, with the growing power of the village elder after Emancipation. Where he had been a mere agent of the collective village will before the reform, after 1861 he was made subordinate to the district superintendent of police, and given police powers in his own village. Since the rural police were underpaid, the *mir*-eaters could frequently buy their cooperation, just as they could ensure the appointment of one of their henchmen to the position of village elder. Thus economic differentiation was accompanied also by differentiation in the ability to affect village decisions.

With the peasant population compressed on reduced amounts of land, the communes began to function as veritable pressure cookers of demand and discontent. The peasants began to buy land and to lease land, frequently from the nobility. The peasant share of total land held rose from 32 to 47 percent between 1877 and 1917, while that of the nobility fell from 22 percent in 1877 to 11 percent in 1917, prompting Treadgold to remark (1957, 41–42) that "if large landholding was the chief culprit of the agrarian problem, then the Revolution may have killed it, but it was already dying." Some peasants bought such land individually, but more than two-thirds of such purchases between 1877 and 1905 were made by communes, acting on behalf of their members. The peasants also found that they frequently did not possess enough pasture and forest land, which often had remained in the hands of the squires after Emancipation. Peasants on their own behalf, peasant associations, and communes thus began to lease both land and such additional and necessary resources. Such leasing merely increased the impression on the part of the peasantry that the nobility served no useful function (Maynard, 1962, 71). In the spring of 1902 and in 1905 in the black-soil provinces disorders would flare most heavily in peasant communes adjoining large estates and linked to them by leases or other economic ties (Owen, 1963, 8). Yet buying and leasing cost money, and for many peasants this remained the rarest of substances. Population was steadily on the rise—a trend reinforced in part by the fact that heads of larger households could claim larger shares in reallotment—but the amount of land per capita available to the peasantry declined by one-third between Emancipation and 1905 (Owen, 1963, 6). Often, moreover, the peasantry had been able to acquire only the poorer land. Many peasants lacked money to buy and lease land and pasture, and were forced instead to buy wood for fuel, straw for fuel, bedding, and roofing, and hay for stall-fed animals. Many of them had to give up animal husbandry altogether. At the same time taxes continued on the rise, drawing increasing numbers into a money economy in which their participation was at the same time curtailed by the scarcity of that rarest of resources. There was a steady increase in small dwarf-size holdings, justifying those critics who had condemned the communes as "national agricultural poorhouses" (Leroy-Beaulieu, 1962, 174).

At the same time, the commune remained for the peasant at once a shield against the besetting problems of the world, and a corporate body capable of acting for him and on his behalf. To the peasant, dreaming of more land and resources in his separate hut (*izba*), it also began to suggest the possibility of collective action. "Even now," prophesied Leroy-Beaulieu in 1876,

> when he as yet turns a deaf ear to all the "nihilistic" preachings, is not the *mujik* inclined to think himself despoiled in favor of the *pomieshchik*, to dream, for himself and for his children, of new distributions of lands? So that, instead of closing forever the door of the villager's *izba* against the revolutionist, the *mir* may very well some day open it for them. It will be in the name of the *mir*, represented to us as the safeguard of society, that the peasant will be invited to "round up" his lot, to gather all the lands into a communal domain. The Russian commune, such as it exists in ancient Moscovia, is in fact an easy means of gaining possession of the soil on behalf of the masses . . . (1962, 186).

Thus it was no coincidence that among twenty governments in which the depredations against landlords were heaviest in the revolutionary autumn of 1905, sixteen showed a predominance of repartitional tenure over hereditary holdings by individual households (Robinson, 1949, 153). They were, moreover, much less common in the non-black-soil areas where there existed alternative sources of employment in artisan and industrial work, but were at their most concentrated in the black-soil provinces which relied so heavily upon agriculture (Lyashchenko, 1949, 742). In 1905, the procurator of the Kharkov Court of Appeals Hrulov wrote that

> there is to be noticed almost universally among the peasant population a conviction amounting to a popular legend, of their having a kind of natural right to the land, which sooner or later must pass into their possession (quoted in Owen, 1963, 2).

Trying to account for the peasant revolts of 1902 and 1905, the government became aware that the realloting commune, far from forming an effective bulwark against social disorder, had in fact furthered it. In 1906 it moved against the commune with a plan for agrarian reform, designed to dismantle the traditional communal structure. Landholdings in communes which had given up land reallotment were converted into the private holdings of individual families. In communes which still reallotted land any landholder was given the right to request at any time that the land to which he was entitled by redistribution be granted to him in personal ownership. Moreover, he was entitled to receive this land in a single block, rather than in widely scattered strips. Finally, entire communes could convert to individual ownership by a vote of their members. The intention was to create a sturdy Russian yeomanry by building—in the words of Stolypin, the author of the reform—on "the strong and sober," in order to

> divert peasants from the division of the land of the nobles by the division of their own land for the benefit of the most prosperous part of the peasantry (Paul Miliukov, quoted in Volin, 1960, 303).

The reform did achieve a measure of success, especially in the west and in the Central Industrial Region where many sold their land and moved into industrial employment, and in the steppe-borderlands of the south where the commune was weak and commercial farming flourished under the impetus of the Western European grain market. In all some three million peasants left the communes. Paradoxically, however, the reform did not succeed in the Russian heartland; there it may have even strengthened the commune by measures designed to slough off the potential dissidents. The reform affected a substantial reduction in the number of the village poor; some 900,000 peasants took out titles to their lands, sold them, and then left the village. At the same time, the reform allowed the more prosperous to "separate" and to set up successful commercial farms outside its limits. The net effect was to leave in the communes some six million peasants unwilling or unable to make the transition to independent individual farming. In most cases they did not have the wherewithal to acquire the land and equipment needed to establish an independent farm; or they continued to pasture their livestock on commune lands, an advantage greatly reduced or absent on independent farms; or they did not wish to forgo the security which came from holding strips in scattered areas as insurance against blight and climatic factors, whereas a consolidated holding meant putting all one's eggs in one consolidated basket. Thus, wrote A. Tyumenev in 1925,

> the communal egalitarianism which Stolypin feared and was determined to destroy, persisted in the parts of the old Moscow Centre where it did not cease to menace the abodes of the squires. Stolypin's policy was most successful on the before-mentioned outer fringes of settlement where its political aim was least in evidence . . . it was the non-differentiation of the Centre, the predominance of a compact phalanx of so-called "middle peasantry" which guaranteed and still guarantees the power of the Communist government (quoted in Owen, 1963, 144–145).

Not only did the reform here work to reduce differentiation in the communes but it succeeded also in setting that "compact phalanx of so-called 'middle peasantry' " against the more prosperous "separators." It greatly exacerbated the invidious comparison between the lands of the prosperous outside the communes and conditions within: "there was a residue of population in the rural areas, which gazed longingly on the new improvements but was powerless to share in them" (Owen, 1963, 71). Envy and hatred of the separators who had withdrawn from the communes' land previously accessible to all and were using it to their private advantage would, in the Revolution of 1917, issue in mass movements to deprive the new yeomanry of their land and to drive them back into the communes by use of force and violence.

The commune thus survived the vicissitudes of change, as did the institution of the village council and of the village, as a self-determining little world, founded on consensus. Centralized at the top, the society was at the bottom an aggregate of innumerable village communes, in many ways beyond the influence, beyond the sphere of vision (Wallace, 1908, 115) of the state. This social autonomy was, moreover, reinforced by considerable autonomy in the religious sphere. Stephen and Ethel Dunn have noted that

> the official religion administered by the Russian Orthodox Church, and the peasant cycle which centered on festivals of pagan origin, were functionally independent. The priest did not take a prominent part in any of the popular festivals, except at Easter, when he made the rounds collecting a stipulated contribution from each household (1967, 29).

Beyond this:

> Due to organizational difficulties and shortages of personnel, the Orthodox Church failed to maintain active control over many rural areas which were nominally Orthodox. Therefore, quite apart from the question of the peasant festival cycle and sectarian influence, peasant religious practice deviated from the official church ceremonies. These deviations sometimes went so far that peasants who considered themselves Orthodox were regarded as schismatics by the Church hierarchy, and were treated accordingly. This is a particularly significant example of the way in which the cultural screen between the peasant and the urban resident operates. The operation of the screen in prerevolutionary Russia produced in effect two cultures in one country, both in point of religion and in other areas of life (1967, 30).

This gap between Church and believer was reinforced still further by the religious schism (*raskol*) which in 1666 divided the Old

Believers (*raskolniki*) from the Orthodox Church. Affected by trends toward centralization and modernization, the Old Believers broke with the Church over such ostensibly minor matters as to whether the sign of the cross should be made with two or three fingers, whether "alleluia" should be recited twice or three times, whether Jesus should be spelled ısus or ıısus. Although a few nobles joined the movement, it remained "overwhelmingly a peasant movement," with "a lay cult depending exclusively on the intellectual and moral resources of the countryside" (Vakar, 1962, 24). The Old Believers were strongly antistate, identifying the tsar with the Antichrist. They came to believe in a Kingdom of Earth in the mythical White Waters, governed by a white tsar, who would one day come forth to rule over Russia. Recognizing no law but their own beliefs and customs, they also gave ready asylum to escaped serfs and other victims of the social order. They held strong ideas of a social and economic egalitarianism which were to blossom in the Revolution in the establishment of egalitarian communes with common property and dedicated to the joys of sharing (Wesson, 1963, 8). Living "within the Russian state, they did not belong to it. They constituted a species of passive anarchists within the empire" (Vakar, 1962, 24). Their absolute numbers before the Revolution are unknown. They are estimated at about one-third of the Christian population in the nineteenth century, and at about one-fourth at the time of the Revolution (1962, 24). In 1928, their number was held to be nine million. There is no doubt that their peasant millenarianism was a strong factor in the success of the Revolution. Leon Trotsky (1932, III, 30) refers to

> the work of the sectarian ideas which had taken hold of millions of peasants. "I knew many peasants," writes a well-informed author, "who accepted . . . the October revolution as the direct realization of their religious hopes."

It must be noted that in addition to the original Old Believers there also existed other sects which had sprung from the main trunk of the *Raskol* movement such as the *Molokani* or milk drinkers, the *Subbotniki* or Sabbatarians, the *Skoptsy*, and the *Doukhobors*. To their influence was added that of the Baptists or

Stundists who burst into activity in 1824. These sectarians numbered six million in 1917 (Wesson, 1963, 71).

The currents of reform created yet another source of opposition to the centralized structure of tsardom, the rural institutions called *zemstvos*. According to the statute of 1864, these *zemstvos* were to be representative bodies entrusted with local functions, previously furnished, at least in part, by the landlords, such as the construction and maintenance of roads, the creation and staffing of educational and medical facilities, and the functions now subsumed under the concept of agricultural extension services. The formal conception of the *zemstvos* stood in curious contradiction to their actual function. They were to be representative organizations within a centralized autocracy without constitution. Hence the central power worked to limit their political functioning in every possible way. Created in part to give a voice to the peasantry, that voice was limited by electoral rules which granted majority representation to the numerically inferior nobility and urban population—the peasants at the beginning held only 40 percent of all seats, a percentage which was further reduced to 30 in 1890. Set up to function on the district level, they lacked any machinery to implement decision on levels lower than the district; for this they had to rely on the civil and police officers of the central administration. Similarly, they could petition the ministry of interior on technical matters but had no direct access to the tsar and could not raise wider political issues. Their presiding officers were appointed and given the right to end discussions and close meetings, a prerogative they came to share with the provincial governor who was gradually empowered not only to suspend meetings but to review elections to the *zemstvos* and pass on appointments made by them, in the interest of weeding out "ill-intentioned persons." Thus the structure was representative in form, but functionally "without foundation—floating in the air," and "without a roof" (Miliukov, 1962, 213).

Politically impotent, the *zemstvos* contributed, however, a number of vital social services, and attracted into these services an enthusiastic and able segment of the intelligentsia. For the first time, secular schools were established in Russian villages, and the rural schoolteachers

> were accustomed to consider their work as a kind of social duty which was to be performed, not as a means of livelihood or as a technical profession, but as a high vocation, chosen by their own initiative, for the good of the country (1962, 160).

In the same spirit labored the physicians and surgeons, the statisticians and agronomists. Yet their roles were necessarily contradictory. The *zemstvos*, islands of self-government in a sea of autocracy, could not but threaten that autocracy by the very example of their existence. Inevitably, men came to hope for an extension of representative government. Inevitably, too, the *zemstvo* intelligentsia—

> men who dealt with actualities, men connected by their day's work with the lowest classes of the population, knowing its wants, sharing its sorrows, sympathizing with all its miseries (1962, 212)

—came to be the chief bearers of that hope, with its promise of greater fruition of their work. Equally inevitable seems to have been the response of the government when the *zemstvos* addressed the tsar with their petitions. "I am aware," said Nicholas II in 1895, shortly after his accession to the throne,

> that in certain meetings of the *zemstvos* voices have lately been raised by persons carried away by absurd illusions ("senseless dreams . . .") as to the participation of the *zemstvo* representatives in matters of internal government. Let all know that, in devoting all my strength to the welfare of the people, I intend to protect the principle of autocracy as firmly and unswervingly as did my late and never-to-be forgotten father (1962, 239).

Equally impressive in the hindsight which history permits us, is the answer of the liberals who had hoped for an expansion of *zemstvo* autonomy:

> If autocracy in word and deed proclaims itself identical with the omnipotence of bureaucracy, if it can exist only so long as society is voiceless, its cause is lost. It digs its own grave, and soon or late—at any rate, in a future not very remote—it will fall beneath the pressure of living social forces. . . . You challenged the

zemstvos, and with them Russian society, and nothing remains for them now but to choose between progress and faithfulness to autocracy. . . . You first began the struggle; and the struggle will come (1962, 240).

In that struggle, many of the disillusioned *zemstvo* "third element"—as the *zemstvo* intelligentsia had come to be known, as a third grouping after the state bureaucrats and the elected representatives—were to throw in their lot with the revolutionaries and the cause of the revolution which would overturn the old regime.

Yet Russia in the nineteenth century was not only a country of peasantry; it was also caught up in a rapid movement toward ever-increasing industrialization. To understand the full impact of this development, we must know that there had long existed a close link between agriculture and industry ever since the seventeenth century, especially in non-black-soil provinces of the north. There agriculture had yielded but little on the prevailing poor soils, and its meager output had to be supplemented by home industries such as weaving, woodworking, pottery manufacture, basketry, or metal-work, or by seasonal employment in lumbering, mining, droving, or hauling freight. By the end of the eighteenth century, between one-fifth and one-third of the adult male population in the non-black-soil provinces had already shifted to nonagricultural means of livelihood (Lyashchenko, 1949, 271). However, the development of a permanent labor force was greatly handicapped by the restrictions on free labor contracts imposed by serfdom. Until 1835 a landowner could at any time recall his serfs from industrial employment to work back on the farm. Thus in the third decade of the eighteenth century workers in textile mills whose parents had also been workers, still numbered only about 10 percent of all workers employed (1949, 286–287).

These limitations reinforced a continuing tie to the land. The prevailing patterns of industrial employment which crystallized under these conditions were either home industry, organized on a putting-out system, or seasonal migration to industrial employment, coupled with seasonal return to agricultural labor. This seasonal swing between farm and factory was known as *otkhodnichestvo,* a pattern which has continued into the twentieth century (Dunn and Dunn, 1963, 329–332). At the end of the agricultural season in the fall, groups of males would set out for work in industry, returning home in time for the spring sowing. These groups developed a characteristic form of organization, known as *artel'*. The members of the group

> contracted with each other, and collectively with an employer, to work at a fixed rate in cash and perquisites to share the proceeds equally. Contracts were concluded by an agent (*artel'shchik*), who acted for the group. All members of the *artel'* performed specific functions; the younger boys served as cooks and general helpers. This form of organization was used also in lumbering and fishing operations, although in these cases the *artel'* did not work as a collective employee but as a collective entrepreneur. But the principle of equal division of proceeds still applied (Dunn and Dunn, 1967, 10).

By 1860, one-third of the 800,000 industrial workers were still serfs; but the Emancipation gave a mighty impetus to the formation of a permanent and free industrial labor force. It created a labor pool of peasants who had no land at all—a number estimated at more than 2.5 million males—who needed to find additional employment. In addition, there were probably about a million peasants who had received allotments of less than one *desiatin*, or 2.7 acres, and who needed to find additional employment to augment their income. By the end of the nineteenth century there were some 3 million persons in industrial employment (Lyashchenko, 1949, 420). The increase of workers in industry was especially striking in the largest factories. Whereas in 1866, there were 644 factories employing more than 100 workers, by 1890 there were more than 951 such factories. At the same time, the number of factories employing more than 1,000 workers rose from 42 factories, employing 62,800 workers, to 99 factories, employing 213,300. The percentage of all workers employed in factories using 1,000 workers and more thus increased from 27.1 percent of the total number of workers in 1866 to 45.9 percent of all workers in 1890.

Such a concentration of workers in giant factories is notable, especially when we compare Russia to other countries. "In the concentration of production," says Manya Gordon (1941, 354),

> Russia as early as 1895 had surpassed Germany. In that year the wage earners in Russian factories with more than 500 employees constituted 42 per cent of all workers, whereas in Germany these large establishments accounted for only 15 per cent of the working population. Workers in establishments with 10 to 50 employees were 16 per cent in Russia and 32 per cent in Germany. By 1912 the workers in Russian factories with more than 500 employees were 53 per cent of the whole. As late as 1925 in Germany the establishments with 1000 or more employees had 30 per cent of all workers in factories with more than 50 hands. Russia as early as 1912 had 43 per cent in factories employing 1000 persons and over. Even more striking is the comparison with the United States. Of all employees in establishments with more than fifty hands the workers in enterprises of five hundred hands or more were 47 per cent in the United States in 1929. They were 61 per cent in Russia in 1912. As a result of foreign capital the backward Slav empire, industrially a pigmy in comparison with the United States, had a greater concentration of production.

This powerful tendency toward concentration of a new working class is also evident geographically. Almost 60 percent of all factory workers in European Russia were concentrated in eight narrow regions: the Moscow industrial region, St. Petersburg, Poland, Krivoi Rog and the Donets Basin in the Ukraine, Kiev and Podolia, Baku and Transcaucasia. Relatively tiny in relation to the total population, therefore, the growing Russian proletariat developed great social specific gravity in a few plants, located in few areas, an important consideration in evaluating the Bolshevik seizure of power in 1917. Similarly there was a great increase in the working force manning the railroad connections between these centers and the hinterland. Railroad mileage increased from 1,488 *versts* in 1861 to 61,292 *versts* in 1906; the number of railroad workers increased from 32,000 to 253,000 (Lyashchenko, 1949, 487, 502).

While this process of concentration was embracing increasing numbers of workers, it was also converting increasing numbers of peasants into part-time workers, and half-time workers into full-time workers.

By the end of the 1890's, one-half of the Russian industrial workers had fathers who had worked in industry before them. At the same time, increasing numbers of workers no longer returned to their village to carry out agricultural tasks. A survey taken in the Moscow industrial region in the 1880's showed that this trend was especially important in the mechanized industries, such as mechanized weaving, cotton printing and finishing, and metalwork. However, in the manually operated trades, such as cotton weaving and silk weaving, the percentage of workers still leaving for field work continued as high as 72 percent and 63 percent respectively (Lyashchenko, 1949, 544–545). Turnover remained high for all workers. These migratory industrial workers provided a continuing link between the towns and the villages, a link that was certainly important in the spread of new ideas and aspirations in the countryside. More indirect, through the channels of trade and commerce, was the connection of the village artisans with the greater world outside. Their number was estimated in 1901 at 4,600,000, working in fifty provinces (Gordon, 1941, 356).

What bearing did these developments have on the structure of Russian society as a whole? What, if any, social realignments did they bring in their wake, and what, if any, consequences did these realignments have for the tsarist edifice? This state had evolved, initially, as a military apparatus. It entered the modern period, first in violent reaction against the invasions of the Mongols from the east, later against the encroachment of Livonians, Swedes, and Poles from the west. In the words of Russian historian Kliuchevski, Russia "became an armed camp surrounded on three sides by enemies." The result was the growth of a great military machine, dedicated to a religious crusade in the name of Moscow as a third Rome. Under Ivan III (1462–1505) and Ivan IV (1533–1584), the Russian nobility lost its former autonomy and was placed completely under the aegis of the tsar. New and old nobles received lands in return for service, and became hereditary "slaves" of the tsar. This military machine further incorporated Mongol patterns of census-taking and taxation, just as it later drew on Western industrial technology to build up an armament industry of its own.

Furthermore, it confronted the modern period with a centralized banking system, in which the director of the credit department of the state treasury controlled the entire financial apparatus of the country (Lyashchenko, 1949, 706). The military budget accounted for 60 to 70 percent of state expenditures in the seventeenth century, and had not sunk below 50 percent by the first half of the nineteenth century.

In such a state, the position of the noble was equivocal and weak. The Russian nobles never were great landowning grandees, able to exert an independent local power against the state. Instead, the tsars labored mightily to make the social standing of any noble at court dependent not upon any autonomous power he might possess, but upon a table of organization in which service defined noble status, while nobility as such did not entail the right to exercise a particular kind of service. Thus the bureaucratic table of organization took precedence over any personal ties of fealty. At the same time, the nobles lived as *rentiers* in towns and cities, rather than as agrarian managers upon their estates; the country *dacha* was a vacation home, not an administrative center. In agricultural matters, they relied in the last instance upon their bailiffs and upon the elected representatives of the village communes. Thus they came to be dependent upon the state, ruling from above, and upon the peasant commune, with its customs and agricultural practices, constraining their ability to make decisions from below (see Confino, 1963). Under orders from above, and constrained from below, they inhabited a kind of social no man's land, in which they substituted for local and territorial solidarities the solidarity of belonging to certain schools and regiments. As Pushkin phrased it at the beginning of the nineteenth century, the boarding school of Tsarskoe Selo had become "the fatherland for us." With the advent of Peter the Great, moreover, increasing numbers of non-nobles were admitted to service and hence to rank. The decision of 1762 to make noble service voluntary rather than obligatory, often represented as a gain for the nobility, in fact declared that the state had found additional strata of the population from which to draw loyal servants (Raeff, 1966, 109), and that the service monopoly of the

G

nobility had been decisively abrogated. Thus the Russian nobility never came to form a

> genuine estate with an autonomous corporate life, whose members, rights and privileges would be based on their creative and socially valuable roles in the economy, the local government, and the expression of ideas and opinions. Failure to create a genuine estate of the nobility perpetuated the average nobleman's rootlessness and dependence on the state; he continued to look to the state for guidance in all that concerned the country's development and transformation (1966, 106).

Instead, they increasingly substituted for their specific service functions the general function of diffusing Western culture—especially French culture—to the masses of "backward" Russia. The noble artilleryman or navigator of the time of Peter the Great became transformed into a "philosopher-nobleman." Kliuchevski describes him bitingly as

> the typical representative of that social class whose task it was to carry Russian society forward along the road of progress; hence it is necessary to point out his chief characteristics. His social position was founded upon political injustice and crowned with idleness. From the hands of his teacher, the cantor and clerk of the village church, he passed into the control of a French tutor, rounded off his education in Italian theatres or French restaurants, made use of his acquirements in the drawing-rooms of St. Petersburg, and finished his days in a private study in Moscow, or at some country place, with a volume of Voltaire in his hands. On *Povarskaia* [one of the fine avenues of Moscow], or in the country in Tula *guberniia*, with his volume of Voltaire in his hands, he was a strange phenomenon. All his adopted manners, customs, tastes, sympathies, his language itself—all were foreign, imported; . . . he had no organic connection with his surroundings, no sort of serious business in life. A foreigner among his own people, he tried to make himself at home among foreigners, and in European society he was a kind of adopted child. In Europe he was looked upon, indeed, as a re-costumed Tatar, and at home, people saw in him a Frenchman born in Russia (quoted in Robinson, 1949, 52–53).

From servants of the state, they had become the inhabitants of a society with which they had little active connection. In the wake of the Napoleonic wars, many of them would come to feel the burden of their "cursed Russian reality." Alienated from the state, alienated from local ties, alienated also from other social groups in their own society, they found their "home" in the end in the proliferating numbers of "circles," lodges, and secret societies which grew ever more critical of the established order. In 1825, these tendencies produced the abortive uprising of the Decembrists, in which military men and some civil servants tried to produce a "revolution from above." Politically impotent, they were also economically ineffective.

> Toward the end of the era of serfdom, the indebtedness of the landlords mounted to huge proportions, and on the eve of the Emancipation two-thirds of all the private serfs had been mortgaged by their masters to State institutions for loans totalling about 400,000,000 *rubls*, or more than half the market value of these serfs at the prices then prevailing—and this does not include the loans from private sources, for which the landlords paid a higher interest (Robinson, 1949, 56–57).

As the nobility declined in effective power, other social groups began to climb the ladder into state employment. The state needed officials: it needed men with skills, such as doctors, engineers, and teachers. To provide these the state began to further education: the cadet school for the sons of the nobility gave way, after 1825, to the university. The growing opportunities for education were to have important consequences for Russian society. Paradoxically, education in Russia "was much less a matter for the rich than in the West" (Berdiaiev, 1937, 67). From 1865 to 1914, the number of students per 100,000 inhabitants increased from 105 to 545, or five times. In higher schools, the increase was even more marked; enrollment multiplied seven times between 1865 and 1914. Moreover, increasing numbers of workers' and peasant children began to receive an education. Between 1880 and 1914, the children of workers and artisans in universities rose from 12.4 percent of all students to 24.3 percent. The children of peasants constituted only 3.3 percent in 1880; but in 1914 they made up 14.5 percent of university students (Inkeles, 1960, 344). Thus it was education which provided the strategic channel for the social mobility of the *raznochintsy*, the people whose rank had not been fixed by Peter the Great's table of ranks, but who furnished the new services needed by the state. It was on the rungs of the educational ladder, leading from seminary to gymnasium on to the university "that the *raznochintsy* climbed to the light of day; without it they could never have existed" (Malia, 1961, 13).

Yet the educational process had unforeseen consequences. The tsarist state could make use of technical talent, but it could not cope with the larger social implications of an educated elite. Education gave rise not only to technical personnel but to a specifically Russian intelligentsia. It was in the universities that members of the nobility—turned writers, critics, or professors—encountered the children of other classes, and it was the universities which spread the antagonism of the educated to the absolutist power of the state. As a result there developed a large group of men and women—estimated in 1835 in the thousands, but by 1897 already between half and three-quarters of a million (Fischer, 1960, 254, 262)—drawn from all classes, but united in a common rejection of the state. They resembled, according to Berdiaiev (1937, 48), nothing so much as a "monastic order or sect," whose attitude toward the existing order was rooted in a quasi-religious sense that "the whole world lieth in wickedness" (John 5:19). Under continuous pressure of state censorship and harassment, large sections of this intelligentsia became a class of "expelled students and censored journalists, who in desperation were driven to conspiratorial extremes" (Malia, 1961, 15), and proliferated, in the latter part of the nineteenth century, numerous conceptions of organized conspiracy of the intelligentsia against the state. Such a multiplication of conspiratorial organizations had begun all over Europe in the period after the Napoleonic wars when

> the political prospects looked very much alike to oppositionists in all European countries, and the methods of achieving revolution—the united front of absolutism virtually excluded peaceful reform over most of Europe—were very much the same. All revolutionaries regarded themselves, with some justification, as small elites of the emancipated and progressive operating among, and for the eventual benefit of, a vast and inert mass of the ignorant and misled common people, which would no doubt welcome liberation when it came, but could not be expected to take much part in

preparing it. . . . All of them tended to adopt the same type of revolutionary organization, or even the same organization: the secret insurrectionary brotherhood (Hobsbawm, 1962, 115).

One such organization had united the young aristocrats, who in 1825, rose against the tsar; but this insurrection was easily quelled. Others, however, followed in their footsteps. If the conspiratorial pattern was pan-European—and even extended into Latin America—

> it had a peculiar attraction for the Russians, and it is this addiction to underground conspiracy, to cloak and dagger methods and programs of terror, that made the Russia of the late nineteenth century stand out from the general tone of European life (Tompkins, 1957, 157).

In the unbroken line of conspirators which link the rebels of 1825 to the revolutionaries of 1917, the figure of Sergei Nechaev stands out, both because he developed the concept of the professional revolutionary and because his writings and activities captured the imagination of educated Russian society, as expressed most clearly in Dostoievski's *The Possessed* which deals with the Nechaevist conspiracy. Nechaev, the son of a serf who had managed to secure enough education to become a teacher and to attend the university in St. Petersburg, is the probable author of the *Catechism of the Revolutionary* written in 1869. In it he depicted the revolutionary as

> a man set apart. He has no personal interests, no emotions, no attachments; he has no personal property, not even a name. Everything in him is absorbed by the one exclusive interest, the one thought, one single passion—the revolution. . . . All the gentle and enfeebling sentiments of kinship, love, gratitude and even honor must be suppressed in him by the single cold passion for revolution. . . . Revolutionary fervor has become an everyday habit with him, but it must always be combined with cold calculation. At all times and everywhere he must do what the interest of the revolution demands, irrespective of his own personal inclinations (quoted in Prawdin, 1961, 63–64).

These professional revolutionaries were to form groups of five, arranged in a revolutionary hierarchy at the top of which was to be the Committee which would

combine the scattered and therefore fruitless revolts and so transform the separate explosions into one great popular revolution
(quoted in Prawdin, 1961, 41).

One hundred and fifty-two Nechaevists were tried for conspiracy in
1871. They were described by one of their lawyers as

the Russian intellectual proletariat. No matter what income any of
the accused may have, collectively they belong to the class of
people who have received a better education, who have tasted the
fruits of science and absorbed European ideas, but who are denied
a corresponding place in life. At best they can earn a livelihood,
but they have no rights, no tradition, no security, and so they are
quite naturally the material in which new ideas can take root and
rapidly develop (quoted in Prawdin, 1961, 69).

The trial gave wide publicity to their views. One secret police
agent wrote that

the trial represents a milestone in the life of the Russian people.
At the moment there is scarcely a spot in all our wide fatherland
where Nechaev's manifestoes are not being read among uneducated
masses who naturally give their particular attention to those points
where there is talk of the suffering of the people and of the men
responsible for it. . . . Until now such teachings had been kept
secret and the distribution of proclamations was punishable as a
crime. Now, all this has become common knowledge, distributed
throughout Russia in tens of thousands of newspaper copies
(quoted in Prawdin, 1961, 75).

The concept of an army of professional revolutionists was to
become the prototype for a number of terrorist movements throughout the last quarter of the century, and strongly resembles Lenin's
concept of the revolutionary party as the general staff of the revolution. What Lenin accomplished, in essence, could be characterized
as the fusion of a Russian concept of an organized band of conspirators with Marxist ideas about the role of the proletariat in
revolution. In Trotsky's words:

In order to conquer the power, the proletariat needed more than a
spontaneous insurrection. It needs a suitable organization, it needs
a plan; it needs a conspiracy. Such is the Leninist view of this
question (1932, III, 170).

In *What Is to Be Done?* written in 1902, Lenin assigned this crucial role of leadership to professional revolutionaries recruited from "the young generation of the educated classes." While workers left to their own devices could only develop trade-union consciousness and peasants only petty-bourgeois demands for land, it would be the guiding intellectuals who would lead the revolution on behalf of the workers and the peasants.

The declining power of the nobility and the rising influence of the intelligentsia was offset only partially by active *political* activity on the part of a growing cluster of entrepreneurs. The development of an independent entrepreneurial class had long been delayed, with trade concentrated either in the hands of traders sponsored by the state, or traders working for nobles and monasteries. It has even been argued that entrepreneurial activity arose on the margins of society, in the schismatic antistate religious communities of Old Believers, rather than in the strategic center of the social order. Driven into the forests of the north by religious persecution, the Old Believers organized monastery-like trading and artisan communes like Vyg, Rogozhsk, and Preobrazhensk; it was these organizations which—in the seventeenth and eighteenth centuries—laid "the foundation of some of the largest fortunes among Russian entrepreneurs" (Bill, 1959, 103). The nineteenth century, with its expansion of trade by ship and railroad, further encouraged the growth of this new class, but it remained strongly marked by its peasant and artisan origins.

> Among the twenty or so families which constituted the top ranks of Moscow's bourgeoisie at the end of the nineteenth century, one half had risen from the peasantry within the last three generations, while the other half looked back to an ancestry of small artisans and merchants who had come to Moscow in the late eighteenth or early nineteenth century (Bill, 1959, 153).

The Emancipation permitted still additional numbers of enterprising and astute peasants to enter the entrepreneurial ranks. Yet, paradoxically, the entrepreneurs remained politically impotent. They found no tie to the nobility which refused to intermarry with them (Ungern-Sternberg, 1956, 53). Their enterprises remained largely on a family basis; corporate arrangements which would have linked the family enterprises and provided the organizational basis for greater class cohesion only developed after the turn of the twentieth century. They also continued to rely heavily on the state, and competed among one another for the perquisites or tariffs, contracts, and subsidies provided by the government. They became increasingly dependent upon foreign capital, which constituted one-third of all capital resources in the 1890's and nearly a half in 1900 (Lyashchenko, 1949, 535), thus causing Trotsky to speak of them contemptuously as a "semi-comprador bourgeoisie":

> the Russian autocracy on the one hand, the Russian bourgeoisie on the other, contained features of compradorism, ever more and more clearly expressed. They lived and nourished themselves upon their connections with foreign imperialism, served it, and without its support could not have survived. To be sure, they did not survive in the long run even with its support. The semi-comprador Russian bourgeoisie had world-imperialistic interests in the same sense in which an agent working on percentages lives by the interests of his employer (1932, I, 17).

Their role in society was given little positive social recognition; the term *kupez* (trader) retained overtones of "scoundrel, cheat"; and they were themselves strongly affected by religious beliefs which held that commercial gain was a kind of sin. Many of them gave away vast sums for religious purposes (Elisséeff, 1956). Nor did they establish any link with the growing intelligentsia which remained hostile to pecuniary pursuits. It is notable that so many of the great Russian writers—Pushkin, Dostoievski, Tolstoi, Gorki—bitterly condemned commercial acquisitiveness, and helped to create that "mood of hostility toward a monetary society which permeated Russia's intellectual and literary world throughout all of the nineteenth century" (Bill, 1959, 181).

We are thus confronted with a society possessed of a vast military machine but with weak classes, as yet uncertain in their ability to articulate their interests meaningfully in a political field; with its educated population largely alienated from its goals and procedures; a society struggling with uncertain success to solve its agrarian problems—and yet in the throes of a ramifying industrial revolution. Involvement in World War I would cripple its military and demonstrate its inability to contain the spread of social disorder, and into the vacuum created by military and political failure would step the armed intellectuals, who could take advantage of mass strikes among the workers and rural rebellion among the peasants to seize power through insurrection.

In the Revolution that was to put an end to the tsarist state and its weak classes three factors were paramount: the development of the mass industrial strike, the growth of peasant disorders, and the mass desertion of the army, composed in the main of peasants and workers called to arms. The success of the Revolution depended upon the successful synchronization of these three movements. All of them were evident in incipient form in the Revolution of 1905, and in developed form in the Revolution of 1917.

The mass industrial strikes of the Revolution of 1905 were preceded by a growing number of strikes from 1880 on. In 1902 occurred the railroad strike of Vladikavkaz in the Caucasus and at Rostov-on-Don in New Russia. The government countered with the establishment of unions under police control which produced paradoxical results. Many workers gained organizing experience in these unions, but quickly went beyond the demands thought permissible by the tsarist police. Throughout this period the workers became acquainted with the tactic of raising strike funds and appointing strike committees. Oscar Anweiler (1958, 28) believes that these first developed among Jewish workers in the western provinces, from where they were introduced into Russia proper in 1896–1897. In May of 1905 there occurred a mass strike of 70,000 workers in the textile center of Ivanovo Voznesensk, located 200 miles northeast of Moscow in the Middle Volga Region. It was here that the strike committee of 150, a quarter of whom were Social Democrats, for the first time called itself a council or *soviet,* and began to assume local political and military functions.

The peasant movement was in part sparked by the industrial uprisings, in part independent of them. In 1902 the railroad strikes in the Caucasus set off peasant disturbances in the area. At the same time, however, and independently of the industrial strike, an uprising took place in Vitebsk, in White Russia, in which the peasants demanded the publication of the "real" Emancipation Proclamation of 1861. From here peasant disorders spread into the Central Agricultural Region. By and large these uprisings were local affairs, but everywhere they produced the same basic demands: abolition of official control over peasant life, termination of redemption payments, mitigation of taxation, and partition of land. Only in the Middle Volga Region was there any link between rioting peasants and urban revolutionaries; in Saratov and Penza provinces the Socialist Revolutionary party had been successful in organizing several armed peasant brotherhoods. Yet as the months went by peasants everywhere began to hear about the mass strikes in the cities from peasant-workers newly returned to the villages, and about the military defeats suffered in the war against Japan. The call-up of reservists further affected peasant life. There was thus increased peasant response to the establishment of peasant unions, stimulated in the summer by zemstvo liberals and revolutionary professionals living in the rural areas. Thus, in Vladimir Province a local schoolteacher, aided by the district clerk and his assistant, organized a peasant union, urged the peasants to occupy landlord-held land and to refuse the payment of taxes. In Saratov Province a local veterinarian headed a peasant movement which organized its own militia, instituted an elective clergy in the place of appointed priests, and turned churches into schools and hospitals (Harcave, 1964, 218). By the end of July, an All-Russian Peasant Union was organized at a meeting of 100 peasants and 25 members of the intelligentsia in Moscow. By November the Peasant Union had 200,000 members in 26 provinces. Within the peasant unions we may note a process that was to be repeated in 1917, with momentous consequences for the distribution of political power: the local peasant delegates proved vastly more radical than the central leadership. At the second meeting of the Peasant Union in early November, these delegates clamored for the use of violence and the seizure and partition of land without compensation. Their radical demands found an echo in the soviet organized in industrial St. Petersburg. "For the first time in the country's history, there was a possibility that urban and rural discontent might be united in action against the government" (Harcave, 1964, 220).

The upsurge of strikes and peasant disorders also affected the armed forces. There were army mutinies in several cities, and mutinies in the fleet, as on the celebrated battleship *Potemkin* at Kronstadt. Here and there sailors' and soldiers' soviets came into existence, yet by and large the army held, and by December of 1905 the government was demonstrating its renewed ability to repress the revolts by force. Between October and February-March of 1906 the number of workers on strike receded from its peak of 475,000 to 50,000. Peasant disorders had affected 240 counties in the summer of 1905; by the fall of 1906 only 72 counties reported trouble; in the fall of 1907 this number had been reduced to 3.

The Revolution of 1905 was to be the "prologue," a prologue in which, Trotsky said, "all the elements of the drama were included, but not carried through." This time the forces of dissolution were still too weak and insufficiently synchronized; the government was still too strong.

After an initial lull, there was a renewal of strike activity. In 1910, 46,623 strikers went out in 222 strikes; in 1912, 725,491 in 2,032 strikes; in 1914, 1,337,458 in 3,534 strikes. During the same period, from 1910 to 1914, peasant disturbances numbered 13,000. The mobilization of workers and soldiers in 1914 naturally slowed the strike movement. Yet by 1915 there were again 928 strikes with 539,500 participating strikers. In 1916, 951,700 strikers went out on 1,284 strikes; and in the two crucial months of January and February of 1917 alone, 676,300 workers struck in 1,330 strikes (Lyashchenko, 1949, 692, 694).

It was again a strike which set off the events of March 8, 1917; but this time the striking workers linked up with mutinous soldiers in ways unforeseen in 1905. On March 8, 90,000 workers went on strike in St. Petersburg. Many of them were women—"the most oppressed and downtrodden part of the proletariat—the women textile workers, among them no doubt many soldiers' wives.

The overgrown bread-lines had provided the last stimulus" (Trotsky, 1932, I, 102). On March 9, the figure of workers on strike had doubled; on March 10, the number of strikers reached 240,000. Police went into action against the assembled crowd, but on the night of March 10 the military garrison of Petrograd mutinied and went over to the side of the workers. A soviet of workers' and soldiers' deputies came into being under socialist leadership, as in 1905, while the national assembly elected a provisional government composed of nonsocialists. On March 14, the tsar abdicated. Thus began a period of competition for power between two rival political bodies, between a weak provisional government, possessed of formal power, and the Petrograd soviet, which controlled the streets of the capital.

The results of this unequal struggle are history. The Provisional Government staked its all on a continuation of the war and on a postponement of internal reform until the war was won. Bolsheviks, under the leadership of Lenin, called for an immediate end to the war. Other parties temporized. Only the Bolsheviks and the Left Socialist Revolutionaries understood that the war was coming to an end because—as Lenin said—the "soldiers were voting with their feet"; in the July offensive staged by the government the soldiers refused to fight and began to desert; the front was collapsing. At the same time the peasants were becoming more and more radical in their demands, far outpacing—as in 1905—their more cautious urban spokesmen. The number of wholesale expropriations of large estates and forests rose steadily from month to month: seizures numbered 17 in March; 204 in April; 259 in May; 577 in June; and 1,122 in July (Mitrany, 1961, 81). By fall the two movements coalesced.

> An army twelve million strong was breaking up, flooding the countryside with peasants in uniform who were returning in bad humor to the villages they had left in bewilderment and despair. In their overwhelming mass they were either Bolsheviks or Left SR's or nonpartisan extremists. They brought back with them a bitter animus against the party whose influence was paramount in the village [i.e. the Socialist Revolutionary party], and a strong prejudice in favor of a man who had released them from the army,

or from the consequences of deserting it. . . . The soldier-peasant's relatives and neighbors deferred to him—usually to his judgment, always to his rifle. . . . It was not the bearded patriarch honoring the Mother of God and hankering still in his heart for the tsar, but the youthful or middle-aged peasant back from the war, accustomed to violence and not loath to use it, who during the last months of 1917 and long thereafter dictated the course of affairs in the village (Radkey, 1963, 278–279).

More than half of these outbreaks of disorder occurred in the crucial region of the Central Agrarian Region and in the area of the Middle Volga (Owen, 1963, 133). Moreover, there was a steady increase in violence. In May less than 10 percent of all disorders involved the destruction and devastation of property. By October, such events numbered more than half (57.5 percent) of all occurrences (1963, 139). Everywhere "separators" were being forced back into the framework of the village communes (Owen, 1963, 172, 182, 210, 223).

Thus in the countryside, all power was passing into the hands of peasants and peasant-soldiers, organized into peasant soviets. But these soviets, in turn, were nothing but the old village councils in revolutionary guise (Anweiler, 1958, 62, 298). In political actuality, this meant a process of complete decentralization on the local level. "The local peasantry," Trotsky quotes a rural commissar as saying,

> have got a fixed opinion that all civil laws have lost their force, and that all legal relations ought now to be regulated by peasant organizations (1932, III, 29).

This view was seconded by a commissar from Voronezh: "Now every village committee dictates to the district committee and every district committee dictates to the provincial committee" (quoted in Owen, 1963, fn. 1, 187). And one year later, the provincial revolutionary committee in Vyatka was to say that

> the happiness of the village consists in not having any officials about trying to see how their orders are carried out. The village therefore began to lead a completely independent life (quoted in Anweiler, 1958, 299).

Where the *mir* had long ceased to exist, seized land was apportioned once more to individuals. But where the *mir* proved to be "living and active though the State was in suspension," the land commune re-emerged. "To this extent," says Owen, "the Revolution of 1917 was a resurgence of old customary land-tenure" (1963, 245).

> The land settlement of the previous decade was wiped out in many parts of the revival of the *mir*. The total extent of land seized by the communes in 1917–18 for redistribution was put at about 70 million desiatins (189 mill. acres) from peasants and about 42 mill. mill. desiatins (114 mill. acres) from large owners. About 4.7 mill. peasant holdings, i.e., about 30.5 per cent of all peasant holdings, were pooled and divided up. The effect of the agrarian revolution, therefore, was in the first place to wipe out all large property, but also and no less to do away with the larger peasant property. In fact, as we have seen, more land was taken away and "pooled" from peasant owners than from large owners, and the levelling and equalizing trend became more marked after October, 1917, and was sanctioned by the law of January, 1918, under which land was socialized (Mitrany, 1961, note 7, 231–232).

A section of the Russian peasant population even entered, in the first enthusiasm of revolution, and under the twin influence of the *raskol* and of socialist millenarianism, egalitarian communes in which

> members worked together without pay, ate at a common table, and lived in a dormitory. They had no use for money; everything but clothing, and sometimes even that, was collective property. According to an early pamphlet, "In the commune, everybody works and is expected to contribute according to his capacities, and everybody receives according to his needs and requirements, that is, equally, since all are equal and are in equal conditions of life and labor." (Wesson, 1963, 8).

Under the circumstances of 1917, the first Bolshevik decrees of November 8, calling for immediate cessation of hostilities and an end to all private property in land, merely gave a stamp of approval to processes that were already going on in the countryside, and which no political party could have resisted even if it wanted to. The criticism of German socialists, like Rosa Luxemburg (1940, 19), that the Bolsheviks had created "insurmountable obstacles to the socialist transformation of agrarian relations" by allowing the peasants to take the land for themselves, was surely beside the point. They were forced to allow this to happen, simply "because the majority of the people want it" (Lenin).

Yet, the Bolsheviks clearly abdicated in the fact of the resurgent village not only because they were unable to do otherwise, but because it was to their political interest to do so, if they wanted to seize power. Land seizures and the restoration of village autonomy meant that the energy of the peasantry and that of the returning peasant-soldiers was directed toward narrow and parochial ends. Bolshevik support of rural rebellion created peasant allies for a Communist take-over, while at the same time absorption in the actual local processes of seizure and reorganization atomized the peasant forces. The dispersion of peasant energies in a thousand rural microcosms cleared the political field for final action. Thus the Russian Revolution embraced on the one hand a peasant movement which led centrifugally away from the sources of power, and on the other hand an insurrection of striking workers and mutinous soldiers under Bolshevik leadership which occupied the strategic heights of power.

> The Bolsheviks overthrew little or nothing. The Government of Russia had for all intents and purposes ceased to function before the Revolution took place. That evening Lenin and his cohorts were climbing atop the wreckage (Lukacs, 1967, 33).

It seems unlikely that this development could have occurred without the collapse of the army and the subsequent participation of the army in the revolutionary process. The disintegration of the army created the power vacuum at the center which was occupied by the coalition of striking workers and insurrectionary soldiers that brought Lenin to power. At the same time, there were no troops in the countryside capable of driving back the peasant rebels; on the contrary, the dramatic impact of millions of peasant-soldiers on the villages brought the peasant rebellion into synchronization with the urban movement. Finally, it was the coalition of workers and soldiers at the center and of peasants and soldiers in the heartland of the commune which was able to withstand the rally of counter-revolutionary forces along the country's periphery.

In contrast to the Chinese revolutionaries under Mao Tse-tung, the Bolsheviks did little—or could do little—during the years of civil war to influence the structure of the village. This was due to their reliance on the urban proletariat and on their desire to identify themselves with the working class. On the other hand it was due to the fact that they fought outward from an established base area which they held through control of the towns and of the communications between towns. The Chinese Communists, on the other hand, were to come to their base area from the outside, forced to flee inland from the cities, and under pressure to sink new roots into an overwhelmingly rural social landscape. The Russian Bolsheviks were content to draw on peasant resources, but did little to change the structure through which these resources were mediated.

They were in need especially of food and, later, of men for their new Red Army. The food crisis was most acute in the summer months of 1918. They met it by organizing Committees of the Poor to requisition food in the countryside. Their primary targets were the food surpluses of kulaks and of rich peasants. These committees were especially active in the black-earth provinces of the Central Agricultural Region. Many of their ten thousand members were former city workers or migratory laborers who had moved in employment between town and country. Theoretically, peasants who used hired labor but raised products mainly for peasant needs rather than for the wider market were also eligible as members. However, the requisitions quickly turned into an undeclared war between the committees and the better-off peasantry, and it became clear that unchecked collections would end by alienating the middle peasants as well. In 1918, there were twenty-six peasant uprisings in July against the confiscations, forty-seven in August and thirty-five in September. In mid-August the Bolsheviks began to warn against violations of middle peasant interests, demanding that the Committees of the Poor must be revolutionary organizations of the whole peasantry against former landlords, kulaks, merchants and priests and not organizations only of the village proletarians against all the rest of the village population (Chamberlin, 1957, II, 44).

On November 8, 1918, the committees were formally abolished and fused with the village soviets. Soviet policy was to be, in Lenin's words,

to reach an agreement with the middle class peasantry, not relaxing for a moment the struggle against the kulak and relying firmly only on the poor (quoted in Chamberlin, 1957, II, 46).

Finally, the Eighth Party Congress, held in 1919, stated that

the party aims to separate the middle class peasantry from the kulaks, to attract it to the side of the working class by an attentive attitude toward its needs, combating its backwardness by means of persuasion, not by methods of repression (quoted in Chamberlin, 1957, II, 371).

Food requirements were covered partly through continued forcible levies, partly through purchases in the private market or through private foraging trips to the villages. While the Soviet regime weathered the major crisis of the summer of 1918, food supplies remained below requirements throughout the entire period of civil strife.

The other Bolshevik demand on the villages was for soldiers, once it became evident that the Revolution would have to be defended against its foreign and domestic enemies by force of arms. Thus the peasantry which in 1917 had voted with "its feet" for a termination of a sanguinary war was again drawn into the battle through enlistment and conscription, this time under the auspices of the newly formed Red Army. The Bolsheviks faced the onset of the civil war with only one division of Latvian riflemen and some 7,000 Red Guards—armed workers—in Petrograd and Moscow (Deutscher, 1954, 404). By August 1, 1918, the Red Army numbered 331,000; by the end of that year, 800,000. At the end of the civil war it would amount to 5.5 million men, about half of whom fought at the expanding fronts, while the other half garri-

H

soned the interior. The first recruits were volunteers, but by late summer of 1918 conscription was decreed. The first conscripts were workers.

> Only when the proletarian core of the army had been firmly established, did Trotsky begin to call up peasants, first the poor and then the *serednyaks* (the middle peasants). These often deserted en masse and their morale fluctuated violently with the ups and downs of the civil war (Deutscher, 1954, 409).

Desertion remained a chronic problem

> in the Red Army, even more in the White Armies. The enormous majority of the peasants, who necessarily constituted the main source of recruits for both sides in the civil war, had experienced all the fighting they desired during the World War. When any government was sufficiently established to carry out mobilization with threats of concentration camps, confiscation of property and shooting for recalcitrant recruits and deserters, the peasants perforce went as soldiers; but they often took the first opportunity to run away and return to their homes. The amount of desertion naturally depended a good deal on the fortunes of war (it increased when the Red Army was losing ground and decreased when it was advancing) (Chamberlin, 1957, II, 30).

Nevertheless, the Red Army held. Deutscher (1954, 409) ascribes this

> to the fact that it was set up in a number of concentric and gradually widening rings, each from a different social stratum and each representing a different degree of loyalty to the revolution. In every division and regiment the inner core of Bolsheviks carried with it the proletarian elements, and through them also the doubtful and shaky peasant mass.

No wonder that Trotsky called the Communists, of whom perhaps as many as half were in the army—180,000 in October 1919; 278,000 in August 1920—a "new Communist Order of samurai" (quoted in Chamberlin, 1957, II, 34).

While the Bolsheviks fashioned the Red Army into a reliable instrument of power, an anarchist movement occurred among peasants in the southeastern Ukraine, the so-called *Makhnovsh-*

china, named after its founder, Nestor Makhno, son of an almost destitute peasant family of Guliai-Pole. Successively a cowherd, a farm laborer, and a worker in a local foundry, Makhno was arrested in his youth for involvement in terrorist activity and sent to prison in Moscow for nine years. Here he met Petr Arshinov, a former metalworker and former Bolshevik turned Anarchist, who acquainted Makhno with the writings of Kropotkin and Bakunin. Released in February of 1917, Makhno returned to his home town to organize a Guliai-Pole Association of Peasants. Guliai-Pole is often described as a village; it was, however, a town of some thirty thousand, with several factories (Avrich, 1967, fn. 16, 209). It was located, moreover, in an area which differed in some major characteristics from the remainder of the Ukraine, the "Ukraine of the steppes," colonized only after it was wrested from Turkey in the first quarter of the eighteenth century. The growth of commercial grain farming in this area of low population had early encouraged the use of wage labor and machinery rather than of serfs (Lyashchenko, 1949, 345–357). In the course of the nineteenth century its peasantry bitterly resisted the spread of serfdom by repeated outbreaks of violence. The area thus differed both from the more industrial eastern Ukraine where Bolshevik influence was strong among urban workers, and from the more agricultural western Ukraine, where more than half of the population had been serfs before 1861.

The Guliai-Pole Association of Peasants promptly seized holdings of local landowners and distributed them among the peasantry. Communes with between one hundred and three hundred members were set up on a voluntary basis. Small factories were turned over to the workers. Grain produced in the agricultural area was exchanged for manufactured products in towns. To defend this new anarchist redoubt, Makhno organized a highly mobile partisan army, making extensive use of cavalry—based on the plentiful supply of horses in the villages—and of machine guns mounted on little horse-driven carts (*tachanki*). Troops could mass quickly, and disperse just as quickly to the villages where they merged unobtrusively with the peasantry until the signal came for the next attack.

Commanders were mostly drawn from the peasantry; a very few were workers; a majority of these came from the vicinity of Guliai-Pole. One was a former schoolteacher. At the height of the Makhno movement in late 1919, this army was estimated variously as possessing between 14,000 infantry and 6,000 cavalry to 40,000 infantry and 15,000 cavalry. By capturing enemy weapons it had come into the possession of field guns, armored trains, armored cars, and 1,000 machine guns (Footman, 1962, 285). Throughout its operations, from 1917 to 1921, it remained an autonomous fighting force, operating as "a republic on *tachanki*" under its own black Anarchist flag. Refusing to accept Bolshevik cession of the Ukraine to Austria-Hungary and its Ukrainian allies in the treaty of Brest-Litovsk, Makhno nevertheless cooperated at various times with the Bolsheviks against the threat of White invasion; in the fall of 1919 he was instrumental in choking off the northward advance of General Denikin. At the same time serious differences separated the Ukrainian Anarchists from the Bolsheviks. In addition to doctrinal differences, they fell out over their respective views of the peasant problem. The Bolsheviks wanted to nationalize all sugar-beet plantations and vineyards, as well as livestock and equipment seized from the local landlords; the peasants held both land and equipment to be their own. These differences caused some of Makhno's peasants to believe

> that a new party had come to power in Moscow. They were, they proclaimed[,] for the Bolsheviks who had given them the land, but they were against the Communists who were now trying to rob them (Footman, 1962, 270).

The Bolsheviks also wished to fan the conflict between poor peasants and kulaks in the villages; the Makhnovites—while recognizing the problem posed by kulak presence—hoped for a voluntary solution to village antagonisms. At the same time the Makhno movement remained purely rural in orientation. They did not understand some of the complex economic problems posed by an urban economy based on specialization and wage payment. Where the peasants could feed themselves by retreating into rural self-sufficiency, urban workers depended on wages paid in an acceptable currency. The Makhnovites, by accepting all currencies—past and present—in use in the towns they occupied, brought on a rampant inflation which quickly turned workers against them. As long as the Bolsheviks needed Anarchist support in their struggle in the south, they willingly cooperated with Makhno. When it became evident, however, that the White armies were going down in defeat, they increasingly severed their ties with the Makhnovites, and in 1921 proceeded to the wholesale elimination of this rival movement in the Ukraine. By that time the peasantry had been bled white, and the strategic supply of horses and food in the villages, on which Makhno had relied up to then in the absence of any supply organization of his own, began to dwindle. After a bloody struggle in which the Bolshevik Cheka summarily executed thousands of Makhno supporters, while the Makhnovites killed Bolshevik party members, Cheka, militia, tax collectors, and peasant organizers, the growing strength of the Red Army proved decisive. Makhno was forced to flee abroad, dying in Paris in 1935.

Certain resemblances—reliance on local support within a circumscribed area marked by a common history and identity; dominance of a libertarian ideology with an emphasis on the organization of communes; lack of a formal organization of supplies; use of guerrilla tactics; inability to understand the problems of urban workers and to establish viable contacts with them—make the *Makhnovshchina* comparable to the Zapatista movement in Mexico. Similar also, in both areas, was the inability—or unwillingness —of both movements to develop an organizational framework capable of sustaining the structure of a state. Final victory in both areas fell to the men who understood the importance of organization: to the Constitutionalists in Mexico, to the Bolsheviks in Russia.

Yet when the Red Army had won its battles, the *mir* had once again become the dominant form of social and economic organization in the countryside and would remain such until the period of forcible collectivization under Stalin (Male, 1963). In 1917, the Bolsheviks had won the heights of power but the "old rural Russia survived till 1929" (Maynard, 1962, 363). "To read the Party records of 1925–26 is to catch something of the flavor of an army of occupation in hostile territory," comments Merle Fainsod, on the basis of Communist party records from Smolensk Province in White Russia (1958, 123). In 1924, in Smolensk Province, for example,

> there were only sixteen Communists for every 10,000 rural inhabitants of working age, or approximately one Party member for every ten villages. Since over 90 per cent of the population of the guberniya [province] was located in rural areas, the extreme weakness of the Party in the countryside becomes readily apparent (1958, 44).

> The situation of the village Communists, the majority of whom were classified as poor peasants, was described as equally deplorable. Many of them were illiterate or semiliterate, and exercised little influence on their neighbors (1958, 45).

> To a not inconsiderable extent, the Party was at the mercy of the villages, of their capacity for passive resistance and silent sabotage. The training of new village cadres was at best a slow and painful process, and even the new cadres had roots in the countryside which made for cross loyalties and divided allegiances (1958, 152).

Thus, for a considerable time, rural Russia found itself in a condition in which overtly and more frequently covertly "every village committee dictates to the district committee and every district committee dictates to the provincial committee." The travail of Russia in the 1930's and after would be a gigantic attempt to reverse this chain of command, and to undo the facts which the first revolution had brought into being. This second revolution would be carried out "from above" by the state apparatus against the "petty-bourgeois" peasantry.

After its successful consummation, the Russian Revolution became—for Communists and non-Communists alike—a hallowed model of how revolutions were made and guided toward a successful conclusion. Yet more features of the society which incubated that revolution are unique than general. Unusual was the strong development of the central autocracy, grown strong at the expense of the various clusters. Unusual, too, was the pattern of conspiratorial revolutionary brotherhoods, of which the Communist party was the latest example. While Russia resembles Mexico both in the persistence of a bound peasantry and its communal organization, neither serfdom nor corporate peasant communities are universal features of peasant society. Similarly, the Revolution itself showed a series of unique features. The army disintegrated in the course of events which accompanied the revolutionary uprisings: few other revolutions have taken place in a similar vacuum of power. There was a simultaneous insurrection of peasants—turned workers in the cities and a peasant rebellion in the countryside—the Russian Revolution was unique in this synchronization. Finally, the Red Army fought outward from the center, rather than in the villages, allowing the peasantry an opportunity to consolidate itself along traditional lines. Such a sequence of causation and events is not universal, and therefore cannot form the basis of a universal dogma. The relations between army and party, between proletariat, peasantry, and middle-class intellectuals, are variably conjugated in different situations and not exhausted in simple formulas.

THREE

CHINA

━━━━━━━━━━━━━━━━━━━━━━━━━━━━━━━━━━

T'i t'ien hsing hao!
Prepare the Way for Heaven!

Rebel slogan from *All Men Are Brothers,*
popular thirteenth-century novel and
Mao Tse-tung's favorite

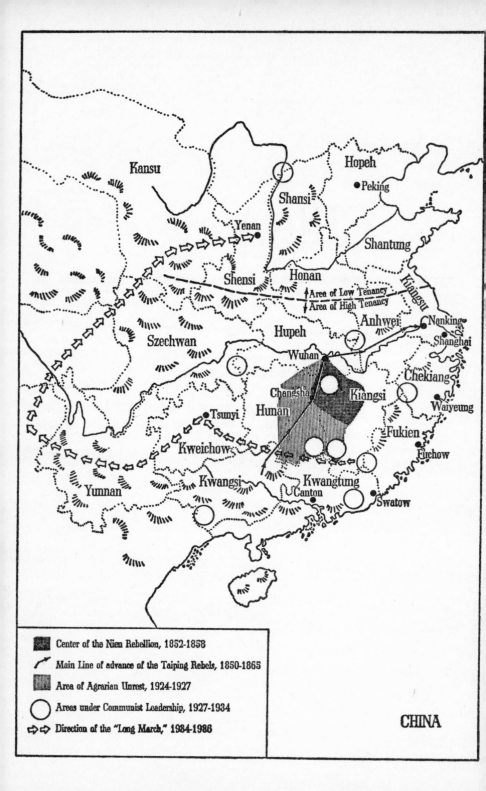

Center of the Nien Rebellion, 1852-1858

Main Line of advance of the Taiping Rebels, 1850-1865

Area of Agrarian Unrest, 1924-1927

Areas under Communist Leadership, 1927-1934

Direction of the "Long March," 1934-1936

CHINA

Mexico in 1910 had a population of 16.5 million, Russia around the turn of the century counted 129 million. China—the society which we will discuss next—however, must be plotted on a vastly larger scale. From Peking to China's western frontier is about as far as from New York to Oregon. Even in 1775 it contained about 265 million people; 430 million in 1850; about 600 million in 1950. Moreover, it is the oldest living primary civilization: the only one still extant of the great societies which crossed the threshold between neolithic tribalism and civilization. Its intensive methods of cultivation, its great waterworks of irrigation and flood control, its bureaucracy of scholars selected by a set of open examinations, its state of technological advancement, its philosophical tradition, and its great art attracted the admiration of the many visitors who came to it from the outside. To the Chinese themselves, it was the Middle Kingdom, the center of the universe, its ruler bearer of the Mandate of Heaven. Invaded frequently by barbarians from the north, it had absorbed them always and turned them into Chinese.

The last major invaders of China from the north had been the Manchu, Sinified Tungus tribesmen from the northeastern frontier.

By 1644 they had won complete control of China for their dynasty, the Ch'ing. The dynasty and their soldiery occupied the top positions of the political order, and maintained a separate military and residential establishment. But they were too few in number to administer a large bureaucratic empire, and hence were forced to rely—as any dynasty had to do before them—on the schooled administrators who had managed China since time beyond human memory. This group of schooled administrators constituted the indispensable hub of the wheels of administration. They were scholars because they obtained their positions through participation in successive examinations and the attainment of academic degrees. They were gentry because—like their English counterpart—they constituted a class of about one million which furnished both the holders of formal political offices and most of the wielders of informal social power in the land. The Chinese state needed to fill about 40,000 official positions, from the central pivot of the state down to the level of the district magistrate, at any one time. Occupants for these 40,000 positions were drawn from a pool of about 125,000 available actual or expectant officeholders. Yet it is evident that an enormous country like China could not have been ruled with so small a number of officials: a district magistrate had to supervise an average of 200,000 people. Between the masses of the peasantry and formal officialdom there stood scholar-gentry, holders not of formal office but endowed with broad social power. They organized and supervised the public works needed to maintain and improve the systems of irrigation and flood control required to sustain agriculture and transportation. They took care of canals and roads. They supervised the storage of surplus grain and its distribution in times of need. They settled local disputes. They had a prominent part in local religious sacrifices and, through their contributions, maintained local Confucian temples and schools. In turn, they might receive special privileges. They could be exempted from corvée; they could wear special clothing; they might be given the right to go accompanied by servants when they appeared in public; they had special prerogatives if they appeared in court. For their services, moreover, they could receive compensation by the state. They might not hold one of the 40,000 offices; but they could receive state funds on a kind of informal subcontract basis. State funds, in turn, went into the purchase of land, to be rented out to peasants. In addition to state funds and agricultural rents, the gentry also drew its income from trade and business. In all, this stratum of high-status persons numbered, at the beginning of the nineteenth century, around one million individuals; by the end of the century they numbered 1.5 million. Together with their families, they comprised perhaps 7.5 million people or 2 percent of the total population of the country (Michael, 1964, 60).

Although the interests of the scholar-gentry were firmly linked to the established state, and the state relied on it to furnish the members of a reliable bureaucracy, the struggle for power and position among various segments of the gentry could provoke individual or sectional dissension or disaffection from the established order. Members of the lower gentry were certainly at a disadvantage in the struggle for offices and the perquisites of office. Many of them never gained access to state funds which could have been used to increase their patrimony. Others never received the special sumptuary and legal privileges. Some sections of the gentry had served the previous dynasty and either would not or could not serve their new masters. Population increase also steadily raised the number of aspirants, drawn from the fast-growing gentry families, while the number of offices remained stationary. Finally, from the end of the eighteenth century on, the state proved increasingly willing to sell scholarly degrees to men willing to make a contribution to state coffers; a virtuous scholar who had gained his degree by successive examinations could find himself bypassed by a newly-rich parvenu. Thus there existed, under any dynasty, a sizable population of scholar-gentry who were potentially antagonistic to a government that refused to grant them their due and would, under given circumstances, support a local or regional reaction against the central power. In such a venture they might be joined by local landowners or other power holders who did not belong to the gentry at all, but who held economic and social power in the village. It may well be that, at any one time, more than half of all gentry went unrewarded by the state and constituted a powerful potential for disgruntlement and unrest. At the same time, such potential dissidence was always concerned more with the distribution of spoils within the state system, than with any effort to restructure the state as such. Only when the Chinese state had become seriously enfeebled by foreign encroachment in the course of the nineteenth century did dissidence begin to call into question the very nature of both state and society in China.

Its entire way of life, its expectations and demeanor, its ideology set off the gentry from the remainder of the population, most of whom were peasants. The Chinese peasant, however, differed significantly from other peasants the world over. First, his access to land was regulated largely through concepts of private rights in landed property expressed in monetary terms. Second, he was potentially mobile: given access to the appropriate literary training, he or his sons could rise into the stratum of the scholar-gentry through the examination system. Third, gentry and peasantry were frequently linked through kinship in so-called clans or *tsu*.

Ever since the time of the Sung (1114–1234) private ownership in land has been the dominant form of tenure in China. The state, at one time or another, reserved for its own use royal lands to sustain the court, banner lands to support the military aristocracy, lands for the purpose of military colonization, lands for the support of temples serving the state cult, and lands in the hands of provincial or district government. At the beginning of the eighteenth century, royal and government land amounted to 27 percent of all land, temple land to 14 percent, military colonization land to 9 percent, while the remainder was in the hands of private holders, either individuals or clan corporations (Institute of Pacific Relations, 1939, 2). During the later phases of Manchu rule, however, the private sector grew ever larger until it comprised about 93 percent of all land (Buck, 1937, 193). Rights to private land could be bought and sold; rights to the subsoil and to the surface of the land could be alienated independently of each other. The result has been that most Chinese peasants had access to land either through inheritance or through a complex set of leases and rents. Landlords and cultivators have been linked, not through a hereditary series of privileges and disabilities, but as "parties to a business contract" (Tawney, 1932, 63). Finally, a peasant could, given propitious financial and bureaucratic circumstances, enter his sons in the imperial examinations and see them rise into the ranks of the scholar-gentry.

When a peasant rose into the gentry, however, he had to leave behind him the ways of the peasantry and adopt the life style of the higher-status group. Where the peasant was illiterate and spoke his local or regional dialect, the gentry was literate, prizing its training in calligraphy and its classical style (*wen-hua*) of literary expression. Where the peasantry saw rice and meat only rarely, and subsisted to a large extent on a diet of sweet potatoes in the south and coarse grains in the north, the gentry ate rice, fish, and fowl, often served according to sophisticated culinary canons. The gentry wore elaborate clothing, the peasant a simple padded jacket and trousers. The characteristic graphic art of the gentry was inspired by its calligraphic skills with all its formal restraints; peasant art, on the other hand, was "more interested in person and symbol, approaches the supernatural directly and without self-consciousness, and stresses violent and unmodulated color" (Fried, 1952, 335). In ancestor commemoration, the peasantry was concerned primarily with the cult of the immediate ancestors in the parental and grandparental generation; the significant peasant pantheon consisted of deities who controlled crops, water, health, and illness. The gentry upheld the Confucian norms of proper filial conduct and paid special attention to elaborate ancestor cults, related to the maintenance of enduring lineages and branching clans. The gentry family was large and extended, with many descendants and their families living under the same roof; peasant families were small and rarely included more than one living member of the parent generation. Marriage was, for the gentry, a major mechanism for social mobility: marriages were carefully arranged between families; women were subject to the decisions of their male guardians; high status was shown by subjecting women to special disabilities, such as the binding of feet, which restricted their movement outside the home. Peasants married to acquire strong and willing workers. Peasants remarried easily; the gentry prized widow chastity. The scholar-gentry looked down upon military pursuits as inferior to their own activity as literati. The peasant worshiped many deities with military titles and looked favorably upon the man of violence, with the knowledge that military activity had often been the key to success. The fact is that the Chinese peasant, far from being the pacific son of the East usually described, has a strong affinity for military heroes, especially for those who emanate from his own social stratum. The characteristic cynosure of the peasant is the social bandit who takes from the rich to give to the poor. This penchant has found literary expression in a popular novel widely known throughout China, the *Shui Hu Chuan*, or *The Water's Edge*, which Pearl Buck translated into English under the title of *All Men Are Brothers* and which deals with 108 heroes who are fugitives from the law wielded by unjust officials. The occurrence of banditry and peasant violence are closely linked to the over-all state of the society. They usually occur during phases of breakdown when a once powerful dynasty has grown weak and unable to manage the affairs of the state, and people seek alternative solutions to the prevalent disorder. During such periods of disintegration, a bandit who successfully consolidates his forces may become a viable contender for dynastic power, sometimes even the founder of a new dynasty. The first Han emperor and the founder of the great Han dynasty (202 B.C.–A.D. 221) had himself been such a bandit who became, in the course of events, emperor of China and bearer of the Mandate of Heaven.

While gentry and peasantry were culturally differentiated, they yet shared a form of social organization, the corporate kinship group or *tsu*, comprising members of both classes in one social unit. These kinship units are usually called clans in the literature. Members of these clans were held to be related to each other by patrilineal descent from a common ancestor; women upon marriage became members of their husband's clan. Where a clan or a clan segment grew prosperous, it would celebrate its common descent and membership by erecting a clan temple, where the genealogies of the clan were deposited and ancestor tablets kept. Where a clan grew large, it might subdivide into sections, each with its own temple and religious paraphernalia. However, the required clan rituals could only be celebrated by a member of the scholar-gentry, and such temples were most often located in towns where the higher gentry maintained its residences. Many villages, inhabited by poorer sections of such clans, lacked clan temples of their own. Clans could also vary greatly in size. Some might comprise as few as four families, others well over a thousand: most appear to have had between forty and seventy families. Clans in southern China were both larger and more important than in the north, and

fulfilled important economic functions, as well as serving ceremonial and social ends: they often owned land and other property
and a whole village might belong to a clan. In the north, a village
might contain several smaller clans, and their functions were
primarily social and ceremonial rather than straightforwardly economic. We shall soon see some of the reasons for this variability.

All clan members might consider themselves related as descendants from a common ancestor, but not all members held an
equal voice in the affairs of the clan. Usually clan activities were
guided by the members with the greatest wealth, education, influence, and status. While this group might include wealthy peasants,
the tasks of making decisions on behalf of the clan were usually in
the hands of gentry. This was especially relevant where the clan
owned land. Land was not farmed collectively, but rented out to
individual tenants. While strangers—nonmembers of a clan—
might be considered as tenants, members had a prior claim to land
allocation, an important privilege in areas where a dense population
competed for available amounts of land. Members and nonmembers, however, paid the same amount of rental once admitted to
tenancy. Income from land rent was used to defray the costs of
maintaining clan temples and graveyards, of underwriting the
annual clan banquet, of providing scholarships for talented children
of the clan, or for defense against bandits. Occasionally, money
income was distributed among all members of the clan; more frequently, however, it was invested again in land or other business
dealings by the clan executives. The clan also acted as an organization in defense of its members, as well as an instrument in support
of claims against rival clans or government officials. The interests of
clan members could thus diverge markedly. The gentry members of
a clan were primarily interested in using the clan structure to
fortify and extend their power; they were the main agents in
maintaining the institution. It granted them effective stewardship
over a wide range of resources and increased their standing relative
to other members of their class and with the government. The
peasant members, on the other hand, benefited mainly by gaining
access to scarce land and by their ability to invoke clan solidarity

I

when they needed protection and influence. This convergence of interests might draw gentry and peasantry together in resisting the exactions of the central government or the competition of rival clans. At other times, however, the gentry executive would treat the peasant members of the clan simply as landlords have always treated their tenants. Often, moreover, clan rules contained provisions which allowed the clan executive to expel members it considered undesirable. These rules could stipulate that continuing clan membership required certain financial contributions or possession of certain ceremonial clothing. They could also demand expulsion of any member who gave his children up for adoption or sold daughters into servitude or prostitution. Such stipulations, by their very nature, discriminated heavily against poorer clan members who lacked the necessary wherewithal to maintain ceremonial expenditures or who were forced to limit the size of their families in times of need.

We have said that the clan was a more important institution in the Chinese south than in the Chinese north. This is due, in part, to historical reasons: the Chinese colonized the south over a long period of time: it is conceivable that this was done by clan groups establishing their own clan villages. Here, too, the southern Sung sponsored a Confucian revival against the pastoral nomadic Ch'itan and Jurchen, an effort which included state support for the development of numerous great branching clans. Later, regional considerations came into play. The south was farthest from the seat of the central power at Peking in the north; hence the local and regional power base of the gentry, as exemplified by the clan, was apt to be stronger here than in the north. Finally, it must be remembered that foreign commercial contact and penetration began in the south and that the opening-up of opportunities for overseas migration drew hundreds of thousands of Chinese to seek their fortune in Southeast Asia and across the Pacific. Contact with foreign firms and governments stimulated the development of clans into quasi-business organizations, while massive remittances by overseas Chinese who wished to be recognized and commemorated in their homeland furnished a great deal of wealth for the support of clan ceremonial and display. As beneficiaries of this inflow of capital, many clans became, as Chen Han-seng has said, like public utilities with numerous shareholders but controlled by a few who appropriate and dispose of most of the profits (quoted in Lang, 1946, 177). As land rent became an ever more important source of capital, and capital was increasingly invested in an ever widening national and international market, the deficits created by exactions from the poorer clan members began to outweigh the benefits associated with continued adherence to the clan. Thus the tendency to consolidate land in the hands of clans also accentuated internal conflicts within the clans between rich and poor. Thus, in 1924 to 1927, Kwangtung,

> the province where the clan system was most intact, was the scene of the most violent peasant uprisings and the seat of the strongest peasant unions, which united poor and middle peasants as well as farm laborers of different clans in the common fight against their clan brothers and clan enemies—the rich landowners and merchants (Lang, 1946, 178).

Still another feature of Chinese society in which both peasants and gentry participated was the secret society. In the middle of the fourteenth century A.D. one organization of this type, the White Lotus, had raised the flag of rebellion against the Yüan dynasty, established by the Mongol invaders, coupling its nationalist appeal with messianic expectations of a new Buddha-Matreya, a savior who would usher in a new reign of justice. The White Lotus, in turn, gave rise to a number of other societies such as the Eight Trigrams, the Nien, the Great Knife, the Boxers, the Society of the Faith, and the Red Spears. Another great society, the Triad—involved in the Taiping Rebellion of the mid-nineteenth century about which we shall have more to say below—spawned in turn such organizations as the Ko-lao-hui (The Society of Elders and Ancients), the Green Band, the Small Knife. All of these societies —and there were many others—drew their members from disaffected gentry, from the peasantry, especially from dispossessed and marginal peasantry, and from artisans, petty merchants, smugglers, demobilized soldiers, and bandits. Organized internally along strictly hierarchical lines, equipped with secret codes and symbols which were learned in complex procedures of initiation, these groups came to constitute veritable "counterorders" to the established order, with their own sets of norms and social sanctions. Politically they directed their efforts against the central government, especially when that government was in the hands of foreign invaders, as had been the case with the Mongol dynasty (1280–1368) and was to be the case again with the Manchus who held sway from 1644 to 1912. Ideologically, they tended to be anti-Confucian and employed Taoist and Buddhist elements in their symbolism. Some societies, for example, maintained a belief in an Old Mother or Old Father-Mother Who Was Never Created, a unitary supernatural being, corresponding to the Taoist concept of a Prior Sky, in existence before the world became divided into the opposing elements of yin and yang. The Taoist orientation held that a putative golden age in the past had given way to the disorder of the present.

The Buddhist orientation foresaw the advent of messianic Buddhas. What these two orientations have in common is their convergent tendency to regard the present as a period of disorder which must be transcended. This brought the secret societies into direct opposition with the Confucianism favored by the state which strove to create a this-worldly hierarchical scheme of proper social relations, built around the axis of filial piety. Many secret societies exhibited further heterodox tendencies. Most of them were strongly feminist, contrary to Confucian thinking which asserted the dominance of male yang over female yin: the secret societies tended to accord equal status to women. They also made use of the colloquial language, *pai-hua*, as against the classical linguistic *wen-yen* forms of the Confucian gentry. Some of them were also strongly puritanical; the White Lotus, for example, prohibited the use of alcohol, tobacco, and opium. The special contribution of the secret society to political life in China, says Franz Michael,

> was their militant political organization. They were formed as brotherhoods of the persecuted and of those who had no voice or power in the existing political and social structure. They formed

underground political organizations, rival and potentially hostile to the existing state organization. Their members were sworn to aid each other in distress, to give refuge to members who were in hiding from the officials, and to support each other in conflicts with outsiders as well as with the government. Loyalty to society brothers was the first obligation, but above the brotherhood of equal members was a hierarchy of officials of the society who could enforce absolute authority and discipline. The societies were secret orders of all those who had no other way to defend themselves against the pressures of the state and the privileged social leaders. They flourished especially in the rural villages and among the peasants but frequently included within their membership lower scholar-gentry (1966, 13).

These societies "therefore provided a model after which a rebellious organization could be patterned." From this perspective, the Communist party of the twentieth century did not violate traditional expectations, but dovetailed neatly with an established pattern of gaining economic and political leverage. Moreover, many Communist leaders—like Chu Teh, Ho Lung, Liu Tzu-tan—had been members of such secret societies as the Ko-Lao and were to use their secret-society connections in furthering the cause of the Communists.

Superficially static, Chinese society was in actuality subject both to repeated rebellions and to periods of disintegration followed by new cycles of consolidation and integration. Many of the recurrent rebellions involved uprisings of the peasantry. These conformed to a patterned sequence (Eberhard, 1965, 102–104). During the first stage of such an uprising, a number of peasants, driven from house and home for any number of reasons, would seek sanctuary in the wilderness. Turned bandits, they would raid travelers or rich landlords. Usually they maintained contact with their home villages and drew continuing supplies from there, while at the same time protecting the villagers against the incursion of rival bands.

During the second stage, the band would extend its radius of action, thus encroaching on the zone of operations of other bands. The resulting conflict would lead to the elimination of the less viable units, and established the dominance of the strongest and best-organized band. When this happened, rivals could no longer threaten the village base of the bandit band; this freed the band for further activity.

During the third stage, the band began to encounter resistance from landowners forced to pay additional amounts of tribute. Attempting to resist, the landowners called on the government of the nearest town. The bandits therefore attacked the town, attempting to cut off this source of assistance to the landowning group. If the government troops succeeded in driving off the attackers, the bandit band withdrew into the hinterland, only to splinter under the impact of defeat. Then the cycle would begin anew. However, government troops could make common cause with the rebels, while disgruntled local gentry would find that cooperation with the rebels in its own best interest in opposing the central authority of the state. As a result, the town might surrender to bandit pressure, offering the bandits an urban pivot for further activities.

During the fourth stage, the victorious band extended its sway over additional towns, and prepared to defend its booty against government troops. To achieve further success, they had to enter into ever closer alliances with the scholar-gentry of the region, since these held the monopoly of bureaucratic and social skills required for efficient administration. The bandits first adapted themselves to the norms of the gentry; later they adopted them as their own. Thus the victorious bandit leader became a general, a duke, or an emperor. Relying on the scholar-gentry for continued support, he became, in turn, a pillar of the established order.

A good example of a bandit who graduated through this four-stage cycle is that of the founder of the Ming dynasty, Chu Yüan-chang. China was then in the hands of a Mongol dynasty, the Yüan. Around the middle of the fourteenth century a series of natural disasters and political failures caused the decay of irrigation and transportation facilities; taxes rose precipitously, while food reserves became depleted. A series of bands formed primarily in the areas of Honan, north Anhwei, and north Kiangsu; they were associated with the White Lotus society, a secret organization which proclaimed that "the empire is in revolt, Buddha-Matreya is to be reborn, an enlightened ruler will appear." The bands extended their sway against a disunited government, unable to bring all its forces to bear at decisive points. One of the recruits to the bandit cause was an orphan from a peasant family who had spent part of his life as a beggar monk. He drew after him a group of supporters from his home village; many of them were actual kinsmen or adopted sons (*i-erh*). Gradually he eliminated the competition of rival bands: one source of his strength lay in his ability to combine a strong antiforeign appeal, directed against the Mongol rulers, with the social grievances and religious motivations which had promoted the uprising. As he extended his power over most of Anhwei and Kiangsu, with Nanking as the center of his power, he increasingly made use of literati drawn from the scholar-gentry of the region. In 1367, he drove the last heir of the Mongol dynasty back into the northern steppe and became emperor of China. The gentry families who had supported him in his struggle took over the positions of gentry that had served the foreign invader. The personnel of the governing elite thus underwent a complete change, while the structure of the system remained very much the same.

Movements which thus began as peasant rebellions frequently became, if successful, the means for a renewed concentration of power at the helm of the state, permitting Chinese society to reintegrate and consolidate itself. The new ruler would favor the gentry in his own following with appointments to official positions, while depriving opposition gentry of offices and landholdings. Frequently such a period of overturn was accompanied by widespread distribution of land taken from the enemies of the regime—distributions calculated to win the support of wide segments of the peasantry and local gentry for the new ruler. With renewed centralization of the governmental bureaucracy and greater efficiency in taxation, it also became possible to consolidate and expand the great hydraulic system on which Chinese agriculture depended for its surpluses, thus also increasing both the quantity and productivity of irrigable land. Yet the very expansion of the system tended to produce contrary forces. Local power holders increased and widened their power; taxes which had fed the central government were diverted once more into private hands; the hydraulic system suffered and fell into increasing disrepair; landholding became more concentrated. Exactions fell more heavily on the local peasantry. Disgruntled gentry who had gone unrewarded became more vocal in their dissatisfaction. Sporadic uprisings would become endemic until a major rebellion produced a new leader who would rise on the crest of peasant support to lead a return to order and centralization. In the course of Chinese history numerous dynasties had thus risen and fallen, with their rise and fall largely prompted by internal causes. In the nineteenth century, however, there was added to these internal causes the heavy pressure of foreign influence which simultaneously weakened the ability of the last dynasty to resist disintegration and made it ever more difficult for the country to achieve a return to social order and cohesion on its own terms.

European traders and missionaries—Portuguese, Spaniards, Dutch, and English—had long traded in the East for silk, spices, tea, and porcelain, and had sought to introduce their respective variants of Christian religion. Yet, before the advent of the nineteenth century, they had accepted the political and religious structure of the Chinese Empire, and even looked upon Chinese culture with a sense of admiration and hope. After the turn of the century, however, British trading interests began to exert ever greater pressure upon the Chinese government to relinquish its monopolies over trade and to allow the free importation of opium and textiles. The so-called Opium Wars (1839–1842) broke Chinese resistance to foreign imports. Successive treaties lowered the barrier to the introduction of opium on a large scale, reduced tariffs on imported goods, and opened a number of treaty ports to foreigners. It also forced the government to pay indemnities to Britain for fighting the war, the first of a series of such payments which were ultimately to ruin the Chinese treasury. An immediate consequence of this opening up of China to foreign traders was the vastly increased outflow of Chinese silver required to pay for the imports. As a result of the outflow of silver, the internal balance of silver to copper—the currencies used for local transactions—changed from 1:2 to 1:3. This greatly harmed the peasantry whose tax and rent payments were rendered in silver, but who received only copper for their salable produce.

The opening up of the treaty ports made China increasingly a satellite of the industrial world. What industrial development took place thereafter was largely concentrated in or near the treaty ports, fed by foreign investments and protected by foreign arms. The treaty ports became veritable bastions of foreign interests within China. Not only were foreigners subject to their own laws, and hence free of restrictions by Chinese law, but Chinese who had legal dealings with foreigners were to be judged under foreign law also. The defeat and the resultant encroachment of foreigners greatly injured the prestige of the Manchu dynasty and its capacity to retain a grip on the country. As it weakened internally, it was forced to rely ever more on outside powers who now had a decided interest in shoring up its internal defenses as a reliable instrument of order in the hinterland. They sought a government "weak enough to accept orders and controls from abroad, but strong enough to give orders and exercise control domestically" (Lattimore and Lattimore, 1944, 104).

At the same time, missionary attitudes toward the Chinese began to change also, especially with the advent of the first nonconformist English missionary in China, Robert Morrison. Where earlier Christian emissaries had looked upon the Chinese with a sense of kinship and admiration, there was a tendency now to see them as benighted heathen who would have to give up a deficient and inferior culture in favor of one constructed upon the patterns of the Protestant West. The treaties which legalized the importation of opium also provided for the untrammeled right of European missionaries to spread their teachings. In the words of the British historian Joshua Rowntree (1905, 242), opium and the Gospel "came together, spread together, have been fought for together, and finally legalized together." It is sometimes said that Christianity had little impact on Chinese society because its norms proved incompatible with Chinese family patterns and forms of ancestor commemoration. Yet it did have both short-run and long-run effects. The short-run effects are clear in the religious syncretism of the Taiping Rebellion, about which we shall have more to say later. The Taiping leader thought of himself as a younger brother of Jesus Christ and made use of the Bible as a sacred book. The movement was Christian enough to cause the churches to send investigators to discover whether its tenets coincided sufficiently with those of orthodox Christianity to be accorded Western aid. The report of the investigation was negative—one is prompted to speculate what would have happened if the missionaries involved had rendered a less fundamentalist and more ecumenical decision. Certainly by 1937 there were some three million Catholic Chinese, recruited mainly from the lower classes, and half a million converts to Protestantism, mainly of middle- and upper-class origins. Yet it is true that the effects of Christian endeavor lay less in conversion than in the transmission of Western ideas and techniques. Robert Elegant has said of this (1963, 86):

> The vast Christian missionary establishment in China was one of the most successful efforts by one culture to influence another. If the missionaries produced few Christians, they encouraged many sceptics; if they did not establish Christian morality, they engendered discontent; if they did not turn men's minds to contemplation of eternity or awake desire for spiritual enlightenment, they made known the material benefits enjoyed by Christian nations.

The fabric of Chinese society was weakened still further by a series of wars carried on by outside powers: the Anglo-French War against China in 1860–1861; the annexation of what is now Viet Nam by the French; the Japanese war against China in 1894–1895; and the Russo-Japanese war of 1904–1905 which was fought on Chinese soil. But there were also two major internal rebellions—among a number of smaller ones—which strained and rent the fabric from within: the Taiping Rebellion (1850–1865) and the rebellion of the Nien (1852–1868). These rebellions are important not only in their historical context, but because they proved to be rehearsals of a still greater event, the peasant-based

Communist revolution of the twentieth century. They exhibit some organizational and ideological themes which were to come into their own a century later. Moreover, many Communist leaders were raised at a time when the memory of these movements was still green. Chu Teh, for example, in his youth heard the story of the Taiping from a wandering weaver who had taken part in the movement (Smedley, 1956, 22–29).

The Taiping Rebellion began in the south, in the provinces of Kwangtung and Kwangsi, a natural unit marked off from the rest of China by a chain of mountains and oriented toward the port city of Canton. It was at Canton that foreign traders had first set foot on Chinese soil, and it was through Canton that foreign influence drove its main entering wedge after the opening of China to foreign trade. The area was ethnically and occupationally highly heterogeneous. It contained—enclaved among the Chinese—sizable minority groups of both Chinese and non-Chinese affiliation. The largest minority was the despised Hakka, Chinese who were later-comers to the area in contrast to the longer-established Han Chinese. Their customs and dialect differ from the Han to this day, when they number about twenty million. There were also tribal people in the area—Miao, Yao, and Lolo—who had once occupied much of southern China and were driven back to marginal and mountain land by the incoming Chinese. There also existed occupational groups with distinctive characteristics and professional organizations under their own leadership, who nursed particular grievances. Among them were the boat people whose services in canal shipping had suffered at the hands of coastwise foreign transportation; pirates whose lucrative activities on the high seas had been curtailed by foreign navies; smugglers of salt who busily circumvented the government salt monopoly by tapping the salt-producing areas of Kwangtung and Kwangsi on their own; miners; and charcoal burners. These readily enlisted in the Taiping armies. The Taiping leader, Hung Hsiu-ch'üan (1814–1864) had been a poor Hakka peasant from Kwangtung. His family had sacrificed itself to pay for his studies which were to make him a school teacher, but he failed the examinations which would have allowed him to enter the bureaucracy. A Protestant missionary tract served as the catalyst in setting him upon an alternative career as a religious leader. In the course of a vision, he came to see himself as the younger brother of Jesus Christ and hence as the second son of God, chosen to destroy the demons on earth in order to create a new Kingdom of God. He also received two months of training in an American mission at Canton under the tutelage of the fundamentalist Reverend Issachar Roberts from Sumner County, Tennessee. The Bible took its place among the sacred books of the new religion. The movement spread quickly through eleven provinces south of the Yangtze River; its geographical distribution markedly coincides with the area in which the Communists first established themselves after World War I (McColl, 1964; Laai Yi-faai, Franz Michael, and John Sherman, 1962). Before it was finally put down by government troops with a loss of an estimated twenty million lives, it had set in motion a whole set of processes which were ultimately to cause the disintegration of the Chinese state from within, much as foreign encroachment had caused the state to disintegrate from without.

The Taiping uprising ended in defeat, yet it made a powerful impression on the Chinese people. The announced objectives of the movement have a strangely modern ring still a hundred years after the bloody events of the rising. They were the first, since the opening-up of China by the West, to announce some of the themes later taken up and developed by the Chinese Communists. It should be no surprise, therefore, that in present-day Communist writings the Taiping appear as ancestors and forerunners of the present-day movement.

What are these "modern" features of the Taiping? First, they envisioned a social order which would do away with the rule of the Chinese gentry. The Taipings, says Franz Michael, "sought to introduce a monist order in which the state would be all" (1966, 7). Instead of the traditional division of society into scholar-gentry, peasantry, and military, peasantry, soldiery, and administrators were to be one. The entire society was to be organized into peasant-soldier cells of twenty-five families commanded by a sergeant. Each family would receive land to work but not to own. Any surplus above the amount required to feed the family would be transferred to a public granary supervised by the sergeant. Four cells, or one hundred families, were to be commanded by a lieutenant; five lieutenancies would form a captaincy, five captaincies a coronelcy, five coronelcies a generalship. Each military officer would be at one and the same time administrative official, judge, and religious guide. A sergeant, for example, would not only head a military unit of twenty-five peasant-soldiers and administer their granary; he would also preside at weekend services and life-cycle ceremonies. Any question he could not settle would be passed up the chain of command for resolution at the next higher level. Good performance would be rewarded by promotion, poor performance by demotion or capital punishment. Moreover, the Taipings directed their attacks not only against the scholar-gentry but also against their ideology, Confucianism, as the religion of a class of enemies; in its place they would institute their own vision of the Heavenly Kingdom as the religion of *all* the Chinese. To the monism which imbued their vision of a new political society, they allied an ideological monism. "This set the Taipings not only against the government but against the defenders of the existing social order itself, the gentry, and all those who believed in the Confucian system" (Michael, 1966, 7).

It is very likely that the Taiping did not create this ideal of a monist society and polity out of whole cloth, but drew on older sources of inspiration for their concepts of what the social order ought to be like. It is generally agreed (Shih, 1967, 253–268) that they made use of the Chou-li, an ancient document purported to have been written by the Duke of Chou, the prime minister of Wu Wang, who vanquished the Shang dynasty in the twelfth century B.C. The Duke of Chou envisaged a tightly organized feudal state in which barons would owe allegiance to viscounts, viscounts to earls, earls to marquis, marquis to dukes, dukes to the Son of Heaven. These five grades of vassals correspond to the five grades of officers envisioned by the Taiping. At the bottom of this pyramid was the peasantry, organized around agricultural units of nine farms, one of which was to be public, while the surrounding eight farms were to be private. The peasants were to till the public farm, as well as their own private lots. The resemblance to the Taiping scheme is intriguing. Nevertheless, it must be pointed out that the Duke of Chou also recognized that his five kinds of feudatories would each be served by five kinds of gentry: minister, great officer, upper scholar, middle scholar, and lower scholar. Moreover, all positions were to be hereditary. In addition, it would seem that peasants were not to bear arms. Yet it may be surmised that there existed a tradition of political thought that could take its departure from such first principles, principles which were clearly divergent and in opposition to later concepts of an Oriental society administered by a nonhereditary scholar-gentry. It is certainly true that in a literary tradition which relies heavily on citations from the classics, anyone wishing to score an intellectual point must fortify it by such citations. It is also curious to note that the Chou-li was also invoked by Wang An-Shih (A.D. 1021–1086), the "New Deal" reformer of the Sung dynasty. Wang An-Shih was himself a believer in the well-field system of eight private farms and one public farm. Yet when he encountered opposition to its restoration, he focused less on agrarian reform as such than on a development of the institution of the public granary which would draw supplies from the peasantry and, in turn, make loans of supplies to them in times of need. At the same time, he also initiated military schemes which made each peasant simultaneously into a soldier. In opposition to the use of mercenaries, Wang An-Shih "would try to train such civilian soldiers, gradually replacing the imperial armies with them, and return to the old way of a farmer-soldiery" (Miyakazi, 1963, 87). He further attacked the literary traditions of the gentry, and advocated a system of technical specialization, thus attacking the ideological justification of the scholar-gentry itself. These reforms failed, but it does not seem unlikely that the concepts of well-field system, public granary, soldier-peasantry, and hierarchical grades of leaders who simultaneously fulfill a number of functions were kept alive in the larger Chinese ideological tradition.

The Taiping had a number of other features which make them forerunners of the revolutionists of the twentieth century. They granted equality to women, including access to the grades of leadership; there were female soldiers in the Taiping army. There were edicts against foot-binding, prostitution, and trade in women. Marriage was to be based on mutual attraction between the partners, not on financial arrangements between families as in the past; the tie was to be monogamous. All of these measures were directed against the gentry with its marital arrangements for purposes of social mobility, the use of female foot-binding as a mark of social status, the employment of concubinage, the assertion of male dominance over women. The Taiping also supported the use of the popular language as against the linguistic forms of the literati. They advocated the introduction of a modern Western-type calendar. Opium, tobacco, and alcohol were forbidden. Finally, the movement was strongly iconoclastic, destroying not only ancestor tablets—which hit at the continuity of lineages and clans, one of the mechanisms of gentry dominance—but aimed also at the elimination of Buddhist, Taoist, and Confucianist images.

Most of this program remained visionary and was not put into practice; a Communist writer, Fei Min, has spoken of the Taiping program as "fantasy socialism" (quoted in Levenson, 1964, 181, fn. 14). Yet there is some doubt if it should even be described as "socialism." The Taiping aim was less to benefit the peasantry than to organize it according to a new social scheme, in which political power would be differently allocated, but in which the peasant would still be the main burden-bearer of the new society. The projected vision of agrarian reform was, in fact, not realized; ever increasing taxation in the end turned the peasantry against the Taiping. This reverse was cleverly exploited by the government troops set against them. The Taiping could in the end not count on the peasantry because they had failed to hold its loyalty (Michael, 1966, 195).

The second major rebellion was that of the Nien, who rose in the millet- and kaoliang-growing north. The Nien were strongly anti-Manchu; their common leader pronounced himself Great Han Prince with the Heavenly Mandate. Their symbols and ceremonials were derived from the anti-Manchu Buddhist White Lotus Society. Their intermediate leaders were drawn in the main from the lower degree holders of the gentry and from their powerful clans. Less ideological than the Taiping, they were, however, more adept at organizing mass support for their venture. Their pattern was to enroll entire communities and to organize them into self-defense corps behind great earthen walls surrounded by a zone of scorched earth to facilitate attack and defense. They opened prisons and staged vengeance trials against officials. They organized production and carried out distributions of grain. They made extensive use of cavalry, using thousands of horses. Their pattern of organization, however, showed three striking weaknesses, cleverly exploited by opposing government troops. They remained primarily rural, unwilling and unable to seize and hold cities. Their efforts were largely decentralized, each community remaining largely concerned with its own immediate gains and defense; and they ultimately alienated the land-hungry peasantry with their scorched-earth policy. The able government leader Tseng Kuo-Fan exploited these debilities by isolating community after community, cutting off cavalry raiders from their home bases, and attracting to the government side many of the peasants who had suffered from the Nien defensive policy.

In historical perspective the rebellions of the nineteenth century were to have a paradoxical effect on the course of Chinese development in the twentieth century. The rebellions were defeated, but only at the cost of raising large regional armed forces under regional leaders. These, usually members of the top gentry and honored officials of the state, thus found themselves in positions of increasing independent power. The state had delegated to them the task of destroying the rebels; yet in so doing it had in fact mortgaged the future of China to officials who were at the same time regional power holders. Moreover, the number of military officials had increased heavily during the rebellions. Some of these new men of power were destined to become the first industrial entrepreneurs in China. They favored industrial development to strengthen their own power as opposed to that of the central government; they also sought to create adequate industrial and commercial instruments capable of resisting the growing foreign impact. Yet as members of the traditional scholar-gentry they also continued to see in these instruments primarily the means to preserving the essence (*t'i*) of traditional, Confucian, agrarian China (Feuerwerker, 1958, 245). They lacked both the technical experience in the management of modern enterprises, and the social vision which would have allowed them to employ landholding as an adjunct to industry and trade, rather than making industry and trade subservient to traditional landholding. Thus, even while they moved toward involvement with Western capitalism, they remained gentry first and entrepreneurs second.

While these great officials were still caught up in the dilemma between Confucian values and modern private enterprise, they were soon outpaced by a large group of entrepreneurs who were much less attached to the old order and more committed to new ways of carrying on business. These were the treaty-port merchants or *compradores,* as they were called in Portuguese, agents of foreign business firms in China. By traditional Confucian values their commercial activity had been held in low esteem; the merchant had held low status in Chinese society, which gave social priority both to the peasant and to scholar. The merchant had

> drained from the peasant the surplus above the minimum needed for survival. At the same time, the merchant was competing for that surplus with the gentry-landlord, and with the entire official bureaucratic structure which was ultimately supported by taxation and multiple customary exactions on the total agricultural product. It followed that in the dominant ideology the merchant was seen as essentially parasitic on the two classes accorded the highest positions in the traditional rank-order of gentry-official, peasant, craftsman, merchant (Feuerwerker, 1958, 50)

Entry into the foreign business world thus gave them a position and esteem which they had not received in the imperial past. Their role within the new commercial-industrial orbit, however, remained subsidiary; in their activities they faced the heavy competitive pressures of foreign business establishments and governments. Most of them remained financially weak and exposed to the vicissitudes of changes in internal and external prices. In 1918, of

956 Chinese firms, 653, or 69 percent, held capital of less than fifty thousand yuan; only 33, or 4 percent of all firms, operated with capital of more than a million yuan (Chesneaux, 1962, 30, fn. 2). Nor was this wealth easily convertible from one business enterprise to another, while European firms mixed banking operations, industrial investment, and management in facile symbiosis. A foreign firm like Jardine & Matheson, tied in with banks in Hong Kong and Shanghai, had simultaneous holdings in shipyards, public transportation, insurance companies, and coal mines. The Chinese firms were also dependent upon foreign firms for much of their fuel and power required to drive the new machinery, as well as upon imports of that machinery itself. They were handicapped by innumerable local taxes charged against the circulation of goods within China, while unable to defend themselves against the competition of foreign goods which were protected by a foreign-imposed limit of 5 percent on Chinese tariffs. In addition, most of their goods traveled up and down the Yangtze River and abroad in foreign carriers. Their own resources were thus insufficient to underwrite an independent base of power; their livelihood depended on their symbiotic relationships with foreign business. They did not care for the ways of the foreign devils, but they were victims of the pact they had signed with them. Their activities affected the entire fabric of Chinese life, but they themselves were not the arbiters of the terms of change brought on by them. They might on occasion bargain for improved contracts, but the basic condition of their existence made them no more than the adjutants of foreign powers on Chinese soil. They were unable to free themselves from the chains which bound them to the bureaucratic patterns of the Chinese past, and yet impotent to assert their independence in the face of forces to which they owed their novel status.

Yet the old order was doomed, and the inherited Confucian bureaucracy with it. Debilitated by foreign exactions and by internal rebellions, increasingly fragmented into regional power blocks of officeholders and soldiers who were beginning to entertain relations with different foreign firms and powers on their own, the Chinese Empire collapsed in 1911 to make way for a disorderly and divided republic. Nationalist rebels, dreaming of a strong and united China, capable of maintaining order at home and of resisting foreign pressure, took over the reins of government. Yet the collapse of central authority had left the road wide open to the assumption of local or regional power by war lords. These were, in Lattimore's phrase, "politicians with private armies." Such soldier-politicians could be found at all levels, exercising their dominions over towns, regions, a province, or several provinces. They collected taxes and gifts, seized loot from political opponents, and were in an ideal position to promote smuggling, gambling, or the production and distribution of opium (for case histories, see Chow, 1966). Frequently they cooperated with the local gentry, now freed from central control, and both found their alliance to their mutual benefit. They also entered into coalitions with each other or fought against each other, often in response to the influence of foreign or domestic business groups which favored now consolidation, now conflict. They recruited their armies primarily from the impoverished peasantry, unable to make ends meet. These were hired as mercenary soldiers; on a few occasions a talented peasant boy might become a high-ranking officer or war lord himself. The process, of course, set up a vicious cycle: the greater the number of war lords and mercenaries, the greater the chances of continued disturbance in the countryside, the greater also the tendency of both peasants and sons of the gentry to enter upon a military career. The line between accredited military activity and outright banditry was a very fine one, and easily erased in the process.

At the same time, with the advent of the twentieth century, Chinese agriculture entered into a state of open imbalance. Experts assign differential importance to one or another factor, but there is no doubt that several of these forces, working in conjunction, augmented the weight of the burden resting upon the Chinese peasant. First, and perhaps foremost, was the age-old problem of how to feed an increasing population crowded on limited amounts of land; population was to increase from 430 to 600 million between 1850 and 1950. Such a rate of population increase would in and of itself have brought on considerable stress. For decades,

Chinese agriculture had proved capable of feeding this growing number of people; yet by 1900 demographic pressure on resources was beginning to exceed tolerable limits. This pressure was intensified still further by the age-old pattern of Chinese inheritance which insisted on equal partition of land among the available heirs. The growing population was thus increasingly compressed on ever smaller plots of land. Second in importance was the decline in effective flood control and water management, and the inability to undertake expansion and the construction of new works. Inability to manage these works on which much of China's agriculture depended had always accompanied dynastic decline; the central power grew increasingly unable to marshal the men and goods required to maintain dikes and canals. Third, as the central power declined, local and regional war lords began to retain taxes which they had previously passed on to the imperial coffers and to exact new and unpredictable levies to fill their own treasure chests and to finance their own enterprises (see Gamble, 1963, 139–141). Furthermore, levies were extracted by excess troops billeted in the countryside or by bandits who were often merely the defeated soldiers of unsuccessful militarists. Fourth, the decline of the Manchu and the advent of the republic put an end to the institution of the public granary in which surplus foodstuffs were accumulated under government auspices against times of need. The remnants of existing stocks were sold in 1912 to defray the cost of the Revolution and were never replaced.

Fifth, the surpluses generated by age-old patterns of tenancy and usury were increasingly converted into instruments of commercial expansion. To some extent, all the factors previously mentioned—population pressure, failure in water control, political fragmentation, depletion of food reserves—had made their appearance before in the course of Chinese history. The twentieth century, however, proved distinctive in facilitating the diffusion of private entrepreneurial capitalism into the rural areas of China and in generating specifically Chinese reactions to this spread.

This statement should not be interpreted to mean that there

did not exist a tradition of private entrepreneurship in China before the advent of Europeans. We have seen that China has long permitted land to be bought and sold. Chinese society also allowed the gentry to amass peasant surpluses as part of their informal subcontractual relations with the state, and the use of credit at high rates of interest was widespread and customary. The state also permitted a modicum of private profit-taking in commercial undertakings, and we hear of merchants in Peking who drew more of an income from pawnbroking, moneylending and shopkeeping than from land rent. But where in the history of Western Europe political power often had to make concessions to the independent merchant groups of the cities, in China the state was overwhelmingly strong. It could rely on an enormous peasant population to furnish it with the sustenance it required and to accomplish this without any labor-saving machinery; in its scholar-gentry it had found a reliable instrument of political and social control. Thus the Chinese state never had a need for a political alliance with private groups of mercantile entrepreneurs. It limited their activity through the operation of great state monopolies and kept their property "weak" and subservient to the state. Moreover, social power and prestige derived from the ownership of land and from possession of scholarly titles; if they wished to gain either, therefore, the merchants had to plow back their gains into the purchase of land and into the educational careers of their children (Balazs, 1964; Murphey, 1962; Wittfogel, 1957).

But the encroachment of the foreign powers upon China and the combined results of the "open door" policy simultaneously produced the disintegration of the state apparatus and the liberation of commercial and industrial activity from traditional political and social controls. Industry grew, though in all likelihood not fast enough to furnish a dependable alternative source of investment for the majority of those who had capital to invest. There was a great increase in the production of crops of high market value, such as tobacco and opium. Food crops, however, were also involved in this development. In Chu Hsien, in Anhwei province, for example, informal estimates indicate that in a good crop year more than fifty per cent of the rice harvested in Ch'uhsien is destined for an outside market. . . . Such is the value of rice as a means of obtaining cash, that many farmers eat their own rice only at special times of the year. They prefer in many cases to dispose of their entire crop with the exception of seed and invest part of their return in cheaper foodstuffs for their own consumption. Thus many Ch'uhsien rice growers eat maize as their staple. . . . Frequently the farmer cultivates no personal garden. Since green vegetables are an important element in the Chinese diet, the farmer who lacks them must get them through trade or purchase. Under normal conditions of production, therefore, it is quite obvious that the Chinese farm family is far from being self-sufficient (Fried, 1953, 129).

In some areas, this produced

the emergence, side by side with small landlords who live in the villages and are partners with their tenants in the business of farming, of a class of absentee owners whose connection with agriculture is purely financial. The development naturally proceeds most rapidly in the neighborhood of great cities, in districts where the static conditions of rural life are broken up by the expansion of commerce and industry, and in regions like parts of Manchuria, which have recently been settled by an immigrant population. The symptoms accompanying it are land speculation, and the intrusion between landlord and tenant of a class of middlemen. In Kwangtung, it is stated, it is increasingly the practice for large blocks of land to be rented by well-to-do merchants, or even by companies especially formed for the purpose, and then be sub-let piecemeal at a rack rent to peasant farmers. Elsewhere, a result of the growth of absentee ownership is the employment of agents, who relieve the landlord of the business of himself squeezing his tenants, browbeat the tenants by threats of eviction into paying more than they owe, and make money out of both cheating by the former and intimidating the latter (Tawney, 1932, 68).

The introduction of commercial crops and the commercialization of land affected land prices, tenure conditions, and rent charges. Prices for land doubled and tripled in some areas, and secure tenure was replaced by short-term contracts. At the same time rents increased outright or rose through the use of such mechanisms as advance collections or the payment of rent deposits to ensure rights of permanent tenure.

Elsewhere the growth of the market brought customary rural handicrafts into competition with industrial products, foreign or domestic. It would seem that this competition did not lead to an absolute decline in handicraft output (Feuerwerker, 1968, 11); a craft industry like cloth manufacture even benefited from the introduction of machine-made yarn. Growing conversion to the use of machine-made products, however, proved a direct threat to the many peasant households who had supplemented their meager returns from agriculture with marginal craft production. It is for this reason that the Chinese anthropologists Fei Hsiao-tung and Chang Chih-I concluded their study of three communities in Yunnan with the conclusion that agriculture alone could no longer feed the Chinese population.

> The industrial revolution in the West at last threatens the peasants in the Chinese villages in their capacity as industrialists. However, skillful they may be, they are fighting a losing battle against the machine. But they must keep on fighting, because otherwise they cannot live. The result is that China is gradually being reduced to an agrarian country, pure and simple; and an agrarian China is inevitably a starving China (1945, 305).

We must not imagine that these novel processes advanced everywhere at the same rate and with the same intensity. Depending on local circumstances, the introduction of commercial crops might favor landowning peasants or landlords or absentee commercial associations engaged in farming. In one locality or one region tenancy patterns could continue on a traditional basis, with landlords of traditional expectations; in another, the spread of tenancy might be associated with commercial agriculture. Handicrafts of one kind might suffer, but handicrafts of another branch, carried on elsewhere, might find profitable outlets. Some areas had banks, others—perhaps too uncertain politically—lacked them. Some landlords would invest their money in commercial enterprises, others—in a neighboring village—would bury their gold in the ground. These differentials produced great local variations and underwrote different social relations in one locality as against another, in one region as against another region. Power relations differed accordingly. As a result, economy, society, and polity grew increasingly disjointed. Yet the same over-all dynamic was everywhere apparent, drawing the resources of differing microstructures into an expanding vortex. The structural controls exercised by the state disintegrated; the prestige associated with owning land and gaining scholarly titles diminished. Conversely new possibilities for investing wealth in commerce and industry grew apace and offered new opportunities to merchants as to the officials and war lords who had inherited the fragments of the shattered state apparatus. It was through a new symbiosis between landlords, officials, soldiers, and merchants—achieved on the local or regional level in the twenties and thirties—that potentially capitalizable wealth was mobilized in the countryside and combined with capital imported from the eastern seaboard. In this symbiosis there emerged what Chen Hanseng called "quadrilateral beings:"

> They are rent collectors, merchants, usurers, and administrative officers. Many landlord-usurers are becoming landlord-merchants; many landlord-merchants are turning themselves into landlord-merchant-politicians. At the same time many merchants and politicians become landlords. Landlords often possess breweries, oil mills and grain magazines. On the other hand, the owners of warehouses and groceries are mortgagees of land, and eventually its lords. It is a well-known fact that pawnshops and business stores of the landlords are in one way or another affiliated with banks of military and civil authorities. . . . While some big landlords practice usury as their chief profession, nearly all of them have something to do with it. Again, many landlords are military and civil officials (quoted in Isaacs, 1966, 32).

Yet land and land rent remained a vital concern to many whose major formal activity was associated with other ways of gaining a livelihood. Even when people had moved to the cities, investment in land remained an important source of income.

Of 391 middle-class people in Peiping, from whom information was secured [in 1936–1937], 191 or 48 per cent owned land; of 21 of our informants (clerks, merchants, and owners of workshops) in Shanghai, 11 or 52 per cent had land. . . .

Extra occupational sources of income have played even a larger part in the economic life of the upper than in that of the middle class. An official with a salary of $200 a month and an income of $100–150 a month from land was not unusual. Informants among merchants often could not say whether their main source of income was business or land. . . . Of 231 upper class families in North China who gave information, 126 or 54 per cent (not including landlords) owned land; many owned houses. Investments in stores, factories, and loans played an important part (Lang, 1946, 94, 98).

To the peasants of even very remote and isolated villages this meant that their surpluses were drawn off through an extensive hierarchy of powerholders who increasingly held the mortgages to their means of livelihood. In Ten Mile Inn, Wu An County, of what became the Communist border region against the Japanese in the north, for example, one big landlord carried on a business in which he advanced cloth to the peasants in the spring in return for cotton deliveries in the fall when prices were low; owned one hundred *mou* of fertile land; and had bought the right to collect debts owed to a landlord in nearby Stone Cave Village. Another farmed and ran a store in which the most profitable items were the sale of heroin on credit, with land as security, and the relending of money, itself borrowed from landlords in a nearby village (Crook and Crook, 1959, 18–20).

Thus the overall picture was one of pyramids within pyramids, one of the smaller pyramids consisting of the smaller landlords themselves. Thus the big landlords used the lesser, and the lesser landlords used those still smaller—or they used rich peasants. These in turn used middle or even poor peasants as their agents. The money loaned out by the Hsin Hsung Shop in Ten Mile Inn, for instance, at 100 per cent interest every twenty days was originally borrowed—by no means interest free—from the landlord Chang "Lao-wantze" of West Harmony (Crook and Crook, 1959, 28).

Mr. Chang, whose nickname means Old Meat Ball, in turn dealt with landlords more powerful than himself. At the top of the pyramid in Wu An County stood Chang Hsin-hai. He had possession of forty thousand *mou* of cultivable land, four hundred times as much as the richest landlord in Ten Mile Inn, in addition to controlling rentals from eighty villages and owning forty courtyards in town (Crook and Crook, 1959, 11).

Yet throughout this period of increasing commercialization of agriculture, China remained primarily, as it had been in the past, a land of peasants with access to land through ownership or rent. In 1930 it was estimated that about half of the peasantry owned their land, another quarter owned some land and rented some, still another quarter was made up of land renters (Tawney, 1932, 34). Ownership was, however, unequally distributed. Studies of four *hsien* or districts in north China in 1936 showed that landlords who formed 3 to 4 percent of the population possessed 20 to 30 percent of the land; poor peasants formed between 60 to 70 percent of the population but controlled less than 20 to 30 percent of the land. In the south, as represented by four southern *hsien*, landlords composed 2 to 4 percent of the population and held 30 to 50 percent of the land (Institute of Pacific Relations, 1939, 3). Tawney estimated in 1932 that "between 40 and 50 percent of the peasant families did not have enough land to provide them with food" (Tawney, 1932, 71). Estimates of the totally landless are hard to come by. A survey of 3,552 families in the 1920's (Tayler, 1928, 106) showed only 16 percent without any land at all. Mao Tsetung gave a figure of 20 percent of the peasant population of Changsha County, Hunan, in 1927 as "utterly destitute,"

> that is, people who have neither land nor money, are without any means of livelihood, and are forced to leave home and become mercenaries or hired laborers or wandering beggars (Mao, 1965, 32).

Most farm labor was still performed by peasants themselves or by their families; only about one-fifth of all farm labor was performed by hired laborers (Buck, 1930, 231–237). A discussion of forms of farm labor in China emphasizes the degree to which farm laborers did not constitute a separate class.

In studying the form of farm labor in China, it is highly

> important to remember that in general the hired agricultural laborers in China are at the same time poor peasants who cultivate land either owned or leased, and in intervals are also hired out as coolies. While the general phenomenon among the rural rich is a trinity of landlord, merchant and usurer, that among the rural poor is another trinity of poor tenants, hired farm hands and coolies. According to a field investigator, who in 1933 worked throughout Honan province, the landless peasants and those with insufficient lands have to change rapidly from one farm to another. One day they do field work on their own land or the land they have leased; the next day they work as hired laborers in someone else's field; and the day after that they work as coolies transporting goods from the shops in the city. These partially hired laborers in Honan far outnumber the full time hired laborers, and the same situation is also to be found in many other provinces (Institute of Pacific Relations, 1939, 71).

The resulting social profile is that of a rural society dominated not "by the hired laborer, but the land-holding peasant" (Tawney, 1932, 34). Yet this landholding peasantry was at the same time struggling fiercely to maintain itself on the land, doubly threatened as it was by pressures of commercialization from above and the prospect of destitution from below.

All these developments—continued foreign encroachment, the infighting of war-lord armies, the spread of industry and trade, and the deepening agricultural discontent—could not fail to create a rising ferment among a population increasingly thrown into disorder and ever more despairing of the hope that order could be restored in the Celestial Kingdom. Ferment was especially marked in three new segments of that population, among the developing Chinese working class, produced by the growth of industry and trade; among students, ever more caught up in contradictions between the conflicting standards of past and present; and among the peasantry, affected deeply by the vicissitudes of agriculture. As the twentieth century wore on, there also appeared new political forms, new parties, and new types of political institutions, which would attempt to incorporate and direct these new elements on the political level.

By 1919 the number of industrial workers had reached 1,500,-000. Three-quarters of these were engaged in transportation or light industry, especially in textile production. Three-fifths worked in Chinese-owned enterprises, two-fifths in enterprises owned by foreigners. Most of them were concentrated in eastern China: Shanghai alone had some 300,000 industrial workers; the area of Hong Kong some 50,000; the twin provinces of Hupeh and Hunan, 100,000. The great majority were former peasants recently recruited into industrial work and transplanted to the city (Chesneaux, 1962, 85; Lang, 1946, 87). They frequently left their families in the countryside, often residing in dormitories or in the workshops themselves while on the job. Often they returned to the countryside during harvest time, causing high rates of industrial absenteeism. They often visited in the country: transportation costs for such visits composed the third highest item on their budgets, following closely after expenditures for food and clothing. Their local and regional ties continued strong. Often they were hired from the same area by the same labor boss; some of them continued local or regional specialties, like ink-making or carpentry, under industrial circumstances. They also showed a tendency to form regional associations or regional chapters of trade-unions. Few of them were skilled workers; most of the positions requiring industrial skills were filled by foreign labor. At the same time, the permanent industrial labor force merged imperceptibly with a much larger urban mass of workers in traditional craftshops, coolies, peddlers, and other middlemen characteristic of the urban scene. This urban mass may have numbered some ten times the number of the industrial workers themselves. Many of these people carried on activities which bordered on the illegal or were in fact against the law, supported by a proliferation of more or less organized clandestine organizations of the poor. These organizations merged, in turn, with the more traditional secret societies which also recruited members of the new working class. There existed, therefore, a whole network of relations, tying the new workers to the peasantry in the country and ramifying through the urban mass, beyond the industrial work force itself. Yet in 1918 the first industrial union made its appearance—as opposed to the craft or regional associations mentioned above—and only a year later workers were already on strike in support of nationalist students. By 1925 one million workers went out on strike in support of political causes. In 1927 union membership numbered three million, and an attempt at urban insurrection relying heavily on worker support came close to success in seizing power in May of that year.

A second element was the movement of nationalist students. The age-old Confucian examination-system had been abolished in 1905; traditional Confucian scholarship was fast losing its traditional prestige. Instead, a new student population eagerly sought to acquire mastery of new techniques and customs in the course of Western-oriented educational careers. Already by 1915 there were some four million Chinese students engaged in studies beyond the elementary-school level, taught by some 200,000 teachers. More than a hundred thousand went to study abroad between 1872 and 1949. By and large

> they were drawn from an economic elite. Even the relatively low annual tuition, room, and board of the government university was equivalent to perhaps five months' wages of a Shanghai textile worker. The same worker would have to spend five and a half years' earnings to put his son through four years of missionary college. In short, a family had to have an upper-middle-class income to send a child to a public college and an upper-class income to send him to a missionary institution (Israel, 1966, 5).

While at first the values of this group were still strongly fettered to the traditional norms of the scholar-gentry, their involvement with the problems posed by their new education and setting made them increasingly resistant to the influence of parental authority, and increasingly open to the influence of new values. Increasingly they reacted against the narrow familism of their parents and in favor of wider social goals. In 1915, Ch'en Tu-hsiu, professor at Peking University and later a founder of the Chinese Communist party, gave voice to their sentiments in his *Call to Youth*:

Be independent, not servile!
Be progressive, not conservative!
Be aggressive, not retiring!
Be cosmopolitan, not isolationist!
Be utilitarian, not formalistic!
Be scientific, not imaginative!

Caught between the conflicting standards of the old and the new; between East and West; between the world of their parents with their more particularistic loyalties, and their own involvements with fellow students drawn from all over China; faced often with uncertain economic conditions and threatened by unemployment; and ever more conscious of the impotence of China in the face of the growing foreign threat, the students reacted to their situation with an accentuated nationalism. They made their presence felt first on May 4, 1919, when students in Peking protested Japanese encroachment and the willingness of Chinese politicians to yield to Japanese demands. The protests spread rapidly to other cities with student populations, and workers began to support the student movement with strikes. Winning wide public support for their actions, the effort of May 4 set the pattern for future student involvement in politics.

As time went by, the older generation of students, especially those who had studied abroad, increasingly accommodated itself to circumstances, most of them entering employment with Western and Westernized enterprises. Yet an active minority of the older generation and an ever growing number of new students would play an important part in the anti-Japanese fight and in the swing to the Left that was to end in the final takeover of the Communist party in 1949.

The growing political involvement of the work force located in industrial and commercial centers, for a long time obscured the other major movement of political mobilization—the formation of politically oriented leagues among the peasantry. The peasant movement of the twentieth century had its origin in 1921 when P'eng Pai, the son of a wealthy landlord turned schoolteacher in his native village of Haifeng and one of the founders of the Communist party in Canton, organized the Haifeng Peasant Association. Haifeng is located in the East River districts of Kwangtung Province: once again the Chinese south began to play its strategic role in raising the flag of rebellion in China. It was here that Chinese had experienced the longest and most intense contact with overseas areas and foreign ideas. It was here that the Taiping had originated, and from the south that they launched their effort to wrest control of China from the Manchu dynasty. It was from the south, once again, that Sun Yat-sen had challenged the imperial rule in Peking to establish the republic in 1911, and it was to Canton in the south that he had retreated to defend the republican constitution against the war lords. Here he and his successors were to receive the support of thousands of overseas Chinese who had sought new opportunities abroad and had come to visualize alternatives to the rule of the past. Now the south had once again incubated a movement of the peasantry which in the course of thirty years was to lend its energies to an effort to transform Chinese society along entirely new lines. By May 1925 the peasant associations in Kwangtung numbered about 180,000 peasant unionists (Isaacs, 1966, 69).

Yet the task of organizing the peasantry was not uniformly successful, and some of the problems raised in the course of the organizational effort were to recur—in one form or another—in all later attempts to organize the Chinese peasantry. Roy M. Hofheinz, who has discussed the process of organization in Kwangtung in detail, has noted two major sources of difficulties. First, not all peasants lend themselves equally well to the task of organization. Contrary to the common belief that

> there was a high correlation between high rates of tenancy and the incidence of rural unrest . . . the facts seem to demonstrate the opposite. It was precisely in those areas where tenancy was the highest—the delta hsien to the immediate south of Canton—that the peasant movement had the greatest difficulty (1966, 191).

Here agriculture was productive, and the vicinity of Canton—with its large demand for produce—made it profitable. Tenants could participate in windfalls during good years or when water levels were adequate. In addition, the prevalence of banditry in this area often made landlords reluctant to collect rents. Hence, they saw little reason to endanger their position by joining the peasant movement. But there was a second aspect to their reluctance. The republican revolution of 1911 had done little to alter the structure of local power. Control was firmly in the hands of local gentry, frequently backed up by private armies (*min t'uan*). Many members of the gentry worked hand in glove with local bandits— "it often occurred that entire villages went over to the underworld" (Hofheinz, 1966, 199). Clan ties were also strong; often a whole village belonged to the same clan. At the same time, villages were linked to each other through the secret society of the Triad. Here the reformers thus faced an entire integument of local power which they would first have to pierce before the peasantry could begin to play an independent political role. Hofheinz has said that the peasant associations

> attempted to grow up in a veritable forest of other social groupings. So long as traditional structures remained intact they had to be competed with. The evidence suggests that in many cases the growth of the peasant movement was severely restricted by such competition (1966, 220).

Where they were most successful was in Haifeng on the eastern seaboard and in Kwangning district in the West River area where the land was mountainous and less productive; here more than 20 percent of the peasant population answered their call for rent reduction.

Yet even here it quickly became evident that the peasant movement would not be able to gain its demands on its own. As long as it adopted no more than what Hofheinz calls a "Christian social action approach" (1966, 209), it could not surmount the political barriers raised against it. Partial success came only when the peasant movement allied itself with the military forces of the Kuo Min Tang operating from Canton, and grew able to call on military support in implementing reform and checking gentry power. In 1925 the movement thus began to expand, making "the transition from moderate reformism to independent local subversion to blitzkrieg pincer attacks combining internal and external force" (1966, 211). Peasant mobilization thus proved impossible without political and military leverage. That leverage was to be furnished by new political and military institutions.

Workers, students, and peasants organized into peasant leagues constituted some of the major new elements which—in the twenties—were incorporated into large-scale mass parties of a type hitherto unknown in China. The first of these was the Kuo Min Tang or Nationalist party, based upon the revolutionary organizations which had achieved the overthrow of the empire and the creation of the republic in 1911. The other party was the Kung Ch'an Tang, the "Share Production party or Communist party," founded in 1921. Casting about for foreign allies which might aid it in the struggle for national integrity against foreign powers already represented on Chinese soil, the Kuo Min Tang in 1923 found such an ally in the Soviet Union, which had in 1920 renounced all territorial and extraterritorial demands on China. In 1923 formal liaison was established between the KMT and the Communist party of the Soviet Union. Under this agreement the Soviet Union sent advisers to shape the KMT into a disciplined party organization with an organized mass following. At the same time, the nascent Chinese Communist party was pressured to yield its autonomy and to merge its forces with the KMT. The aim was to create an organization capable of mounting an effective anti-imperialist struggle and to introduce liberal reforms within China, to create a national democratic state, but to eschew revolution. The effect was to transform the Kuo Min Tang

> into a rough copy of the Russian Bolshevik Party. Bolshevik methods of agitation and propaganda were introduced. To create the basis of an army imbued with Kuomintang ideas and to put an end to the previous dependence on old-style militarists, the Russians in May 1924 founded the Whampoa Military Academy. This academy was supplied and operated with Russian funds, staffed by Russian military advisers. Before long, shiploads of

L

Russian arms were coming into Canton harbor to supply the armies which rallied to the new banner as soon as the Kuomintang began to display the new strength with which all these activities endowed it. The Chinese Communist party, chief organizer of the new movement, confined itself religiously to building the Kuomintang and propagating its program. Its members were the most indefatigable party workers, but they never appeared as Communists nor presented any program of their own. The Communist party, became in fact and in essence, in its work and in the manner in which it educated its own members, the Left-Wing appendage of the Kuomintang (Isaacs, 1966, 64).

The two major institutions which developed in the course of the KMT-CP alliance were Whampoa Military Academy and the Farmers' Training Institute. The Whampoa Academy, organized in 1924, provided the military staff for the effort to break independent war-lord rule in China, and to provide a military basis for an effective centralized government. Its graduates were to become responsible for the triple northern expeditions which were to carry the Kuo Min Tang government from Canton to Nanking. Its personnel were mainly drawn from rural *hsien* of the southern provinces, with a disproportionate percentage from Hunan, Kwangtung, and Chekiang. Strong participation from Hunan proved especially significant in the successes of the northward military movement. Eventually the academy would provide military leaders to both the Kuo Min Tang and the Communist party after their early period of collaboration came to an end.

The Farmers' Training Institute was also set up in 1924, and operated from 1924 to 1926. Its purpose was to train rural leaders who would return to their home areas and organize the local peasantry. Most of these areas were located near major economic and transportation centers, especially along the main avenues of attack which would carry the northern expeditions from the south northward to the Yangtze Valley in 1926–1927. Political organization of peasants in this area and armed uprisings by the organized peasantry furnished the logistic basis of the northward drive (McColl, 1967, 41–44).

Especially significant in this northward expansion of the

effort to mobilize the peasantry was to be the Communist attempt to set up peasant organizations in Hunan. Ever since the mid-nineteenth century Hunan "had been a center of creative and sometimes aggressive reaction to the Western impact" (Landis, 1964, 158). Tseng Kuo-fan had successfully led Hunanese troops against the Taiping rebels and organized them into an army that was to serve as a prototype for regional and provisional war-lord armies down to the mid-twentieth century. Thus, Hunanese had been caught up early in the political fragmentation of China and developed habits of reacting regionally to the centralism of Peking. In the early twentieth century Hunan had then undergone some industrialization and commercialization of its own, and by the early twentieth century Hunanese financiers began to express increasing opposition to foreign influence (Landis, 1964, 159–160). There was thus an indigenous basis for a rising antiforeign nationalism. Nationalism was also an issue in early mass mobilization in the area. In 1923, the Communist party had begun successfully to organize railroad workers and miners in Hunan and to expand its drive for organization into the villages with the slogan of "over-throwing the foreign moneybags." Peasant mobilization here centered, initially, less on the specific issues raised by relations between landlords and tenants and more on struggles to prevent rising rice prices caused by exports of rice from the province (Hofheinz, 1966, 225, 233). Further impetus to peasant organization came with the arrival of the southern army, represented locally by the Independent Division of the Fourth Army, under direct Communist leadership. Contrary to Kwangtung where the most commercialized area near Canton proved most impervious to peasant organization, in Hunan the Communists scored their greatest successes in the commercialized areas, notably east of Changsha. Here gentry control seems to have been weak, and landlords lived in the city rather than on the land. There were no bandits, and gentry defense organizations were also feeble. The Communists, on the other hand, established good relations with the locally dominant secret societies, in this case the Ko-lao-hui. The main slogan utilized was not that of rent reduction, as in the south, but attempts to guarantee the "people's food" through seizure of warehouses and lowering prices (Hofheinz, 1966, 242–257). The entire integument of control appears to have been weaker, giving greater latitude to the movement for peasant mobilization.

The military leader who carried through the northern expedition and who was to wrest the fruits of the Kuo Min Tang-Communist coalition from the Communists was Chiang Kai-shek. In his favored position he could draw freely on Russian support and arms as well as on the strength of the worker and peasant organizations sparked by the Communists. As director of the Whampoa Academy, he commanded the Whampoa cadets and knew how to harness both those with traditional sympathies and those who favored the Left into an effective fighting force. At the same time he began to build up his own political machine, financed by contributions from Shanghai compradors who thus hoped both to guarantee his eventual ascendance over the Communists, as well as to buy their own safety. The northern expedition proved a major military and political success; in its wake Chiang was enabled both to seize control of Canton, subordinating Communist influence to his own, and to couple the conclusion of the campaign with the expulsion of the Communist party from the Kuo Min Tang and its virtual liquidation in the major cities. Expecting the victorious entry of troops from the south, workers in Shanghai had begun a series of strikes which ended on May 21, 1927, in the seizure of the city. At the height of the insurrection more than half a million workers were involved in the strikes, while the task of seizing the city was delegated to a workers' militia of some five thousand men. On March 26, Chiang entered the city. Writing in Moscow, Leon Trotsky—then already in opposition to the main Communist line—correctly forecast the shape of events to come when he wrote that

> the policy of a shackled Communist Party serving as a recruiting agent to bring the workers into the Kuomintang is preparation for the successful establishment of a Fascist dictatorship in China.

The strikes had barely placed Chiang in command of the city when he enlisted the cooperation of its financial elite and of the gangster organization called the Green Gang to turn the seizure of power to his own advantage. On April 12, 1927, the blow fell. In the resulting massacre some five thousand Communists lost their lives, and the Kuo Min Tang under Chiang achieved undisputed domination.

The seizure of Shanghai marked the end of worker participation in the political movement and of Communist hopes that the revolution could be won by the nascent working class of China. That hope was to flicker on until 1930 when the Communists attempted still another uprising, based on urban insurrection coupled with rural support, only to go down in a final defeat in the cities. From then on the party would turn ever more resolutely to the peasant movement as the only and final base for victory.

From the debacle of 1927 there emerged a new Communist strategy, this time based firmly on the mobilization of the peasantry. There had always been peasant discontent, but for the first time it was to be harnessed to a massive attempt to create a new power structure which would fill the political vacuum left by internal disorder and foreign intervention. The protagonist of this new approach was Mao Tse-tung—son of a rich peasant from Hunan, then a student and one of the founders of the Communist party. As early as December 20, 1926, Mao had declared that the peasant problem was the central issue of revolution in China, and initiated land confiscations and redistributions by peasant associations in Hunan (Rue, 1966, 53). He emerged from the destruction of the Communist party in Shanghai to become the foremost spokesman for a policy of independent Communist action, backed up by peasant support rather than by reliance on the workers of the cities. In 1938, he would write that in capitalist countries, characterized by bourgeois-democratic regimes, it was appropriate to use a long legal struggle to mobilize the proletariat. Insurrections should not be started until the possibilities of the legal struggle were exhausted. Once, however, the time for uprisings had arrived, "cities should be taken first, and only later the villages, not the opposite." But

> in China, it is different. China is not an independent democratic state, but a semicolonial and semifeudal country . . . there is no

legislative assembly to make use of, no legal right to organize the workers to strike. Here the fundamental task of the Communist Party is not to go through a long period of legal struggle before launching an insurrection or civil war. Its task is not to seize first the big cities and then the countryside, but to take the road in the opposite direction (Rue, 1966, 283).

There were three requisites for this new strategy. First, the revolution could no longer rely on alliances with the Kuo Min Tang; it had to create its own base of political power in the countryside, independent of the Kuo Min Tang bureaucracy. Second, it had to win the support of the peasantry. Third, it had to create its own Red Army. Its task was, according to Mao, to render possible

the recruiting of new troops, the Sovietization of new rural areas and above all, the consolidation under thorough Soviet power of such areas as already had fallen to the Red Army (Snow, 1938, 180).

The geographical setting for this new strategy was first south central China, notably the areas of Kiangsi-Fukien and the Oyü-wan (Hupeh-Honan-Anhwei). Driven from these areas in 1934, the Red forces marched northward over a distance of six thousand miles to establish themselves anew first in Shensi, and later expanding into Shansi and Hopeh where their arrival in Shensi had been prepared by army commanders with strong Communist sympathies who had sponsored numerous uprisings in the traditionally rebellious hills of northern Shensi ever since 1925.

In winning the support of the peasantry, Communist strategy went through several distinct phases. During the first months of the retreat into the hinterland there was much talk and some action aimed at radical land reform which would confiscate all land and pool it in newly established collectives. This early phase, however, soon gave way to a more considered strategy, aimed at enlisting the sympathies of middle and rich peasants on the side of the revolutionaries. Mao believed that the party had

to make a correct assessment of the vacillating character of the intermediate classes, and . . . devise policies to take full advantage of the contradictions existing in the reactionary camp (Rue, 1966, 105).

Complete confiscation would only alienate the intermediate categories of the peasantry, and serve to isolate the poor peasants (1966, 115). In Mao's judgment

> the agrarian policies of the first year had been too radical. Because the party had attacked the small landlords and rich peasants unremittingly, these classes had "incited the reactionary troops to set fire to large numbers of houses of revolutionary peasants." In Mao's judgement the poor peasants were isolated in Red areas by CCP policy. Mao believed the solution to this problem lay in a more lenient policy toward the intermediate classes, who in the villages he defined as small landlords and rich peasants. The major political task of the party, as long as it controlled only a small and weak base, was to win the support of these classes. Here we have the wellspring of Mao's "rich peasant line" (1966, 110).

This "rich peasant line" was, if anything, too successful. In 1933 Lo Fu, the secretary of the Central Committee of the party, wrote from Juichin, the Soviet capital, that

> the land was divided, but the landlords and rich peasants also received land and better land at that. A number of landlord and rich peasant elements still retain their authority and position in the villages. . . . Not a few of them are in control of party and government institutions and use them to carry out their own class interests. . . . In many places the land problem seems to be fully solved, but upon close scrutiny it appears that even landlords are found to have received land and the rich peasants still retain their superior land (Isaacs, 1966, 344).

Mao Tse-tung himself wrote in a similar vein that

> facts from innumerable places proved that they have usurped the provisional power, filtered into the armed forces, controlled the revolutionary organizations, and receive more and better land than the poor peasants (Ibid).

This brought the Communists to the realization that land distribution, as such, was not sufficient to build firm support among the peasantry. In order to win peasant support adequate to their aims, they had to gain a direct foothold within the social unit where the struggle for resources was being fought out at first hand. That social unit was the village. In the 1930's they experimented with village cooperatives as one means of penetrating the village but found that such organization "from the top down" did not furnish an answer to their problems. This answer they found after their Long March to the northwest. It lay not in land redistribution as such, but in the establishment of political controls in the villages. This task was facilitated in their new home by the fact that floods and other natural disasters had often resulted in large-scale dislocations and relocation of population, so that village relations possessed less traditional strength and resistance than elsewhere. Risings against landlords and other upheavals had caused many landlords to take their departure, even before the advent of the Communists. Others were soon to flee before the threat of Japanese invasion. Their departure left a political vacuum in the villages which the Communists were able and willing to fill.

In the northwest, in fact, they became even more liberal in their handling of land reform than they had been earlier on the basis of Mao's rich peasant line. They did expropriate some landlord land, especially that of landlords who remained in political opposition, as well as the land owned by officials. With this land and land reclaimed from wasteland they rewarded poor peasants, thus creating

> an entirely new class. These were the men and women who had risen from the ranks of the once-debt-burdened poor to become owners of land and a force in their village. They were known as "new middle peasants" (Crook and Crook, 1959, 73).

Yet they did not wipe out all landlords, and they scrupulously guarded the land of rich peasants who worked their own land, albeit with agricultural labor. Instead, they relied on a progressive land tax to introduce greater social equity, and they sharply curtailed the ability of the upper crust of the village to exact peasant surplus through loans and indebtedness. They remitted all peasant debts for a year and then began to offer government loans at 5 percent, while still allowing private loans to be made at rates up to 10 percent. This relatively mild reform program was probably facilitated because many landlords had taken their departure, and also by the fact that landlord power in the northern area had been generally weaker than in the south. While amounts of land rented to tenants in the south composed between 42 and 47 percent of the area in farmland, in the northern wheat-growing area these percentages fell between 12 and 17 (Buck, 1937, 195). Forty-six percent of the peasants were tenants in the southern rice region; in the northern wheat region only 17 percent were tenants (1937, 196). Reform here could also benefit the middle peasants and raise numerous poor peasants to middle peasant stature (e.g., Crook and Crook, 1959, 121).

Three features of Communist success in the north are thus closely connected with the area in which they built their new redoubt. First, they built their new edifice of power among an impoverished but landowning peasantry. "In 1934 the available data indicate that the Communists were concentrated in those areas where land reform was most needed. In 1945 they were concentrated in those areas where land reform was least needed" (Moise, 1967, 12). They were situated in a marginal area, which had yet possessed great strategic significance since the earliest history of China. And, finally, they moved into an area relatively free of domination by superior power holders. Their reforms still further loosened the grip of the few landlords who had remained.

The reform also introduced new forms of organization—village councils, work teams, peasant unions—which gave the poorer peasants and the landless political leverage in influencing the course of village decisions. The Crooks, describing this process for the village of Ten Mile Inn in the T'aihang Mountains, show how these organizations became

> a training ground for the development of a capacity of leadership and for independent organized action on the part of the masses themselves. Little by little a dual power was to be established in the village. And though at the outset the peasant union was to be only the shadow or secondary organization, its objective was to produce leaders who would take over the village government (1959, 52).

The new organizations often made use of quite traditional mechanisms for mutual aid and cooperation, usually based on the cooperation of kin or friends; but they were made to serve the new purposes of village organization and defense under peasant leadership. When the new young leaders proved their mettle, they were taken into the party or into party-controlled mass organizations.

> This "penetration of the natural village" was, in essence the great achievement of the Yenan period. The work and battle teams had arisen on a traditional foundation of work cooperation, but, through their Party cadre leaders, had been transformed into a new type of organization that served the political-military and socioeconomic aims of the Chinese Communist Party. The team was indissolubly a part of the village, yet at the same time transcended it (Schurmann, 1966, 427).

Thus, if village organizations furnished one basis of support among the peasantry, another means of enlisting that support was to be the Communist party itself. Oriented first toward work in the cities, it acquired peasant support only gradually. Its membership had expanded from 57 in 1921 to close to 16,000 in 1927; it had been reduced to 10,000 by late 1927—after the split with the Kuo Min Tang. Some sources claim that it had again reached 300,-000 in 1933–1934, but after the transfer to the northwest it again numbered only 40,000. When the war had ended and the Communists stood poised to take over all of China, membership had attained more than 1,000,000 members (Schurmann, 1966, 129). Socially, the top Communist leadership resembled that of the Kuo Min Tang.

> In both parties, the leaders have been drawn most frequently from a relatively thin upper layer of the Chinese population. In both parties these men were often the sons of landlords, merchants, scholars, or officials, and they usually came from parts of China where Western influence had first penetrated and where the penetration itself was most vigorous. All of them had higher educations, and most of them had studied abroad. The leaders of both parties, despite a relatively high status in private life, showed a reluctance or perhaps an inability to establish private careers. The majority were alienated intellectuals, men and women whose Western educations isolated them from the main currents of Chinese society. . . . Whichever party they belonged to, Communist or Kuomintang, they differed from the Imperial elite . . . in that they were drawn from a much wider circle . . . recent

revolutions in China have brought forward the sons of the nouveau-riche compradors, other business classes of coastal cities, the sons of landlords, and recently, even, the sons of wealthy peasants (North, 1965, 376–377).

However, there were also characteristic differences:

The characteristic Communist leader was the son of a landlord or rich peasant, whereas the characteristic Kuomintang leader was the son of a merchant or other urban person (1965, 395). . . .

The Kuomintang elite came more extensively from the coastal areas, particularly around Shanghai and Hong Kong, while the greatest concentration of Communist leaders was from Central China—the basin of the Yangtze (1965, 402).

Moreover, the struggle between Left and Right accentuated this profile; "the decline of the left and the rise of the right was one of the factors that made the Kuo Min Tang increasingly a merchant's party and decreasingly a landlords' or rurally oriented one" (1965, 409). In contrast, the migration of the Communist party into the hinterland furthered the replacement in party personnel of intellectuals of middle-class and upper-class backgrounds by sons of the peasantry. The Red Army notably became a channel for peasant mobility. Thus it is not surprising that in 1949, when the Communists stood ready to take over all of China, about 80 percent of the party members were peasants. In 1956 peasants still accounted for close to 70 percent of membership; three-quarters had been poor peasants, one-quarter middle peasants (Lindbeck, 1967, 89; Schurmann, 1966, 132).

The third element in the new parallelogram of forces destined to emerge from the years in the hinterland was the Red Army. It, too, went through a number of different stages in development. The first stage was marked by the mutiny of several crack regiments of the Kuo Min Tang National Revolutionary Army which had carried out the northern expedition, the so-called "Ironsides." These—20,000 strong—revolted at Nanchang on August 1, 1927. They were joined by 3,000 military cadets, miners, and other workers. At the same time, Mao Tse-tung was organizing a partisan army in Hunan from miners, peasant guards, and mutinous Kuo Min Tang soldiers. Contrary to later patterns of recruitment, workers were heavily represented in this first Red Army. Especially notable was the participation of miners from the biggest iron mines in China, the Hanyehping mines near Wuhan, which had closed down in 1925 and thrown a hundred thousand miners out of work. Miners were also represented in Mao's Hunan army (Wales, 1939, 244). Yet this early Red Army was decimated in the first fruitless phase of insurrection when the Communist party still hoped to seize the cities and had not yet decided to withdraw into the hinterland. Of 25,000 participants in the Nanchang uprising, only 1,200 remained (1939, 244). Mao reached sanctuary with only a thousand survivors of his Hunan army (Snow, 1938, 169). Yet by recruiting peasants—once the policy of relying on the hinterland had been decided on—the army once more regained strength in its new redoubts in the interior until it numbered once again 200,000 regulars in 1934. These were supported by an equal number of Red Guards and guerrillas. It recruited numerous peasants, but it also received reinforcements from further mutinies among Kuo Min Tang troops. Some 600 to 700 *min t'uan*, acting as auxiliaries to the Kuo Min Tang, deserted to the Reds at Kian in 1929, and 20,000 KMT troops came over at Ningtu in 1931 (Wales, 1939, 129–130, fn. 55). These troops held out in the Central Soviet area until 1934 when overwhelming military pressure forced them to evacuate and undertake their six-thousand-mile-long march to the northwest. Of the 310,000 only about 100,000 survived the rigors of the Long March (Wales, 1939, 61). Yet by 1945, the army was bigger than ever, numbering close to 500,000 (Johnson, 1962, 74). During this entire cycle of decimation and resurrection, peasant participation in the army had greatly increased. Nym Wales provides percentage figures for the First Front Red Army from the Central Soviet in Kiangsi:

> 58 per cent of the men in this army came from the peasantry; 38 per cent came mostly from the "rural proletariat," which included farm laborers, apprentices, craftsmen in village industry, trans-

portation workers and such, while part of this 38 per cent was made up of industrial workers from city factories, mines, pottery works, etc. The remaining 4 per cent came from the petty bourgeoisie and were usually the younger sons of small landlords, merchants, intellectuals, and such (Wales, 1939, 56–57).

The mobilization of the village for party and army and the occupation by Communists of the significant ganglia of communication and control was greatly intensified and speeded up by the Japanese invasion in 1937. In contrast to the Kuo Min Tang, which tried to buy time for a military build-up by yielding space to the aggressors, the Long March had placed the Red Army squarely in the way of the Japanese thrust. This move had been made consciously to escape Kuo Min Tang encirclement, but also to show that the Red Army was prepared to defend China against her foreign enemies, while the Kuo Min Tang frittered away resources and men in an internal struggle against fellow Chinese. Chalmers Johnson has argued that the Japanese invasion provided the major catalyst in rallying the peasantry to the Communist cause:

> it succeeded because the population became receptive to one particular kind of political appeal; and the Communist Party—in one of its many disguises—made precisely that appeal: it offered to meet the needs of the people for leadership in organizing resistance and in alleviating war-induced anarchy in the rural areas (1962, 7).

In the process of the war the relations between village, party, and army were consolidated, the Red Army expanded to embrace half a million men, and the Communists ended the war with control over a population ten times the size than the nine million they controlled in the northwestern provinces in 1938. The establishment of the northern redoubt in an area of landholding peasantry permitted the construction of an apparatus of power that was to serve as a springboard for the expansion of revolutionary power throughout China in 1949. We may assign the success of the Communists in building this base of power to their success in rallying this tactically mobile peasantry to their side under conditions of warfare, first against the Kuo Min Tang, later against the Japanese.

Without warfare as a catalyst, it is unlikely that the Communist-led coalition with the peasantry could have scored the notable success that it did. This success is, moreover, in striking contrast to the failure of the part of China which remained under Kuo Min Tang control. Numerous and divergent explanations are available for Kuo Min Tang failure (Loh, 1965). Kuo Min Tang armies failed where Communist armies succeeded; attempts at land reform by the Kuo Min Tang regime came to nothing, where reform in the Communist areas proved a rousing success; where war and inflation fatally weakened the regime of Chiang Kai-shek, it strengthened on every level the capacity of the Communists to survive. This success was possible because it enlisted the participation of a particular type of peasantry in a marginal zone of China. At the same time, the Communists did not become a "peasant party," even though they recruited peasants into their organization until these provided the vast majority of the membership. They were able to harness peasant energies, but for ends never dreamed of by the peasantry.

The Revolution has reversed the structure of Chinese society, and made the millenarian dreams of past peasant rebellions a social reality. The new Chinese state claims to be an offspring of the Taiping, rather than that of the Confucianist scholars. Yet there are also continuities. The traditional concept of the ruling elite as a nonhereditary and open class recruited by examination has much in common with the Communist concept of a party recruited from the population at large. Similarly, with its great tradition of hydraulic management and public works, the state always saw itself as the primary and ultimate source of decisions. Finally, the state was not only a political entity, but the bearer of a moral order, expressed in ritual and ceremonies. "Ceremonies are the bond that hold the multitudes together," states the ancient Book of Rites, "and if the bond be removed, those multitudes fall into confusion." In Communist China, ideology has been given a role of crucial importance, quite at variance with Marxist tradition (see Fried, 1964).

> Mao and his comrades-in-arms successfully implanted themselves in one of the least endowed regions of China, traditionally in the grip of famine, by demonstrating to the semi-literate peasants that

they were the bearers of a new ritual which was collectivist and beneficial to all (Karol, 1967, 25).

The past was marked by the Confucian definitions of significant social relationships. This task has fallen in the present to the Thought of Mao, with its insistence that the ultimate sanctions in the new society are less the result of force than of moral suasion.

FOUR

VIET NAM

We fear your valor, but we fear Heaven more than your power. We vow that we shall fight everlastingly and without respite. When we have nothing else left, we will arm our soldiers with branches. How then can you live among us?

> Anti-French manifesto, 1862

If we have to fight, we shall fight. You will kill ten of our men, and we will kill one of yours, and in the end it will be you who will tire of it.

> Ho Chi Minh to French negotiators, Sainteny and Moutet, 1946

M

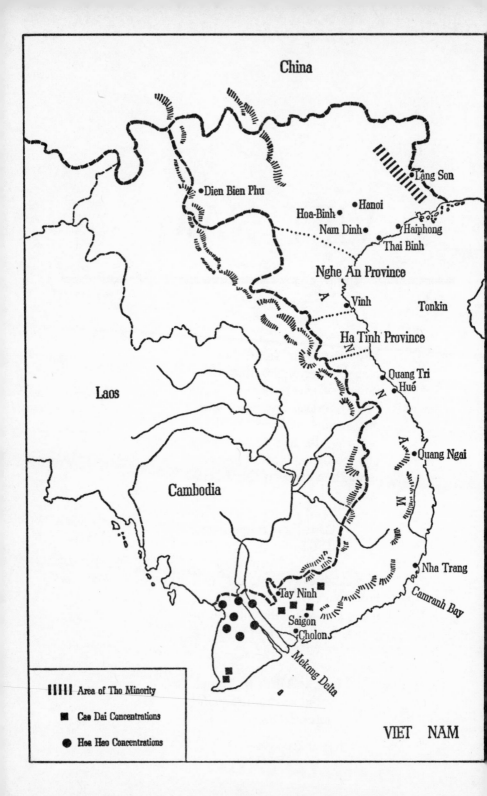

China

Dien Bien Phu

Hoa-Binh   • Hanoi
Nam Dinh • Haiphong
          Thai Binh

Nghe An Province

A   • Vinh   Tonkin

Ha Tinh Province

• Quang Tri
  Hué

Laos

• Quang Ngai

Cambodia

• Nha Trang

Tay Ninh

Saigon   Camranh Bay
 •Cholon

Mekong Delta

Lang Son

||||| Area of Tho Minority

■ Cao Dai Concentrations

● Hoa Hao Concentrations

VIET NAM

The Vietnamese are the product of a fusion of populations once settled farther north, in what is now southern China below the Yangtze River, and the indigenous population they encountered in Viet Nam proper. This fusion was the product of Chinese expansion which had pushed some of the population elements that were to become Vietnamese ever farther south, beyond the confines of the Yunnan Mountains. Chinese domination of their new homeland followed. It was only thrown off in the tenth century A.D., though a symbolic tribute paid by the Small Dragon Emperor of Viet Nam to the Bigger Dragon Emperor of China continued until the arrival of the French.

What the Vietnamese may have been like before their Sinicization is shown by their linguistic and cultural relatives, the Muong, of whom about 200,000 still inhabit the highland area on the southwestern fringe of the Red River valley. They are divided into an elite of noble families, *tho lang*, and a peasantry. The *tho lang* are descendants of the first settlers of the land. Each first settler was deified as an ancestor of the area he occupied, and their descendants in the patrilineal line hold title to the land settled by their ancestor. The *tho lang* families maintain their ancestor cults, with special altars and lacquered plaques containing the names of their ancestors, as an outward sign of their privileges. The peasants do not hold title to the land; title is vested in the local headman who claims the appropriate *tho lang* descent. Local village headmen and higher nobles form a hierarchy of hereditary lords who are at once priests, administrators, and soldiers. As Chinese influence spread among the Vietnamese, they steadily modified this pattern in the direction of Chinese models. As in China, the state became the main sponsor and organizer of irrigation works. The concept of the scholar-gentry was introduced. A fixed hierarchy of state officials was established in 1089; an academy of training officials was set up in 1076, and examinations were initiated in 1075.

Nevertheless, Viet Nam was riven by continuous tensions between attempts by the emperor and his staff to centralize the state and the efforts of local power holders to make themselves independent. The members of the upper class had learned Chinese ways: this ultimately gave them "the ability to govern and the ambition to rule without the Chinese through a training, a world of ideas, and a way of life imported by the Chinese" (Buttinger, 1958, 109). They would thus back a Vietnamese ruler of their own in an effort to win greater autonomy from China. But

> their personal desire to be free of all restrictions in dealing with their own subjects proved to be stronger than the wish to assert the claim of the country to its whole produce and the right of the Vietnamese to their own way of living and of settling their public affairs. The structure of Vietnamese society created by the Chinese was obviously quite to the liking of the semifeudal and semimandarinal local bosses once the central authority of the state was removed. Their main objection under the Chinese had been to the taxes required for a national administration, and to interference with their local rule in the interest of national economy and defense. But this was precisely what aroused them also against their own monarchs after the Chinese had left, and why they created a state of political anarchy fraught with dangers that were greater for Viet Nam than another century of Sinization (Buttinger, 1958, 139–140).

The peasant, on the other hand,

> clung to his pre-Chinese customs and religious ideas, and he would cling to some of them to this very day, under an outer cloak woven of later importations. He continued with his un-Chinese habit of chewing the betel nut. He kept his host of village genii and spirits of the house, of the rivers, and of the mountains. He rejoiced in his ceremonies and festivals that originated in a pre-Chinese past. He stuck to his special form of ancestor worship. And he even preserved the memories of Van Lang and Au Lac [pre-Chinese Vietnamese kingdoms in the Red River area before 200 B.C.], into which he poured his yearning for a life of peace and plenty, free from the vexations of foreign rule. He was, in fact, more of a Vietnamese in the year 900 of our era than he had been in the first century B.C. (1958, 108).

Nor did the Sino-Vietnamese upper class disturb the cultural patterns of the peasantry, as long as the peasants worked the land and paid dues to their overlords. The villages retained considerable autonomy; they "preserved their originality and became the breeding places for a nation apart" (1958, 108–109).

The state, on the other hand, bent its efforts toward the construction and management of hydraulic works, and toward the acquisition of new lands. In this effort, southward expansion, carried through in continuous warfare against rival Cham and Cambodian kingdoms, proved especially important. The area around Hué was reached in the early 1300's and Central Viet Nam was settled in the fourteenth and fifteenth century. Cham power was broken in 1471. The Bassac River was reached in the first half of the eighteenth century. This slow advance was

> carried on primarily by a type of peasant-soldiering for which this people seems to have developed an aptitude at a very early time. The peasant became a soldier whenever an enemy approached either for plunder or to drive the Vietnamese from a newly settled territory (Buttinger, 1958, 38).

The enemy population was either absorbed or driven into marginal areas. Thus to this day there remain scattered remnants of Chams in Viet Nam, and a Cambodian population of about 350,000.

In addition to expansion by military means, the ruler—as in China—frequently tried to improve the lot of the peasantry and to curtail the power of the overlords through such means as dividing the land of families who collaborated with the Chinese; confiscating idle land for redistribution to cultivators who would render it productive; ensuring periodic redistribution of communal land among needy peasants; and the creation of military colonies whose members would farm in peacetime and fight in times of war. Yet only rarely was the state able to counter the tendencies of chieftains to seize and hold power in the provinces, and to check the autonomy of the Vietnamese village. The last cycle of renewal and unification set in at the end of the eighteenth century and the beginning of the nineteenth. By this time, the Europeans had already arrived in Southeast Asia and were making their presence felt along its entire maritime perimeter.

Unification was spurred, in the main, by two factors. One of these was undoubtedly the conquest of Cochin China completed in 1757 which opened up new land and resources for the Vietnamese. The second set of factors involved a series of military and political events which served to introduce Western military equipment and military techniques into Viet Nam. These events may be divided into two phases. The first phase was marked by the Tay-Son Rebellion, an uprising led by three brothers whose native village gave a name to the event. In a series of successful military sweeps they successfully wrested power from both southern and northern factions and dynasties (1771–1786) and in 1789 were able to turn back a Chinese army sent against them in support of the discredited rulers. Their rule, however, was, in turn, brief; they were overthrown once more in 1802. The social roots of the rebellion are not well understood. The grandfather of the three brothers had been a member of the upper class, deported to Tay-Son. The rebellion began when the oldest of the brothers took to the woods, at the head of a typical bandit band. They drew their following from dispossessed and downtrodden peasantry, smarting under the loss of land and heavy taxes and labor dues; the movement was financed by independent merchants who wanted to widen the ties of national and international commerce, and also wished to eliminate Chinese commercial competition. Several features of the rebellion are reminiscent of Chinese popular rebellious movements: their use of military rather than civilian officials at all levels of administration; their employment of the vernacular language, *nom*, as against Chinese, in translating the Chinese classics and in the works of a florescent Vietnamese literary movement; their friendliness toward Catholic converts; their support of the Triad Society which had risen in rebellion in Chinese Szechwan. However, they failed to improve the lot of the peasantry in any way; the peasants merely suffered a change of masters and in the end did nothing to support the Tay-Son in their hour of need. The anti-Confucianism of the Tay-Son also set against them the Chinese-oriented Confucian scholar-gentry. They were defeated by Nguyen-Anh who reunified the country, this time with French military assistance. As early as 1615 the Portuguese had equipped one of the rival contenders for rule with a foundry for the local production of heavy guns. Such foreign armament and advice by foreign military advisers, naval officers, and engineers, was in all probability responsible for the success of the new ruler. This monopoly of new weaponry also allowed him to take the next decisive step, that of severing control over land from occupation of public office. Where previously officials had also been owners of land or beneficiaries of tribute paid by the rural population, the new dynasty made the official examinations the sole road to office and put all officials on salaries of rice and money. These measures limited the tendency of officials who were also landowners to build up local power blocs, the phenomenon that had caused Viet Nam's repeated relapse into periods of disintegration and anarchy.

The measures, however, produced contradictory results. They not merely curtailed the power of the wealthy and of the nobility; they eliminated from competition for power all power holders except those who were "employees of the state and responsible only to the emperor" (Buttinger, 1958, 287). Within this official class, power was strongly concentrated. Some

> 20 top mandarins held most of the high positions in the civil administration and in the armed forces, a dozen of them residing in the provinces with the remainder working or serving in positions as advisors to the emperor in the central government at Hué (Jumper and Nguyen Thi Hue, 1962, 16).

Some key officials held several offices concurrently. It was not unusual "for a single high official to function simultaneously as a provincial governor, minister, and military chieftain" (1962, 16). The top three grades of the mandarinate—in contrast to the six lower ones—moreover, were at one and the same time civil and military positions. This meant that power in the top ranks of the bureaucracy was as much military as it was based on Confucianist learning. The Nguyen had indeed unified the state against the rival claims of feudal overlords; but "the real basis for their power was military might and not legalization of imperial authority" (1962, 66). While it was true that the state was more centralized than it had been in the past, reliance on powerful civil-military mandarins in charge of the various provinces inevitably produced strong centrifugal tendencies, as well as continuous competition at court for the stakes of influence over the emperor. Such dispersal of authority was further reinforced by the existence of numerous secret societies which connected leaders on the national level with local or regional groups. Many of these were, as in China, at once religious and secular, combining mutual aid and security functions with participation in ritual or in political manipulation. There thus existed a shadowy underworld of clandestine linkages, often more significant and important than the social and political charades of the visible overworld. Habituation to subterranean activity, here as in China, would provide a basis for revolutionary activity in the future.

A second result flowed from the nature of mandarin recruitment. The qualifications for office were established by an examination system which demanded knowledge of the accumulated wisdom of the past, as exemplified by the Chinese philosophers. Perhaps because it represented a provincial offshoot of the prototypical Chinese tradition, the Vietnamese system appears to have been even more formalistic than the Chinese original. Of this the emperors were themselves aware. Minh-mang opined that

> for a long time, the examination system has warped education. In the essays one makes use only of outworn clichés and hollow formulae, one tries to shine only through the parading of a useless knowledge (quoted in Le Thanh Khoi, 1955, 363).

But he was also aware "that the habit is set and that it is difficult to change it at once." Rendered intellectually immobile by their adherence to the canons of the past, the Vietnamese mandarins also proved unusually rapacious. The assigned salaries proved ridiculously low (Jumper and Nguyen Thi Hue, 1962, 55); but authority yielded the power to exact fines and gifts. Thus furnished with a strong vested interest in the system which gave them authority, the

Vietnamese mandarins were at the same time equipped with a kind of understanding of the world less and less adaptable to circumstances that made new demands upon them.

In 1850 began the second phase of foreign involvement in Viet Nam when the French—spurred on by a desire for imperial grandeur—took decisive steps toward the opening up of Viet Nam by force of arms. In 1861, they seized the three eastern provinces of Cochin China; in 1867 they occupied the western provinces. After a war of ten years, Hanoi was taken in 1882. Treaties signed in 1883 and 1884 confirmed French rule over Cochin China and established a French protectorate over Tonkin and Annam. Annam was to remain nominally autonomous under French supervision; Tonkin was to be administered, with the aid of Vietnamese mandarins, by a French resident commissioner. Resistance, however, continued, mainly led by the mandarins who were determined to prevent any kind of change.

> If the West penetrated Vietnam, it would set into motion developments bound to destroy the basis of mandarinal rule. . . . The defense of mandarinal power and privileges became identical with the defense of Vietnam (Buttinger, 1967, 116).

An uprising, led by mandarins, began in 1885 and continued in northern Annam until 1896; in Tonkin a rebel band held out till 1909. But the days of the mandarins were numbered. When their attempt at restoring the dead past failed, it became clear that "if national resistance ever was to gain the strength necessary to oust the French, it had to aim beyond the mere restoration of ancient Vietnam" (Buttinger, 1967, 143).

One of the immediate consequences of French occupation was to turn rice into a major export commodity. Before the advent of the French, rice had not been sent abroad in any appreciable quantity; exports in 1860 amounted to a mere 57,000 tons. Exports in 1937, before the onset of World War II, amounted to 1,548,000 tons. To make this increase possible, there arose a class of large landowners, capable of producing large surpluses of rice, in contrast to the small landowners who consumed most of what they grew.

These new landowners were the direct beneficiaries of French efforts to reassign old land or to colonize new land, as part of their new colonial mission.

Some of the land handed to the new landowners had been owned by those killed in the uprising of 1862, or had been deserted temporarily by their survivors.

> When the displaced peasants, usually long after the fighting had stopped, returned to their villages and began to replant their old fields, they were astonished and appalled to learn that these lands now belonged to someone else. Those who insisted on their property rights were treated as thieves and chased away. They could remain only if they accepted the offer of the new owners to work on the land, or to rent a small portion of it at an exorbitant price—generally no less than half the crop (Buttinger, 1967, 164).

Such expropriation was especially characteristic of Tonkin. The result was that in Tonkin 500 large landowners—both French and Vietnamese—came to own 20 percent of the land; another 17,000 held a further 20 percent. The remaining small holders, about one million in strength, divided the rest among themselves; the average holding amounted to less than half a hectare per family.

The other source of landholdings for the new large landowners was land drained and irrigated by the French in the Vietnamese South, through the construction of new hydraulic works. The land so obtained was then sold in lots and at low prices, in the hope of recovering the cost of the waterworks. By 1938 about half of the arable land in the Vietnamese South was in rice. Of this nearly half was in the hands of 2.5 percent of all landowners. Seventy percent of all landowners owned only 15 percent of arable land. Still larger was the class of landless tenants in the South, numbering some 350,000 families and constituting about 57 percent of the rural population. Most of the large landowners of Viet Nam were Southerners. Of about 7,000 large landowners in Viet Nam before World War II, more than 90 percent were located in the Vietnamese South.

This new landed bourgeoisie invested mainly in agriculture; its participation in manufacture, trade, and banking was severely limited by discriminatory French regulations. Its main income came from the land in the form of rents paid by their tenants, as interest from loans advanced to the peasantry, and from the sale of rice to French and Chinese exporters in Saigon. Powerless on the national level, they became, however, "the political masters of the Vietnamese people on the village and community level" (Buttinger, 1967, 165), the new notables. Beneficiaries of the French occupation, many of them acquired French citizenship and had their children educated in France. Politically, they favored cooperation with the French, although they supported a greater measure of autonomy for themselves. Their political instrument in the power struggles after World War I was the Constitutionalist party founded in 1923.

The commercialization of rice linked the population of Viet Nam to the vicissitudes of the world market. Thus the prices paid for rice in the Saigon market fell by two-thirds between 1929 and 1934; the buying power of a given amount of rice measured against other goods fell by one-half (Le Chau, 1966a, 55). During the inflation which followed the Japanese occupation of Viet Nam in World War II and the resultant Allied blockade of the country, rice prices again rose by 25 percent, but could not keep up with prices paid for other scarce goods, which increased as much as 200 percent (1966a, 57). We must also remember that the gains from rice cultivations were unevenly distributed. An inquiry made in 1936 showed that the profit from the sale of rice exported from Saigon was apportioned as follows: 26 percent went to the primary producer, 33.6 percent to the middlemen, 21 percent to the carriers, 5 percent to the processors, 14.4 percent to the public treasury (Robequain, 1944, 346, fn. 1). At the same time, the per capita consumption of rice fell from 262 kilograms in 1900 to 226 kilograms in 1913, and to 182 kilograms in 1937. It is estimated that between 220 and 270 kilograms are necessary to feed an adult individual.

Another agricultural endeavor sponsored by the French was the production of rubber on plantations located in Cochin China and in parts of Cambodia, beginning in 1897, when rubber plants were introduced from Malaya. Rubber became the colony's second largest export, furnishing all the rubber required by the metropolis. Before World War II the crop was grown on 1,005 plantations; twenty-seven companies, however, owned 68 percent of the area planted; moreover, many companies owned numerous plantations, and were in turn interrelated in holding companies. Capital and credit for rubber production were thus tightly concentrated. Since rubber was grown primarily in the Vietnamese South which until then was but sparsely populated, the new enterprises needed to import labor from elsewhere. This need was met by intensive labor recruitment, especially in the densely settled Red River valley of the North. First, local notables were empowered to enlist potential workers in their villages; later this became the function of labor bosses or *cais*. The *cai* thus became a figure of major social significance. According to Virginia Thompson,

> the function of the *cai* varied—he might be a recruiting agent, a foreman, or an estate shopkeeper—but he was always interposed between the employer and his employees. As a subcontractor the *cai* engaged and paid the required number of workers and he organized their output. On other estates he might only recruit laborers. In still other cases, he simply directed their work. At times the *cai* was the laborers' only provisioner of food. But in each of these capacities he had opportunities to make illicit gains; he was often brutal and unscrupulous in forcing deductions from wages, withholding provisions, etc. The government intervened only to check the abuses perpetrated by the *cai* as recruiting agent and to prevent his profiteering at company stores. The government justified its continued toleration of the *cai* in his other capacities on the ground that it was obviously to the employers' interest to eliminate the whole system so that with time the *cai* would be voluntarily dispensed with (1947, 201).

Compulsion, however, remained the essence of this system of labor recruitment, not merely an occasional excrescence. Conditions on the rubber plantations of Cochin China were notorious. Men worked from dawn till dusk for a pittance paid out to them by the *cai* from whom they later had to purchase their food. They lived in barracks, packed like sardines, and were frequently subjected to fines and corporal punishment for putative infractions of labor discipline. Consequently, the rate of desertion from the rubber plantations remained high; every second worker seems to have escaped the labor regime by running away. Every kind of force and trickery had to be used to entice replacements for the deserters. It is estimated that "in order to maintain a labor force which has never at any time exceeded 22,000, nearly 75,000 individuals had to be recruited between 1925 and 1930" (Goudal, quoted in Robequain, 1944, 81). Only in the 1930's did the rate of desertion decline to one or two in five. The impact of the world-wide depression on an area of high population growth, such as Viet Nam, caused opportunities for work to be at a premium. Labor legislation sponsored by the Popular Front governments of the period may also have helped to improve work conditions in the colony.

Just as the *cai* proved to be a key figure in the recruitment of labor for the plantations, so he proved an indispensable middleman in drawing peasants into industrial employment. Industry remained limited due to restrictions placed upon the development of the colony by the metropolis. The mainstay of the colonial industrial sector was the extraction of coal, zinc, and tin; workers in mines and quarries were estimated at roughly 55,000 in 1928. Most of the miners—nine-tenths—came from Tonkin or northern Annam; 60 percent of these came from Thai Binh and Nam Dinh alone (Robequain, 1944, 266, 269). Another 80,000 to 90,000 workers manned the remaining industrial establishments. Among these were some 10,000 (1938 figure) textile workers, especially strong in Nam Dinh; workers in railroad yards and repair shops (10,279 in 1931); workers in electric power plants (3,000); as well as workers in distilleries and other processing plants. Although the industrial work force in such modern industrial establishments increased at an annual rate of about 2,500 since 1890 (Robequain, 1944, 304), many of them retained strong roots in the peasantry. Not only were most of them former peasants, the majority would return to the peasantry before long. Turnover continued strong, at once postponing the emergence of a stable working class from the rural population, while at the same time spreading the effects of industrial employment far and wide (Robequain, 1944, 82).

For those who could or would not find an outlet for their labor in modern industry, there remained traditional artisan work. Full-time artisans may have numbered 218,000 (Le Chau, 1966a, 46), but the total population involved in traditional handicraft industries has been estimated as high as 1,350,000 (Robequain, 1944, 249). In contrast to China, metropolitan goods did not compete with native products to ruin this traditional bulwark of village existence. Nevertheless it is doubtful whether it could have been carried on in isolation from native agricultural endeavors. An artisan employed in handicraft industry earned only a third of what he would have earned as a worker on a plantation. An independent owner of a textile shop, working with his wife, might obtain between 1.5 and 5 times the wages of a plantation worker but had to buy his own raw materials. It is notable that handicraft employment remained more important in the North and in the Center, with their densely packed populations, than in the more commercialized South.

Still another consequence of French colonial rule in Viet Nam was the growth of a heavy tax burden on the native population. Railroads and roads built were paid for largely from increased revenues. Taxes were raised from 35 million gold francs before the French conquest to more than 90 million (Chesneaux, 1955b, 155). Salt, alcohol, and opium were made government monopolies, with prices raised six times above what they had been before the occupation. Revenues from these sources made up 70 percent of the general budget. From time immemorial, the local population had made rice alcohol for family consumption and ceremonial. Now, a continuous battle developed between the government, trying to control and to monopolize alcohol production, and the smaller producers. Most important for the native population, however, was the taxation of salt. All salt had to be sold to the state at prices fixed by the state; salt workers had to pay prices for salt bought on the market from six to eight times higher than those which they received upon delivery. Salt is an indispensable ingredient in *nuoc mam*, the highly spiced fish sauce which forms an essential part of the Vietnamese diet. Many native salines were ruined, as were many fishermen who needed salt to preserve fish and to produce *nuoc mam*. Unable to distribute the salt adequately, the state leased the right to distribution to Chinese dealers. While it is estimated that a Vietnamese needs 22 pounds per capita of salt to maintain an adequate diet, in 1937 per capita consumption was 14.8 pounds (Buttinger, 1967, 467, n. 32).

All these changes affected the internal structure of the Vietnamese village. In its traditional form, the village could be likened to a corporation of family heads who held rights to land within the village orbit. The names of these landowners were listed in a village register. In addition to plots assigned to individual families, the community as such also held communal lands; only those inscribed in the registers, however, had the right to receive assignments of such land. The village also contained people who held no land, and were hence socially and politically disprivileged. These village landless were the target of much imperial legislation against "vagabonds," empowering notables to draft them for corvées or for military service, especially in the military colonies along the expanding Vietnamese frontier which served as a safety valve for land-hungry peasant-soldiers.

The village itself was managed by a council of notables (*hoi dong ky muc* or *hoi dong hao muc*) composed of men of high status. High status here signified either diplomas held as the result of imperial examinations passed or respected old age. Until the fifteenth century the emperor had appointed communal mandarins (*xa quan*) to manage village affairs; after that time, primary authority lay with the council. The village headman (*xa truong*) was more of a go-between, mediating between the village councils and the district chief, than an executive in his own right (Nghiem, 1966, 149). Each village was thus run by an oligarchy, "tempered by the fact that the members of the ruling class were recruited, not by co-optation, but by mandarinal recruiting procedures, literary examinations, or privilege of age" (1966, 149). Rules of precedence among the various grades of notables were laid down in a village code or customary: some of these codes gave precedence to age over mandarin rank; others emphasized imperial rank over age.

The village councils were not wholly autonomous. Through the village chief they received requests for taxes or corvées from higher authorities, and each village was held corporately responsible for satisfying these requests. Each village council was, however, autonomous in the ways in which it met these requests.

> Village custom did not really block imperial orders; however, the imperial order was expected to stipulate only the ends desired; it was the prerogative of the village to find the means for realizing these ends (Nghiem, 1966, 150).

This relation between imperial jurisdiction and village autonomy was expressed in the proverb that "the power of the state stops at the bamboo hedge of the village." The council could take its own measures with regard to internal security, the building of pagodas, the digging of canals and the construction of dikes. These decisions were taken formally at the *dinh* or communal temple of the village. Here local disputes were settled and judicial oaths taken; here the guardian spirit watched over the prosecution of the case. Here a peasant who could not pay his taxes might be whipped (Le Van Ho, 1962, 87). Here the village codes were read during celebrations of ceremonies dedicated to the tutelary supernatural of the village. An interesting built-in check on the power of the notables was the institution of the *dau-bo,* or oxhead, the village speaker for the opposition who had a formal right to speak up in the village council in favor of disadvantaged parties. The *dau-bo* was so-called because the head of an ox is hard; the village speaker "did not fear the menaces of the rich nor the power of the mandarin" (Nguyen Huu Khang, 1946, 203), often representing the cause of the poor.

The *dinh* or communal temple which housed the spirit was the "uncontested center of village life in traditional Viet Nam then" (Le Van Ho, 1962, 86). The guardian spirit represents the moral unity of the village; he watches over the maintenance of moral rules and sanctions. Nguyen Huu Khang says of him that "his role is essentially the same as that of a terrestrial mandarin" (1946, 59). Often he is a founder of the village or an important villager now dead, or a hero selected from the local or national pantheon. The selection of a guardian spirit had to be confirmed by the emperor. Thereafter the sacred objects pertaining to the spirit and the decree confirming him were kept in the central room of the communal temple. Annual ceremonies are held to honor the guardian spirit. The most important of these—called assembly (*hoi*)— was held in spring. Secret rites (*hem*) commemorated the deeds of the guardian spirit; "on their more or less faithful observance depends the happiness and prosperity of the inhabitants" (Le Van Ho, 1962, 92, 98–99). *Hem* was always accompanied by a great village feast, by dramatic presentations, by music, by hand-to-hand fights, by cockfights, by fights between nightingales. Girls and boys sang songs; it was an occasion for the young to look for spouses. Le Van Ho says, appropriately, that "the traditional civilizations of Viet Nam, in which the majority of people participate, is none other than a civilization of the *dinh* festivals" (1962, 117).

In addition to the local tutelary spirit, confirmed by the emperor, more special cult practices were held at the *dinh*. One of these was the cult of Confucius and of his disciples, celebrated in biannual rituals by the holders of degrees, organized as an association. This association

> formed the most powerful party in the village. The chief of this association is at the same time the *tien chi* or *thu chi*, that is to say the first personage of the community whom the notables never fail to consult in important affairs (Nguyen Huu Khang, 1946, 208).

This local cult of Confucius was paralleled on the national level by an imperial celebration at the royal court at Hué. Village cults of tutelary deities and mandarin sages were linked to the imperial sky cult, with its cosmic magic and seasonal calendar thus serving as the "crowning event of peasant society" (Mus, 1952, 237). Paul Mus has said of this cultic linkage that it does not symbolize a Western type of social contract between men, such as Rousseau might have envisioned, but a concept of a supernatural equilibrium between Heaven, Earth, and the ancestors, maintained through the proper functioning of men. The proper functioning of men was thought to guarantee the maintenance of cosmic order; hence

N

"where we say system, they say virtue" (1952, 28). Social disturbance might threaten that equilibrium; the return of order signified
also the return of virtue.

In addition to the associations of the holders of degrees (*cac-
tich*), there were also associations of old men above the age of sixty,
of soldiers, of trade guilds with their own trade secrets and guardian
spirits, of singers, of raisers of songbirds, of cockfighters, of students
of the same teacher, of men linked by common descent or by residential propinquity or by moral affinity. Each of the associations
would have a chief, maintain a list of members and a treasury, and
act as mutual-aid associations in cases of marriage, funerals, or
other religious ceremonies. The most important of these ceremonies
were the feasts which followed the formal religious rituals and
which exhibited and validated status within the community. At
such occasions each rank held a special place at the rituals and was
accorded a special position in the feasts. When buffalo was sacrificed the parts of the sacrificial animal were distributed according to
rank. It was the ambition of every villager sooner or later to participate in sponsoring a feast for the entire village.

French rule affected the Vietnamese village in two ways. The
powers of the village chief were greatly enlarged to allow him to
become the local representative of the hierarchy of colonial administration. At the same time, the autonomous ranking system and the
recruitment of notables on the basis of internal village status was
superseded by stricter norms established by the occupying power.
"In general," says Nghiem Dang,

> the modifications concerned the election or at least the co-optation
> of the elders, instead of automatic elevation to the rank of elder or
> the fulfillment of certain conditions of age, academic degrees, or
> mandarinal rank. These elections or co-optations were subject to
> the approval of the province chief, whereas previously the acqui-
> sition of the rank of elder by right had not required any approval.
> The number of elders was more and more restricted, and the
> specific function of each varied according to the title conferred
> upon him. A certain automatic advancement was assured among
> elders who were classed by order of precedence according to their
> functions. On the whole, *this tendency consisted of eliminating*

the natural leaders and replacing them by men who were sup-
posed to be more devoted to the cause of the central government
(1966, 150–151; emphasis mine).

Secondly, French rule affected village patterns of ownership
and access to land. Cultivated land in the hands of the Vietnamese
peasantry had suffered an absolute decline since the French conquest. By 1930, colonists held close to 20 percent of all cultivated
land, much of it taken from indigenous owners. Communal lands
had also declined, or were used by local notables to obtain share
rents. Although in 1930 such lands still covered 20 percent of all
land in Tonkin and 25 percent in Annam, in Cochin China they
composed only 3 percent. Bernard Fall has said that

> one can see now that one of the greatest errors of French agrarian
> policy has been to allow the communal lands to fall into the hands
> of speculators and dishonest village chiefs, despite the admonitions
> of the experts of the importance of maintaining, even extending,
> the communal rice fields (1960, 265).

Sixty-one percent of all families had come to own no land whatso-
ever and had joined the growing class of *ta dien,* or sharecroppers.
While dependent workers before French occupation were often
treated as dependent members of the household rather than as
laborers, the *ta dien* worked on the basis of an annual contract,
renewable at the discretion of the landowner. He paid half of his
crop to the landowner; he also made presents to the owner twice a
year, once on the fifth day of the fifth month, the second time at
Vietnamese New Year or Tet. It is estimated that half of all the
land remaining in the hands of the native population was farmed
by such sharecroppers; a fourth of the total agricultural product
produced on Vietnamese holdings constituted share rents (Le
Chau, 1966a, 50).

The strategic social stratum of the villages comprised the
owners of between 2.5 and 10 hectares. Nguyen Huu Khang says
of them that they

> belong to the well-to-do class of the village. They often cultivate a
> portion of their land by employing wage-labor which they limit

themselves to overseeing; they lend out the rest for rental or share-cropping. They generally own oxen and buffalo that are used to do the work, and lent out by the year or by the season to small cultivators. The owners of middle-sized farms are in an enviable situation. They have ready cash. In general, it is they who run the affairs of the village, because the notables are recruited from this class (1946, 169).

The competition of this status-conscious group, in turn, served to drive up land prices. The result of this is

> that, in a heavily populated village where there is little land, these fetch exorbitant prices which bear no relation to invested capital and to possible yield. Due to this one may find in neighboring villages with rice fields of equal quality price differences of twice or three times as much (1946, 171–172).

Such competition of course shut out the peasant of slender means, who was increasingly unable to purchase land. At the same time, high interest rates weighed ever more heavily on the rural population. The Vietnamese peasant

> often borrows both the seeds and the work buffaloes necessary to farm his land. When the harvest is bad he must also find funds with which to pay taxes and fulfill his religious and family duties. A money lender, whether merchant or big landholder, will readily advance a loan, but on very harsh terms. The debt will be repaid with difficulty, often at the cost of pawning the harvest, or even of the fields (Robequain, 1944, 168).

Loans were obtained from local notables or from Chinese money-lenders who also managed the rice market, with its major outlet in Cholon, the Chinese suburb of Saigon. In Cochin China, Indian moneylenders were also active. Frequently, moneylenders borrowed money from government credit institutions, only to loan the money out again to peasants in need of credit. Interest rates were high. The crushing burden of rural indebtedness prompted frequent attempts at reform; most of these, however, proved ineffective.

All of the factors enumerated were accentuated in Cochin China. Land was more completely concentrated in the hands of large landowners, including foreign companies. Sharecropping was more pronounced. The commercialization of the rice crop was further advanced and moneylending more widespread and exorbitant. There was a larger group of landless laborers, many of them working on exploitative contracts. Communal lands were scarce. At the same time the villages in this frontier region lacked the social cohesion characteristic of the North and Center. Villages were formed under frontier conditions by various population elements, comprising refugees, adventurers, soldiers, outcasts. Here also direct French impact was at its maximum. Villages lacked the historical depth of association among fellow villagers characteristic of areas further North. Attachment to patrilineages and lineage ancestors was less functional; the role of the *dinh* in communal life was less central. Settlement pattern was more diffuse. Kinship ties were relatively narrow; local government was more often imposed from the outside. Perhaps the large landowners also feared the possible creation of strong nuclei of native populations in this area of their control (Robequain, 1944, 72). What James B. Hendry says of Khanh Hau, a village in the southern delta, may thus be said of all villages in Cochin: it was "not a village whose people are tightly oriented to the past or strongly bound by tradition" (1964, 260). At the same time, it is probably no accident that Cochin China also witnessed, in the first third of the twentieth century, the emergence of large and powerful millenarian movements. Millenarianism would have special appeal to populations confronted with major cultural changes, but atomized in their social relationships and hence limited in their capacity to respond collectively to them.

There were some seven thousand Vietnamese who became owners of large estates; but there was no Vietnamese middle class of any consequence, as defined in terms of involvement in middle-sized economic enterprises. Most modern industrial plants were in the hands of Europeans. The rice trade and the credit operations connected with it were largely in the hands of Chinese. Chinese had begun to immigrate into Viet Nam in large numbers in the early nineteenth century; the French colonial government further encouraged this immigration. The French—like the Vietnamese government before them—"found the Chinese indispensable, first as provisioners to the army of occupation and then as farmers of indirect taxes, and finally as money-lenders and middlemen serving as a link between themselves and the indigenous population" (Robequain, 1944, 183). The 1936 census listed some 171,000 Chinese in the South where the commercialization of rice was most advanced; 35,000 in Tonkin, and 11,000 in the Center. The Chinese were organized into self-regulating organizations or *bangs*, according to the dialect and province of their place of origin. These *bangs* served as mutual-aid associations for newcomers, supporting and placing them in positions of employment. The rice trade became largely a Chinese monopoly; they were also prominent in the trade of fish, hides, and forest products. Army and navy posts were in the hands of Europeans; 10,779 soldiers and sailors made up more than 50 percent of all Europeans before World War II; another 3,873, or 18.9 percent of all Europeans, occupied government positions. Most of the economic alternatives open to a potential Vietnamese middle class defined in economic terms were thus closed.

What remained open for the Vietnamese with the proper educational background, however, were the professions and the lower positions of the government bureaucracy. This tendency to choose white-collar positions in the professions and administrative hierarchy was reinforced by the French educational system which made the granting of a French-style diploma the decisive point in the life of a young Vietnamese seeking employment under the new conditions. At the same time, there were always more applicants for professional and government employment than there were positions open to be filled. Moreover, the salary differential between French officials and Vietnamese officials was often gross: it is said that the French caretaker of the University of Hanoi earned more than three times the salary of a Vietnamese engineer (Le Chau, 1966a, 43).

These contradictions provided some of the fuel for a growing nationalism among the Vietnamese. Acquaintance with French writers whetted appetites to know more; but many of the writers of the French Enlightenment and of the European socialist tradition became available first in Chinese translations rather than in the French originals. The sons and daughters of former mandarins who had a sense of past glory but had seen their fathers go down in defeat before the foreigners, reacted against the mandarin style but now found in Western teaching a new weapon to use against a colonial power that did not grant them equal privileges with the colonists. The sons of families who had strained to send their sons to school but who found little or no employment in the structure for which their education fitted them, soon grew to be dissatisfied with the conditions of their life. Even the sons and daughters of the rich who had been sent to school in France often returned to find that back in Viet Nam

> they were denied citizenship in their own country; the absence of all liberties which they had enjoyed in France, including the freedom to travel, weighed more heavily on them than on those who never left the country. Instead of the equality in their relations with others which they had enjoyed in France, they were again exposed to the scorn of Vietnam's colonial masters in their own country (Buttinger, 1967, 203).

Rising expectations, confronted with impediments to development on all sides, drove many of them into the various nationalist and socialist movements which began to spring up in Viet Nam after 1900.

A forerunner of these efforts was Phan Boi Chau (1867–1940). Like the Chinese "self-strengtheners" of the late nineteenth century, he had understood that a return to the past was impossible.

> The East's entire intellectual heritage would be useless in the struggle for freedom and a better life in Asia unless revitalized by the knowledge and the ideas developed in the West during the still young age of modern science and industrialization (Buttinger, 1967, 145–146).

In this vision, Chau expressed the aspirations of a new set of entrepreneurs, still potential rather than actual, who could envision a future of economic development somewhat like that of Japan; and it was to Japan that Chau's movement turned for inspiration and support. Never more than a movement of the educated elite, it developed little contact with the population at large, in spite of a kind of Asian Fabian socialist rhetoric. Chau himself spent the rest of his days in exile. His movement, in turn, gave rise to the Dai Viet which still exists in South Viet Nam and which combined a strongly pro-Japanese stance of "Asia for the Asians" with an ideology of authoritarian socialism. It probably never numbered more than one thousand members.

A second movement, the Vietnamese Nationalist party (VNDQQ), was organized in 1927, on the model of the Chinese Kuo Min Tang, with a membership drawn largely from civil servants, small businessmen, tradesmen, and company-grade officers in the armed services. According to French sources, more than 50 percent of its members were employed by the colonial government. Never more than 1,500 members strong, the organization was in essence a nationalist secret society, not a political mass party, and relied for its activity on a small group of initiates without the benefit of effective organization. In February 1930, the movement unleashed an uprising among Vietnamese native troops at Yen Bay, a military post northwest of Hanoi. Subject to fierce French repression, the remnants fled to China where they survived only under Chinese Kuo Min Tang sponsorship.

The third political movement of importance was formed by the Communists. The actual formation of a Communist party had been preceded by the organization of various Marxist groups most of whom appealed to teachers, students, and petty officials in the administration of Annam (Sacks, 1959, 118–120). About a fifth of its membership had participated in revolutionary activities in South China before 1927: its greatest regional strength lay in the provinces of Nghe An and Ha Tinh. Here it sponsored an uprising in 1929. Like the Yen Bay Rebellion this attempt, too, was suppressed by the French. Unlike the Vietnamese Nationalist party, however, the Communists, in the course of the uprising, sought the support of workers and peasants, and attempted, for the first time and under the impetus of the rising, to develop revolutionary mass organizations.

Nghe An, the site of the uprising, possessed an old tradition of rebellion. Its population, eking out a bare living from agriculture, had from early times on adopted two subsidiary patterns to add to its income. One was out-migration with the result that its inhabitants possessed wider horizons than many another peasant area in Viet Nam. The other was scholarly achievement in order to push super-numerary sons into official employment or teaching. At the same time, the court at Hué had always discriminated against the literati from this region; they possessed a well-deserved reputation for independence of mind and a penchant for rebellion.

> In this region inhabited by poor peasantry there had already been born numerous movements against foreign occupation or oppression by the central power: the revolt of the Le-Loi against the Chinese in the 15th century, the peasant insurrections of the 18th century against the Trinh lords, the uprising of the literati against the colonial regime in 1885-95 and again in 1907-1908 (Chesneaux, 1955a, 275).

Here the French had also introduced textile plants, railway repair shops, and other industrial establishments. This labor force of some three thousand men located in the towns of Vinh and Benthuy had been recruited primarily from the local peasantry. At the same time the cadre of the Communist party in this area (between 1,100 and 1,700 strong) was largely of local origin; Ho Chi Minh and Vo Nguyen Giap—the future conqueror of Dien Bien Phu—both stem from this area. Most of them belonged to the "French-educated intelligentsia, by class origin largely mandarinal, gentry and bourgeois" (Benda, 1965, 430). They first directed their organizational efforts at the industrial workers; a strike in the match factory set off mass demonstrations which, in turn, brought on riots which drew strong peasant support, due in part to a poor harvest in the region, and in part to the proselytizing efforts of their kin in the factories and railway shops. In all some fifty thousand people are said to have participated, just under 10 percent of the population (1965, 429). The movement brought on the collapse of local civil authority; to replace it the Communists organized soviets, which included seventeen villages. Red Guards were formed, and new officials appointed. Funeral expenses, gambling, and religious expenditures were curtailed. Land was redistributed. For the first time women were allowed to speak in public meetings (Nguyen Duy Trinh, 1962, 16, 18–19). French retaliation was swift; many Communist leaders were executed; by 1932 some ten thousand political prisoners were in jail, and until the beginning of World War II the party was forced to remain relatively quiescent. At the same time the attempted rebellion had gained it wider sympathies among the population, together with the knowledge that it would need a wider social and geographical base for any future activities. Ho Chi Minh—who is said to have opposed the Nghe An uprising from the beginning—emerged with a much enhanced personal reputation.

The Vietnamese Revolution itself may be divided into three stages. The first stage, that of incubation, took place during the Japanese occupation of Viet Nam between 1940 and 1945. The second stage began when French armed forces returned at the end of World War II, and attempted once again to bring the country under the jurisdiction of France. This stage ended with the defeat and departure of the French in 1954. The third stage began with the partition of Viet Nam into two parts, one dominated by the victorious revolutionaries, the other by an anti-Communist regime increasingly sustained by the United States. In 1960 outbreaks of violence in this southern portion culminated in a renewal of warfare which is not yet at an end at the time of this writing.

The first stage of this prolonged struggle—which was to endure for more than a quarter of a century—opened in midsummer in 1940 when France had been overrun by the German war machine and forced to sign an armistice with Germany on June 25 of that year. At this point, Germany's ally Japan addressed a demand to French Indochina for common control of the Indochinese-Chinese border. The Japanese were eager to cut off all southern routes of supply to the beleaguered Chinese Kuo Min Tang government. When the newly installed French rump regime at Vichy delayed response to additional Japanese demands for transit rights through northern Viet Nam, the Japanese attacked French border fortifications, bombed the port of Haiphong, and landed troops. By the end of July the Japanese had won control of all vital port and harbor facilities; at the same time Thailand, acting in alliance with the Japanese, occupied parts of Cambodia and Laos. From then on Indochina was to form part of the East Asia Co-Prosperity Sphere; its raw materials supplied Japan for as long as Japan remained in control of the seas. The French retained nominal control of the internal affairs of the country, but under Japanese overlordship and supervision.

There were minor uprisings in scattered locations, one on September 24, 1940, near Lang Son, shortly after the Japanese attacked that border post; another in Cochin China, spurred on by the Thai invasion, in the Plaine de Joncs where veteran Communist Tran Van Giau had organized paramilitary units during the Popular Front days of the 1930's; a third when a native garrison staged an uprising at Do-luong. There were also riots induced by poor rice harvests and rice requisitions. Of all these events, the first proved to be the most important, not so much for its military importance, but because it led to cooperation between the Communists and an ethnic minority dominant in this area, the Tho, an alliance which was to prove strategic in the Communist victory in North Viet Nam and in the ouster of the French at the conclusion of the second stage of the Revolution.

By 1942 Vo Nguyen Giap had formed a small guerrilla band in the mountains. This became the first unit of the League for the Independence of Viet Nam, the Viet Minh. The uprising at Bac Son by the Tho ethnic minority gave him an opportunity to enter into a viable coalition with the leaders of this group. The Tho were not only the largest ethnic minority group in North Viet Nam, they were also the group most completely subjected to Vietnamese acculturation. They were led by a hereditary elite, the Tho-ti, who were the descendants of Vietnamese mandarins sent in to control the mountain people, but who retained control over the commoners through a continuation of hereditary rights with certain ritual functions, rather than through the traditional Confucian examination system. This Tho-ti elite had been replaced by appointed officials and was thus strongly anti-French and perfectly amenable to a political coalition with the developing Communist guerrilla bands.

> Since they were the only Vietnamese-speaking elite of any mountain minority, they were in an unparalleled position to work with the Viet Minh to organize a highland guerilla base within their traditionally defined territory. Moreover, because the Tho-ti had suffered at the hands of the colonial regimes, their interests tended to coincide with those of the Communists. This attitude was in sharp contrast to the elites of other mountain groups who looked upon the French as protectors from Vietnamese encroachment (McAlister, 1967, 794).

Three Viet Minh generals were of Tho origin, and Tho came to make up about 20 percent of all Viet Minh regulars in 1954 (McAlister, 1967, 796).

It is also important to note the prevalence of men drawn from the Vietnamese middle class within the ranks of the Viet Minh. A Special Operations Research Office case study says on this point that

> the revolutionary leadership came primarily from the emergent middle class, as did much of its early following. Although the rank and file of the Vietminh's guerilla and regular army forces were for the most part peasants and urban workers, the intermediate and lower echelon leaders—the so-called "linking cadres"—were from the lower middle class and all had some degree of Western education and experience. Often these leaders at village level were, or had once been, local civil servants in the colonial administration (1964, 10).

Similarly, a researcher for the Rand Corporation reports on a study of the social composition of the Viet Minh forces initiated by the French in the following words:

> The results of the inquiry showed that 46 per cent of the army was composed of peasants and laborers, with laborers in the majority. . . . According to the inquiry, 48 per cent were petty officials, and the remaining six per cent came from miscellaneous professions and trades. If this breakdown is correct, the petty officials provided nearly half of the recruits for the army, although peasants made up the majority of the total population. These

percentages are especially interesting, as the French controlled most of the urban areas where the largest number of petty officials were likely to reside. They suggest that these officials were more attracted by Communist propaganda than were the peasants (Tanham, 1961, 58).

In the same vein, a self-study initiated by the Communist party after the war showed that of 1,855 key positions, 1,365 were held by intellectuals or sons of the bourgeoisie, 351 by peasants, and 139 by workers. In 1965 Truong Chinh, a leading member of the North Vietnamese Communist party, would still point out that

> our party was born in an agrarian country where the working class was numerically weak. In the great majority our cadres and our militants originated in the petty bourgeoisie (quoted in Arnault, 1966, 230, fn. 1).

Another factor favoring the developing mountain redoubt was access to China where a number of Chinese Kuo Min Tang war lords had hopes of winning the rich resources of Viet Nam for themselves and were willing to sponsor a client movement of their own against the French and the Japanese. The small guerrilla force in the mountains was thus allowed to grow and to extend its network until it became the only force in Viet Nam actively engaged in guerrilla action against the Japanese, in rescuing Allied airmen downed in their territory, and in providing information to the Allies. Nevertheless, the scale of military effort remained minor. The only major armed attack occurred relatively late in the war in an assault by five hundred Viet Minh against forty Japanese gendarmes at the mountain resort of Tam Dao on July 17, 1945.

The end of Japanese rule thus found the Viet Minh in a preferred position to stake out a larger claim in the struggle for Indochinese independence. The Allies had decided at Teheran that Indochina down to the sixteenth parallel was to be occupied by Chinese troops, while the southern half of Viet Nam was to be held by the British. British troops were far too few to impede the movement of Viet Minh into the thinly held hinterland, while the Chinese were mainly interested in pillaging the countryside and evidenced little interest in who controlled the sources of political power. In late August a Viet Minh-led uprising took place in Hanoi, and on August 29 a provisional government of the Democratic Republic of Viet Nam in which the Viet Minh held all the seats took power in Hanoi. The Kuo Min Tang Chinese sold the new government substantial American, French, and Japanese arms in exchange for gold, opium, and rice. The Viet Minh obtained the gold from the population during a "gold week." The Chinese agreed to take their departure in February 1946. The scene was cleared for a return of the French. In March French troops reentered Hanoi.

In 1946 fighting broke out between Viet Minh and French forces. It is not necessary to give a blow-by-blow account of the war to realize that throughout most of the war the Viet Minh area of control lay in the mountains, while the French continued to hold the lowlands and the cities. This pattern was evident as early as May 1949 when a French military mission recommended the immediate withdrawal of all French forces from the peripheral mountain areas to the low-lying rice-producing areas of the *Viet Nam utile,* the useful Viet Nam, which would be the ultimate prize of the battle (Fall, 1967, 108). This proposal went unheeded; French outposts continued to hold outlying positions along the periphery, positions which put them at a marked disadvantage while granting all advantages to the Viet Minh. By January 1950 the Viet Minh had sealed off the Thai highlands from the Red River delta, and by September of that year cut off the delta from both the northern and northwestern mountains. Viet Minh attempts to advance into the flatland itself, however, invited bloody reverses in January 1951. Similarly a French attempt in February to seize Hoa-Binh, which controlled the approach to the highlands in the West, proved equally unsuccessful, merely eating up vitally needed reserves of manpower and matériel. At this point the Viet Minh shifted its emphasis to the conquest of the Thai highlands, Central Laos, and the Southern Mountain Plateau, causing the French to disperse their troops in terrain least suitable for a modern army and most advantageous to guerrilla forces. In the Thai highlands the French found support among the White Thai, while the Viet Minh enlisted the aid of Black Thai and Meo minority groups. The final battle of Dien Bien Phu took place in what was the traditional battleground among tribal groups for dominance in the Thai-speaking zone. John T. McAlister has said wryly that the battle of Dien Bien Phu "could be regarded as a fight for the Sip Song Chau Tai, in which the antagonists again enlisted external aid as they had in the past" (1967, 832). Yet never before had the battles been fought with such large-scale external aid, or with Vietnamese allies so far away from their home base. The story of the battle at Dien Bien Phu from March to May 1954 is history. The French suffered a defeat of such magnitude that it impaired their ability to continue the war. In June the French retreated toward Hanoi and Haiphong. On July 21, 1954, control of North Viet Nam formally passed into the hands of the Viet Minh.

From the beginning of the resistance against the French, the Viet Minh shelved any radical program of land reform. Instead, it followed the pattern of the Chinese Communists in putting the struggle against foreign invasion above any immediate implementation of class conflict. The major emphasis economically was placed upon raising agricultural production, socially upon a reduction in rents and rates of interest paid. Since peasant proprietorship was more widespread in the North than in the South, while the main complaints of the peasantry concerned high land rents and usury, such a policy was in line with the immediate interests of the peasant population. Moreover, the Viet Minh recognized that a major change of social and political structures would have to precede the mobilization of poor and middle peasants against the rich in the villages, rather than follow it:

> In order to carry on anti-feudal struggle in Viet Nam it was indispensable to promote as a prerequisite the radical transformation of social structures which would permit the exploited peasantry to break the vicious circle within which it was confined (Le Chau, 1966a, 72).

Nevertheless, a modicum of land reform was carried through, in part by confiscating lands belonging to the French and to enemies of the Viet Minh, in part by occupying lands held by religious groups hostile to the insurgents, notably the Catholics. Between 1945 and 1953, the Viet Minh distributed 310,210 hectares, or 15 percent, of the total cultivable land in North Viet Nam, with about 17 percent of peasant households in the North receiving land (Le Chau, 1966a, 108–109). This increased the percentage of land held by middle peasants from 30.4 percent in 1945 to 34.6 percent in 1953, by poor peasants from 10.8 percent to 15.6 percent, and by agricultural laborers from 0.0 to 2.1 percent (1966a, 110). Rents were reduced by 25 percent, usurious debts contracted before August 1945 were abolished, and interest rates were fixed at 13 percent for monetary loans and 20 percent for loans in kind. At the same time, artisan production, which had already received impetus during the prolonged period of isolation from world markets marked by World War II, received strong Viet Minh support; increases in textile production were especially marked. Such increases allowed the Jungle Republic to trade surpluses even with the zone occupied by the French, a trade that showed especially rapid increases from 1952 to 1954 (Le Chau, 1966a, 96). The Viet Minh also laid hands on all industrial establishments within its area, transporting and dispersing skilled workers and machines within the mountainous interior where the equipment was relatively safe from enemy attack.

Organizationally, the Viet Minh proved equally adept at adapting itself to the exigencies of the peasant population. Much has been written about Communist sponsorship of "parallel hierarchies," in which territorial units—such as the village, village group, district, province, and zone—were crosscut by associations based on function—such as associations of peasants, workers, or intellectuals, women, or youth. In fact, territorial organization in the North was more flexible than indicated in the formal table of organization, while the establishment of functional associations simply followed the traditional patterns in the North and Center of the country. The territorial organization

> consisted chiefly of a horizontal chain of village-level committees. . . . At all times the basic unit was the village, and the basic

administrative and judicial organ was the committee, whatever its name. These committees during the Viet Minh war were joined like spokes in a wheel to the provincial-level committee, and the provinces were directly linked in the first years to Minister of the Interior Vo Nguyen Giap (Pike, 1966, 47).

These committees exercised judicial control, opened schools, carried through the economic policies of the Viet Minh, such as rent and interest reduction, and land distribution, and organized the military and paramilitary efforts of the communities. In the South —where French control was stronger—organization took on the form of a network, rather than of revolutionary communities; these proved successful primarily in the North (1966, 47).

The use of customary village patterns and symbols allowed the Viet Minh to build a bridge between past and present, rather than severing its links to the past. Paul Mus, the noted French scholar of Buddhism has pointed out the traditional connotations of *xa hoi hoa,* the Vietnamese phrase for socialism. *Xa* is

> the village, the traditional village community, with its spiritual and social connotations . . . the key word *xa* has a central value. It depicts a landscape; not an external landscape, but a sociological landscape.

Hoi connotes "union, assembly, society." The verb *hoa*

> completes this semi-Confucian imagery. Far from implying a revolutionary convulsion, it is applied specifically to the action in depth through which the "mandate of heaven," through the sovereigns who are its bearers, civilize a country and bring into flower all that the social character of man contains.

These words thus

> put the future of Viet Nam under the constraint of its past and of a tradition anterior to that of the French (Mus, 1952, 253, 261).

Similarly, Nguyen Khac Vien points out that

> Marxism never disconcerted the Confucians in centering human thought on political and social problems; the Confucian school did not do otherwise. In defining man in terms of the totality of his social relations, Marxism did not even shock the literati who

o

thought that man's supreme purpose is to correctly carry out his social obligations. . . . Bourgeois individualism which put one's own individuality above society, petty bourgeois anarchism which recognizes no other social discipline are strange to both Confucianism and Marxism. In moving from traditional society to socialist society, Confucian Man adopts a new social discipline, but at the bottom of his heart he had never been hostile, as the bourgeois individual has been, to the same principle of collective discipline, believing it to be indispensable to the development of his personality (quoted in Chesneaux, 1968, 49).

With the French defeat and the signing of the Geneva Agreement, the Viet Minh took over Viet Nam north of the seventeenth parallel, and proceeded to carry out a major program of land reform and social reorganization in the countryside. The execution of the program fell into two stages. During the first stage, 1954 to 1958, land was to be taken from landlords and redistributed among the remainder of the peasantry; at the same time, political control was to be taken from landlords and rich peasants and to be transferred to the poor and middle peasantry. The regime therefore embarked on a policy of class struggle in the villages which would

base oneself without reservation on the poor peasants and the lower stratum of middle peasants, unite strongly with the middle peasants, limit the economic exploitation of the rich peasants in order to liquidate it in the end, educate the middle peasants ideologically, keep the landlords from raising their heads, allow them the chance of changing themselves into new men through work (Truong Chinh, quoted in Le Chau, 1966a, 173).

At the same time, occasional mutual aid which was an old pattern between members of the same village and neighboring villages, was to be transformed into regular and organized mutual-aid teams. In a second stage, land reform was to advance from simple redistribution of land to the organization of cooperatives as well as to the establishment of collective farms set up on the Russian model.

The first stage of land reform, however, unleashed a wave of terror which almost destroyed the chances for a reorganization of agriculture. The classification of the population into various class groups was carried out by party cadre with the utmost ferocity, and—frequently—with great arbitrariness. Public denunciations, organized to air grievances against landlords, often denounced the innocent with the guilty, middle peasants along with their wealthier fellow villagers, until as the North Vietnamese paper *Nhan-Dan* admitted: "Brothers from the same family no longer dare visit each other, and people do not dare to greet each other when they meet in the street" (quoted in Fall, 1967, 156). Many were executed, others imprisoned; one estimate puts the number of men killed at 50,000, those jailed at 100,000 (1967, 156). The campaign provoked serious splits between rural Communist leaders, many of whom were veterans of the resistance, and the higher echelons charged with carrying out the program. These, often urban in origin, came to be known in the villages as "cadre with lacquered teeth (a folk practice, hence symbolic for 'ignorant') who murder" (Le Chau, 1966a, 151). A full-scale revolt broke out in Nghe An Province, the "mother of the Revolution." While it was put down by force, it served as a signal for the regime to halt the campaign, and to "rectify errors" in an orgy of self-criticism.

The attempt to spur the class struggle in the villages had nearly wrecked efforts at agrarian reform. Production declined and mutual-aid teams decreased by more than 50 percent (Le Chau, 1966a, 148). In the wake of the "rectification campaign," an effort began in 1958 to move the peasantry into "semisocialist" or "socialist" cooperatives. The semisocialist cooperative pooled land, livestock, and equipment of individual members, paying them rent for the amount contributed, as well as a share of the remuneration received for the total product. It thus constituted a compromise between individual ownership and collective operation. Retaining the inequalities in amounts of land and stock owned, it paid differential amounts of rent to participants. In contrast, the socialist cooperative—or collective farm of the Russian type—made all property the property of the collective, and rewarded participants by wage payments in proportion to their input of labor. It was in the main the semisocialist cooperative that came into being during the renewed effort at agrarian reconstruction. Between 1958 and

1960, 85 percent of farm units and 76 percent of the land in North Viet Nam were collectivized. Of land collectivized by 1959, 694,800 hectares were held by semisocialist cooperatives and only 39,600 hectares by socialist cooperatives (Le Chau, 1966a, 184–186). Alongside of this socialized sector, individual holdings were also maintained. Moreover, it was recognized that the society could not produce enough without the incentive of individual proprietorship and appropriation in the near future. In 1959 it was estimated that as much as 50 percent of all revenues of peasant households still derived from individual enterprise, such as keeping livestock (16 percent), "secondary" activities (17 percent), and cultivation of family plots (17 percent) (Le Chau, 1966a, 358–359). In contrast to the turbulence generated by the "population classification" campaign, the agrarian reform itself seems to have produced little disturbance, perhaps because it did not go on to outright collectivization and perhaps because it proceeded in an atmosphere of relaxation after tension according to the dictum ascribed to Ho Chi Minh that

> to straighten a curved piece of bamboo, one must bend it in the opposite direction, holding it in that position for a while. Then, when the hand is removed it will slowly straighten itself (Hoang, 1964, 211).

Events took a different course in the South. While the French concentrated their military effort largely in the North, the Viet Minh in the South came into control of much of the rural area largely by default. By the end of World War II they ruled at least half of the villages of Viet Nam south of the seventeenth parallel; some estimates put the villages under their control as high as 90 percent (Kahin and Lewis, 1967, 102). Of outstanding importance in this unimpeded expansion was their program of freely distributing land owned by both French and Vietnamese landlords to the peasantry; some 600,000 hectares are said to have changed hands in this way (Le Chau, 1966b, 58).

Yet despite these successes the Viet Minh hold over the South remained more tenuous than in the North. This was in part due to the more atomized social structure; village level organization was much less cohesive than in the North. While this offered opportunities for penetration by individuals or small groups which could form part of a larger organizational network, it also rendered more difficult organization of the entire village community. In the South, moreover, the Viet Minh also faced competition from two major religious-military sects which had no intention of yielding control in the countryside to the revolutionaries. These sects had grown up as quasi-millenarian movements, offering a cohesive ideology and organization to the more individualized and less solidary peasantry of the southern frontier zone.

The first of these was the Cao Dai—the name standing for "High Palace"—a synonym for God who reigns over the universe. In Vietnamese the movement is known as "the Third Amnesty of God." The first two amnesties granted to the world are thought to be those of Moses and Jesus; the third is Oriental and represented by Buddha and Lao-Tzu. God, however, speaks to men through the largely Vietnamese pattern of spiritistic mediums. The first message was said to have reached a mandarin prefect in 1919; his disciple, a former merchant, organized and institutionalized the movement. Like the Catholic Church, it possesses a hierarchy headed by a pope, but it also owns a secular arm which is responsible for local administration, welfare functions, and the armed forces of the movement. By 1926 the Cao Dai had twenty thousand adherents, many of them holding posts in the French administration; others had belonged to nationalist organizations like Young Annam, but merged with the Cao Dai when that organization was suppressed by the French. After 1934 the movement split into numerous rival segments. In general anti-French before and during World War II, they turned against the Viet Minh during the years of resistance, largely to secure their independent domains. However,

> military units of the sects were primarily concerned with acquiring larger fiefs. Hence, a military unit constituted—as formerly in the case of the warlords in China—a considerable commercial asset that could not be squandered on a sudden military operation. This made the sects highly reluctant to fight the Viet Minh effectively

and their troops could seldom be used except in or near their own living area (Fall, 1955, 241).

The Cao Dai claim more than a million and a half followers, most of them concentrated in the Mekong delta of the South, in Tay Ninh Province close to the Cambodian border, and in Saigon itself.

The other major sect was the Hoa Hao, organized in 1939, with its stronghold in Mien-Tay Province. Claiming roots in the anti-French movement of the nineteenth century which produced two local rebellions—in 1875 and 1913—its main orientation is that of a Buddhist "Protestantism." The cult requires no temples, pagodas, or ritual objects, curtails expenditures at ritual occasions like marriages and funerals, and frowns on gambling, drinking, opium smoking, the sale of child brides, and arranged marriages. Strongly pro-Japanese and anti-French in World War II, they were quite unwilling to yield the areas under their control to the Viet Minh and supported the French during the period of resistance. Their greatest strength lies again in the area to the south and west of Saigon. The Hoa Hao fiefs, says Bernard Fall,

> were first and foremost exceedingly profitable economic enterprises for their leaders, many of whom have acquaintances in high government circles. Soai and his fellow leaders [controlling the oldest Hoa Hao group], for example, controlled the bulk of rice purchasing and milling operations in the Bassac area, through the SOCACI, his own corporation, duly incorporated by the Viet-namese government after a series of highly irregular but very successful interventions by influential persons. The crop was sold by the farmers to Soai below market prices and the latter stored it until the end of the season (when prices are high) and then sold it to big enterprises in Saigon at a huge profit (1955, 249).

The movement claims about a million adherents and possesses its own militia of twenty thousand men.

The two religious-military sects received further reinforcements after the Geneva Agreement by the wholesale migration to the South of 700,000 Catholics. These had been located primarily in the area south of the Red River since the middle of the nineteenth century.

Here you could behold religion with all its urge for power and domination. It was a geometrical world belonging wholly to the faith, one in which the land, the men and everything else had been created by the priests as God created the earth. In the last century nothing existed but marshes, a permanent flood where the reddish waters of the estuaries merged imperceptibly with the tidal flow from the sea. But in this region of mud and brine missionaries dug canals, bringing into existence a checkerboard of green islands and attracting a population which they christened in bulk. Later the clergy became entirely Vietnamese, and then very quickly there grew up still another feudal domain, an ecclesiastical fief in the name of the Lord. The very landscape was clerical. Every main square, with its church in the middle, was a parish; the curé was the Lord and the parishioners his serfs (Bodard, 1967, 211).

Refugee Catholic peasants from this area, led by their priests, settled in new villages in South Viet Nam, some just south of the seventeenth parallel, others in the highland area inhabited by non-Vietnamese ethnic groups, and still others in a cluster of villages around Saigon. Catholics with professional skills would lend their support to the new anti-Communist regime in South Viet Nam, and carry on the battle against the Viet Minh in its new southern guise of the National Liberation Front.

The Geneva Agreement arranged for the evacuation of Viet Minh troops from the South; some fifty thousand went North, taking with them some twenty thousand civilian sympathizers, most of whom came from the eastern coast, long a Viet Minh stronghold (Pike, 1966, 47). They also retained a series of bastions which had served them well during the resistance, and which would come to form bases for the new guerrilla effort soon to break out in 1958. These were located in Quang Nghai Province on the east coast; in the mountains above Nha Trang city, north of Camranh Bay; Northern Tay Ninh Province along the Cambodian border; Zone D, in Phuoc Tanh and Binh Duong provinces north of Saigon; Ban O Quan in Kien Phong Province in the Mekong delta; and An Xuyen Province at the southern tip of Viet Nam (Pike, 1966, 80). Moreover, they retained in their favor the memory of land distributed freely and without payment to the peasantry in all areas where they had won control before 1954. This factor would play an important role in all of the events to come. One informed estimate has it that the Communists left behind a network of some ten thousand persons who could be activated in time of need (Pike, 1966, 75, note 3).

That time was to come sooner than expected, and when it came the Viet Minh would have equally unexpected allies. Just as the Viet Minh had gained adherents by rallying Vietnamese against an external force, the French, so the revolutionaries in the South would soon be able to rally support for their cause against a common enemy, this time the new regime headed by Ngo Dinh Diem. Diem came to power as a result of a power vacuum. The Viet Minh was withdrawing northward, in accord with the Geneva Agreement. Diem inherited from the French an army of Vietnamese auxiliaries, 250,000 men strong (Shaplen, 1966, 134). He had active United States support; and had the backing of many anti-Communist Vietnamese, including the Catholics. The regime scored two early successes. To begin with, Diem was successful in turning his army against the military-religious sects, the Cao Dai and Hoa Hao, united with a third "mafia"-like group in Saigon into a United Front of Nationalist Forces. These had made ready to challenge the authority of the new government, apparently with covert French support. Their defeat strongly aided the centralization of goverment power. Diem was then able to deploy his new army over much of South Viet Nam, especially in the Camau peninsula and in the Quang Nghai and Binh Dinh area which had served as traditional Viet Minh strongholds.

These early military successes, however, reinforced the conviction of the regime that its key mission

> was to consolidate truncated Viet Nam into a viable anti-Communist state; to establish unchallenged control by the central government; and to prepare the non-Communist area for an eventual showdown with the Communist area. In other words, Diem may have considered his own position to resemble that of Emperor Gia-Long who, at the end of the eighteenth century and with the help

of foreign advisers, defeated the usurpers, reunified the Vietnamese state, and gave it the codes and laws that ruled it for fifty years (Fall, 1967, 238).

In 1955, this government refused to hold free elections, in contradiction of the clauses of the Geneva Agreement, which had stipulated the holding of elections, and to which the Viet Minh in the North had given its approval, in the belief that such elections would redound in its favor. In June 1956, the southern regime moved to abolish elections also for village chiefs and municipal councils, thus ending at one stroke the traditional autonomy of Viet Nam's villages, and angering the peasant electorate. The ostensible reason for this move was that the Viet Minh would win many of these elections. Local and municipal offices were made appointive. To strengthen still further the hand of the central government, a new political party, the Can Lao, came into being. Its main function was less that of a mass party than of a "political intelligence agency" (Shaplen, 1966, 130) set up to detect Communists or other dissidents. By the end of 1956 more than fifty thousand people were in jail (Kahin and Lewis, 1967, 100). To add further fuel to the flames, the new government also sponsored an agrarian program which antagonized the peasants who had won more than 600,000 hectares of land (Le Chau, 1966b, 58) through Viet Minh land distribution. Tenants of lands belonging to landlords who had not paid rent for nine years were asked suddenly to pay rent once more, even though at a reduced rate of 25 percent. Later in 1958, the government began a program of land distribution in which peasants were asked to buy, in six annual installments, land which many of them had come to regard as their own. The reversal in land policy under Diem had a special effect on the mountain-dwelling non-Vietnamese populations. These had received French-owned estates as their own during the Viet Minh period. At the same time the Viet Minh had made a special effort to grant the ethnic minority groups significant administrative and cultural autonomy. The Diem regime reversed this policy by abolishing ethnic group autonomy and by taking over land distributed to them, and by settling 210,000 coastal Vietnamese in the mountain uplands which the tribes had historically regarded as their own. Finally, the government, drawing heavily on refugee Catholics from the North, strongly favored Catholics who constituted about 10 percent of the population.

> Many of the district and province chiefs as well as many village leaders were Catholics, as were many of the important military leaders. Catholic villages, through the influence of this burgeoning hierarchy, benefited most from relief and aid programs. They got the most land grants to build schools and hospitals with the help of assigned soldiers, were given priority for loans under the government's agricultural credit system, received official permission to cut and sell lumber from carefully protected national reserves, and obtained export and import monopolies, including exclusive rights to deal in such new and profitable products as kapok and kenaf (Shaplen, 1966, 191).

While supporters of the Diem spoke of his "one-man democratic rule," others called the regime "a quasi-police state" (Fishel, in Gettleman, 1965; Henderson, speaking in 1957, 1968, 183).

The years 1957–1958 witnessed a slowly rising tide of dissatisfaction with the regime; by 1960 much of Viet Nam south of the seventeenth parallel was in open rebellion. The causes of this rebellion—in civil war or in "aggression from the North"—represent not only academic questions, but are germane to any discussion of United States policy in Viet Nam. It will be remembered that the Viet Minh was not the only anti-regime group in Viet Nam south of the parallel: there still existed bands of Hoa Hao and Cao Dai who had not accepted integration into the Vietnamese army. Some of these were not pacified until 1962. There also existed clandestine nationalist groups, such as the Dai Viet party, which maintained armed units in the field, particularly in Quang Tri Province. At the same time, says Douglas Pike, a leading expert on the National Liberation Front and a defender of the thesis that the rebellion was strongly supported from outside,

> in terms of overt activity such as armed incidents or the distribution of propaganda leaflets the period was quiet and the Communists within the remnant Viet Minh organization relatively in-

active. In addition, much of the activity that did take place apparently was the work of impatient cadres operating in the South independently of Hanoi's orders (1966, 75).

There is additional evidence, moreover, that North Viet Nam—in the continued belief that free elections would be held and return a majority for the Viet Minh—urged sympathizers, through Radio Hanoi, to fulfill the Geneva Agreement and to adopt peaceful tactics. After 1956, when the hopes for elections had faded, North Viet Nam became increasingly committed to its program of social transformation and agrarian reform at home, and involved in all the difficulties of which we have already spoken. As Southern militants began to clamor for action, Radio Hanoi warned against resumption of hostilities. It also took sharp issue with demands that a new rebellion not only aim at the destruction of the Diem regime and at national unification, but also adopt a program of radical socialism (Kahin and Lewis, 1967, 110–112). By 1958, however, there is evidence from particular local areas such as the village of Khanh Hau in Long An Province, of a new political movement, called the National Front for the Liberation of Viet Nam,

> referred to by the South Vietnamese government as the Viet Cong or Vietnamese Communists . . . and invariably called the Viet Minh by the villagers. In the vicinity of Khanh Hau the initial efforts of the Viet Cong were largely confined to anti-government propaganda (Hickey, 1964, 10).

In 1959, clandestine groups made their appearance in Quang Nghai, a former Viet Minh stronghold and during the Diem regime an area of fierce repression (Lacouture, 1965, 70). A split was developing between Northern leaders and Southern rebels. The Northerners

> had to listen to bitter remarks that were made to them about the inability of the North to do anything about the Diem dictatorship. The overriding needs of the world-wide strategy of the Socialist camp meant little, or nothing to guerilla fighters being hunted down . . . in 1959, responsible elements of the Communist Resistance in Indochina came to the conclusion that they had to act, whether Hanoi wanted them to or not. They could no longer

continue to stand by while their supporters were arrested, thrown into prison and tortured, without attempting to do anything about it as an organization, without giving some lead to the people in the struggle in which it was to be involved. Hanoi preferred diplomatic notes, but it was to find that its hand had been forced (Devillers, 1962, 15).

In March 1960, a group calling itself Former Resistance Fighters of South Viet Nam launched an appeal to "all social strata, all milieu" to intensify the struggle against the regime (text in Kahin and Lewis, 1967, 384–387); in September 1960, the Communist party of North Viet Nam put the seal of approval on a "broad United Front directed against the U.S. and Diem and based on the worker-peasant alliance." On December 20, 1960, the National Liberation Front of South Viet Nam (NLF) formally came into being.

Douglas Pike describes the original membership of the Liberation Front as follows:

> Members of the original NLF, and its most ardent supporters in the early years, were drawn from the ranks of the Viet Minh Communists; the Cao Dai and Hoa Hao sects; a scattering of minority group members, primarily ethnic Cambodians and montagnards; idealistic youth, recruited from the universities and polytechnic schools; representatives of farmers' organizations from parts of the Mekong delta, where serious land tenure problems existed; leaders of small political parties or groups, or professionals associated with them; intellectuals who had broken with the GVN [government of Viet Nam] (particularly members of a network of Peace Committees that had sprung up in 1954 in both the North and the South); military deserters; refugees of various sorts from the Diem government, such as those singled out by neighbors in the Denunciation of Communism campaign but who fled before arrest (1966, 83).

These were soon to be joined by southern Viet Minh who had gone North after the Geneva Agreement (1966, 83).

What do we know about the social origins and previous occupational commitments of NLF leaders and followers? Of thirty-eight names in the NLF high command, I have been able to ascertain the social origins of only eight: three are the sons of mandarin families, one is the son of a rubber plantation manager, one is the son of a civil servant, one is the daughter of a business-man, another is the daughter of a well-known nationalist leader. Only one has working-class parents. We know something of the previous occupational history of twenty-two out of thirty-eight: seven were schoolteachers, one was a doctor, one a pharmacist; while one each were, respectively, an architect, an electrical engineer, a lawyer, a newspaperman, a labor organizer, a writer, a French militiaman, a Buddhist monk, and a colonel in the Bin Xuyen "mafia."

Some information is available (Pike, 1966) on holders of lower-level positions, though it is cast in uncomparable categories. Province-level chairmen, vice-chairmen, and secretaries-general, for example, are listed as Viet Minh cadre (9), Cao Dai (8), peasants (10), youths (10), Buddhist bonzes (4), women (4), workers (3), teachers (2), village notables (2), and businessmen (1). These categories do not exclude each other; it is possible for a peasant to belong to the Cao Dai, and for a young man to be a teacher. Moreover, it is more than likely that many members listed as Viet Minh were once peasants; the salient appeal of the movement to many young peasants is precisely that they can rise from their lowly stations to positions of some importance and influence. Nevertheless, the clumsy categories are indicative of attempts to grant representation to certain salient groups. Counting only those groups represented by 10 percent or more of the seats on provincial central committees, we find Cao Dai, 13 percent; other religious groups—Buddhists, Hoa Hao, Catholics—23 percent; youths, 12 percent; intellectuals, 11 percent; women, 11 percent. Surprising is the low percentage of people listed as Viet Minh (6 percent) and peasants (6 percent). Among district chairmen 67 percent are listed as Viet Minh, 19 percent as peasants; among vice-chairmen peasants compose 17 percent; Viet Minh, 14 percent; women, 13 percent. Secretaries-general are mostly youths (53 percent), peasants (28 percent), and Viet Minh (11 percent) (Pike, 1966, 222–224). For the village headman, NLF directives specify that "he must belong to the peasant class . . . must have good political background . . . must have good and close relations with the villagers" (quoted in Pike, 1966, 228). Given the qualifications stated above, three conclusions emerge: men described primarily as peasants decrease as we move from the lower to the higher echelons; representation is granted to many different groups at levels above the village; and Viet Minh are represented on all levels, but especially as "linking cadre" on the level of the district.

A recent study isued by the Rand Corporation (Mitchell, 1967) also tells us something about the appeal of the NLF in various rural areas of South Viet Nam. Edward J. Mitchell has found that

> From the point of view of government control the ideal province in South Vietnam would be one in which few peasants operate their own land, the distribution of land holdings is unequal, no land redistribution has taken place, large French landholdings existed in the past. . . . It is suggested that the greater power of landlords and relative docility of peasants in the more "feudal" areas accounts for this phenomenon (1967, 31).

> Moving across provinces and holding other variables constant, we find that as the percentage of owner-operated land rises, control decreases; as the coefficient of variation increases, control increases (1967, 15).

On this point his findings are quite consonant with conclusions which we have drawn elsewhere in this book. We have already found in other cases we have discussed—Mexico, Russia, China—that revolutionary movements among the peasantry seem to start first among peasants who have some access to land, rather than among the poor peasants or those deprived of land altogether. We shall find this to be true also in the case of Algeria and Cuba. Possession of some land grants the property-owning peasant a measure of independence not possessed by the peasant who depends for his livelihood primarily on his immediate overlord. The property-owning peasant thus has some independent leverage which he can translate into protest more easily than a man whose options are severely restricted by a situation of total dependence. Yet Mitchell forgets to mention in his presentation a vital additional factor, namely, that the tendency to rebellion on the part of the Vietnamese peasant has been reinforced by the *kind* of land redistribution carried out by the government of South Viet Nam. The government-sponsored program of land distribution superseded an earlier and more benevolent distribution of land by the Viet Minh. While it is thus true that land distribution increases the options available to the recipients, participation in rebellion is only *one* of these options. Presumably another kind of government, operating under other circumstances with different means and different aims in mind, could have sponsored a scheme of land distribution which would have provided a wider range of choices for the peasants affected *and*, at the very same time, decreased the desire for participation in rebellion. Mitchell's general statement that "the proposition that land redistribution has had a positive effect on control is sharply contradicted" (1967, 15) should therefore not be read as a prediction holding for all cases of land redistribution, but only as an adequate description of the Vietnamese case. The areas where the government can feel secure are also the areas where the Viet Minh has not succeeded in the past in shaking the unitary power domains of powerful landholders.

Within the congeries of diverse elements making up the NLF, it was certainly the Communists who possessed the widest organizational experience, gained during the days of the Viet Minh, as well as the greatest ideological momentum. Such previous experience allowed them to develop an organizational blueprint. It also provided them with ready-made organizational foci in areas where they had always remained strong. They did not have to start from scratch. This ability to create an organizational framework from the very start is sometimes interpreted as evidence for the Northern origin of the NLF; but there was nothing new in its organizational pattern. It simply applied the concept of parallel hierarchies, of territorial units crosscut by multiple associations, which had already served the Viet Minh well in its past struggles. What was new about the NLF was its particular strategy for organization building and its impact on the specifically Southern social scene.

It will be remembered that the social cohesion of villages in the Vietnamese South was markedly less than that characteristic of the North and Center. Their settlement pattern was less concentrated and more extended. There were fewer peasant proprietors and many more tenants. Communal landholdings were unimportant. Craft production was nearly absent, and so were the village-based guilds of craftsmen found in the North. The population had come from elsewhere and moved to this frontier region only within the last 150 years.

> Kinship groups that were to a large extent starting de novo had much narrower circles of relationship to begin with, and subsequently followed a much looser pattern of kinship obligations and ritual observance which are reflected in a rather widespread failure to maintain family genealogies (Hendry, 1964, 260).

The village was an administrative unit, but at Khanh Hau, for example, in Long An Province,

> the most important events in the lives of people living in the village . . . either extend beyond the village in scope or are limited to groups or activities that are less extensive than the boundaries of the village or even of the hamlets therein. Thus, heavy dependence on "exports" of paddy from the village and exchange for a wide variety of things not grown or produced in the village has already tied inhabitants of Khanh Hau to the national economy as commercial agriculturists and anticipations beyond their own village; the population pyramid offers strong evidence that young adults have left the village . . . ties of kinship now extend well outside the village. . . . Add to this the fact that years of fighting and insecurity in the delta have awakened some sense of nationality and identification with something more extensive than the village; they have also put heavy strains on intra-village relationships of all kinds and generated bitterness and hostility that does not disappear easily (1964, 261).

All of these processes were intensified further by the French presence, which was more immediate in Cochin China than elsewhere in Viet Nam.

If cohesion was weak in the villages, cohesion was equally weak at the level of political elites. There were the various religious-military sects, now including the Catholics. There were several highly personalistic "parties" or splinter groups, with strong regional orientation and an inability to enter into viable political coalitions. South Vietnamese society was heavily fragmented; its polity, disunited and weak.

Into this relatively atomized social setting the NLF launched its organizational effort. As during the days of the Viet Minh, they organized a hierarchy of committees linking the village to the district, the district to the province, the province to the zone, the zone to the central committee. At the same time they organized functional associations, of which the most important were the Farmers' Liberation Association, the Youth Liberation Association, and the Women's Liberation Association. The Farmers' Liberation Association (FLA) was to fight for lower land rents, protect land granted to peasants by the Viet Minh against the government, protect peasants who had taken land on their own, oppose rice merchants, fight government exactions for taxes, corvée labor, and the military draft, resist government security forces, and uphold prospects of eventual national unification. At the core of these tasks lay "land and land tenure problems" (Pike, 1966, 168). Similarly, the women's association was to fight for women's rights and to carry on propaganda among opponent forces. The youth association was set up to harness the special energies and enthusiasms of youth for the revolutionary effort. Together the territorial and the functional units furnished the framework for an alternative government organization in the areas under NLF control.

To this extent there was nothing novel about the NLF effort. What was new was its ability to activate and extend these organizations in the course of a specific strategy—the political struggle—in which people were gradually mobilized to express their specific grievances in public meetings, petitions, and mass protests. Organized with a great sense of realism, a NLF handbook called on the organizers to

> set clear purposes and realistic goals for the struggle in terms of the people's interests. Use realistic slogans that reflect the people's demands. Choose the form of struggle most suitable to the degree of enlightenment of the people. Use the correct forces from

P

among the people, that is, those most directly involved (quoted in Pike, 1966, 96).

Thus the movement enlisted masses of people, organized them as they proceeded from target to target, and then utilized the emerging organizations as effective channels for NLF interpretation of both events and goals. As John Mecklin, a former high official of the U.S. Information Agency in Saigon has said,

> the wrongs that counted in a Vietnamese hamlet were those committed by corrupt local officials, or a greedy landlord. All too often the regime condoned this kind of wrong, while the Viet Cong [NLF] promised to put it right. The Diem regime could not be faulted on principle, but it was a sorry match for the Viet Cong in a struggle where the decision would go to the side that could win the people (1965, 36).

At the same time, military and paramilitary forces extended the areas under NLF control, and squads of terrorists spread through the countryside, with the special mission of assassinating government officials, especially the newly appointed government village and district chiefs. There is evidence that at the beginning the NLF saw the political struggle as primary, the military struggle only as supplementary.

> The NLF initially approached the entire Revolution not as a small-scale war but as a political struggle with guns, a difference real and not semantic. It maintained that its contest with the GVN and the United States should be fought out at the political level and that the use of massed military might was in itself illegitimate (Pike, 1966, 91–92).

The end result was conceived as a general uprising within both the government-held areas and the areas under NLF control which would paralyze the government and allow for an NLF take-over. As it became ever more evident, however, that the government drew increasing United States support in armament and manpower, the emphasis in strategy grew increasingly military. North Vietnamese troops in the South increased correspondingly, and the early emphasis on political struggle over military involvement was reversed. Yet it was ultimately the great organizational success of the NLF in building village bases and mass organizations which guaranteed the continued ability of the insurgent effort to maintain itself and even to grow, even in the fact of a vastly escalated "special war."

This success may, in fact, have been due to the circumstance that the NLF alone, among other organizations in the South, offered a viable organizational framework and ideology for an atomized society striving to attain greater social cohesion. In the beginning some of its appeals may even have been similar to those which brought peasants flocking to the cult groups of the Cao Dai and Hoa Hao. Atomized and segmented social relationships in the villages stood in contradiction to an ever widening network of social relationships outside. Old ideologies no longer furnished security and predictability under new circumstances. Just as the military-religious sects offered a wider organizational framework and a new ideology, so the NLF now mobilized people in wider parallel hierarchies and for more transcendent ends. But where the Cao Dai and Hoa Hao had remained essentially segmented and regional, the NLF held out a universal appeal. To this date, it constitutes the only such organization in South Viet Nam. In the midst of the Viet Minh struggle against the French, Paul Mus commented on the great paradox that a European would find himself most at ease psychologically and ideologically among the Vietnamese Marxists who were his political enemies, while his political allies—the Confucian traditionalists and the members of the military-religious sects—were also those with whom he could be least at home in both emotional and cognitive terms (1952, 251–252). At the time of writing—sixteen years later—this paradox remains apparently unresolved.

FIVE

ALGERIA

The Arabs with great insight
understand very well the cruel
revolution we have brought
them: it is as radical for them
as socialism would be for us.

> General Bugeaud,
> the conqueror of Al-
> geria, 1849

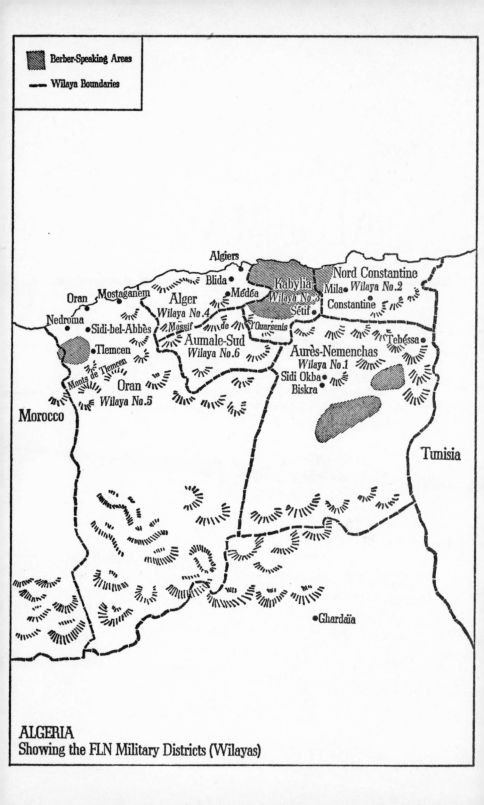

Berber-Speaking Areas

Wilaya Boundaries

Algiers

Oran Mostaganem

Nedroma

Sidi-bel-Abbès

Tlemcen

Monts de Tlemcen

Morocco

Blida

Médéa

Alger
Wilaya No.4

Massif de l'Ouarsenis

Aumale-Sud
Wilaya No.6

Kabylia
Wilaya No.3

Sétif

Oran
Wilaya No.5

Mila

Constantine

Nord Constantine
Wilaya No.2

Tébessa

Aurès-Nemenchas
Wilaya No.1

Sidi Okba
Biskra

Tunisia

Ghardaïa

ALGERIA
Showing the FLN Military Districts (Wilayas)

In 1830, an altercation between the Turkish governor of Algiers and the French consul brought French armies to Algiers. At first, France merely established a protectorate; but in 1840 the French government decided on the wholesale conquest and colonization of the entire country. The conquest was carried out by General Bugeaud who combined warfare carried on by flying columns with a scorched-earth policy of total devastation. "In Europe," Bugeaud had written,

> we not only fight armies, we also fight vested interests. When we have beaten the belligerent armies, we seize the centers of population, of trade, of industry, the customs, the archives, and soon the vested interests are forced to capitulate. There is only one interest one can seize in Africa, the interest vested in agriculture . . . well! I have found no other means of subjugating the country than to seize that vested interest (quoted in Julien, 1947, 65).

Begun as a military operation abroad in order to divert French attention from the growing unpopularity of the regime of Charles X at home, the occupation of Algiers soon became an end in itself. Its first effect was to deprive the native population of much of their land and to transfer this land into the hands of Europeans. Algeria, like most other non-Western areas of the world, had not known the European institution of absolute private property before the advent of the Europeans; rather there existed a complex hierarchy of use rights. Rights to land were divided, first of all, between those held by the bey as ruler and those held by the tribes. The bey's lands were of three kinds. One kind, *melk* (from *malaka*, to rule) was granted to individuals, but with the sovereign retaining ultimate title. The recipient peasants could inherit their use rights, fence their plots, and transfer their rights through gift-giving or sales. Nevertheless, sales were rare because they had to have the approval of the entire local community—which had priority rights of purchase in such a case—and was associated with a loss of honor and shame for having alienated the basis of one's livelihood. A second kind of land pertained to each of the three administrative districts (*beylik*) into which the Turks had divided Algeria. These district lands comprised the best land available and the land most suitable for irrigation; they were cultivated under the direct administration of the bey himself, either by corvées drawn from neighboring dependent tribes, or by sharecroppers who received oxen, plow, and seed, and retained a fifth of the yield. A third kind of land, called *azel*, was either land confiscated from rebellious tribes or purchased by the bey. It was granted in lieu of salary to particular officials or families or to compensate tribal units that furnished soldiers to the ruler or pastured his herds with their own. Some of these lands were pasture, but agricultural lands were in turn farmed by sharecroppers or leaseholders who retained hereditary use rights to these lands. It is estimated that in Algeria more than fifteen thousand families were involved in these derivative cropping arrangements.

In contrast to these lands, under the ultimate jurisdiction of the governor, stood the tribal lands, *bled el'arsh*. Titles were vested in the tribe as a whole, but once again any tribesman who worked the land with his plow was entitled to heritable use rights and to private appropriation of the produce. These lands were unfenced and open to all claimants: labor invested in the land served as a guarantee of continued occupation or as a primary claim to it.

All of these lands were subject to taxation which amounted to 2 percent of total yield. At the same time the cultivator had complete security of tenure; it was unthinkable that "for some whim of the government he could lose the land which is his livelihood" (Nouschi, 1961, 93).

After the conquest the French state, as successor to the rights of sovereignty, seized the *beylik* lands outright, and parceled them out among French settlers. "Since the arrival of the French who have occupied the beylik lands," complained the natives through their chiefs,

> we have been pushed back on land most of which is yet uncleared. We have not been so unhappy since the time of the Turks, because a large part of our people were established on these beylik

lands which have always been the best and the best irrigated. It is true that we had only use rights to these lands; but certainly we cultivated them and they always produced a great deal more than the terrain we occupy today. These we work, but we have not yet succeeded in putting them into proper condition for cultivation (quoted in Nouschi, 1961, 386–387).

At the same time, the French also seized the lands belonging to religious foundations, the *habus*. This seizure, too, violated a complex set of use rights. Many individuals and organizations, such as guilds, had granted their lands to mosques or schools, in return for perpetual use rights to portions of it. The French also increased taxes on land. Within one year (1839–1840) tax income tripled (Nouschi, 1961, 181). Finally in 1863 the French applied Western European concepts of private property in land to Muslim holdings. This legal act accomplished two things. On the one hand it destroyed in one blow the entire pyramid of overrights which had guaranteed the livelihood of the lowly cultivator but which had stood in the way of making land a freely circulating commodity. On the other hand it threw all land held by Muslims upon the open market, and made it available for purchase or seizure by French colonists. Some French observers foresaw the consequences. Before the institution of private property

there was at the bottom of that chaos some guarantee for work, a certain sentiment of equality. With the beginning of individualization it will no longer be the same. Once the land is definitely acquired, inequality begins: on one side the owners, on the other side the proletarians, exactly as in our civilized societies (quoted in Nouschi, 1961, 313).

The *Colon* press, nevertheless, acclaimed the step (L'Independent of Constantine, 12 April 1861, quoted by Nouschi, 1961, 282):

Thanks to the constitution of property which proceeds from this, the greater part of Algerian territory passes immediately from the condition of dead value to the state of real value; millions spring from nothing. . . . The countryside will become populated and the cities will witness in their midst the flowering of all aspects of commerce and industry.

The new legislation, wrote Frederic Lacroix to his friend, the Emperor Napoleon III, in 1862, will "civilize, perfect, gallicize the Arabs."

The wholesale transfer of land from the Muslims to the European population affected not only agriculture; it also interfered with the complex symbiosis between cultivators and pastoral nomads. The pastoralists were shut out from pastures in the settled zone which they had previously used during fallow seasons. At the same time attempts of coastal communities to pasture their herds in the nomadic hinterland quickly drove up prices for the remaining pasturage, and made livestock-keeping unprofitable as an adjunct to agriculture; herd size per individual decreased by four-fifths (Yacono, 1955, II, 326). The danger of this resettlement on marginal land was seen as early as 1845 by General Bugeaud who predicted that "the colonization cannot but help provoke the discontent of the Arabs who feel themselves shut up in too narrow a space" (quoted in Nouschi, 1961, 194–195).

The imposition of French norms of private property in land went hand in hand with a program for the dismemberment of the great tribes whose chiefs had been the main supporters and beneficiaries of Turkish rule. These tribes were not homogeneous kinship units, of equal members, all tracing descent from a common ancestor. Quite the contrary, they often consisted of sections of diverse origins and social status which had become aligned with each other through common ties to the dominant lineage of the dominant section. When we speak of tribes here we are thus speaking of coalitions, organized around a group of power holders. The French understood this well when they proposed to abolish rights to land in terms of tribal affiliation not only as a means for instituting private property in land, but also in order to break the independent power of the great lineages. They accomplished this in part by stripping the core lineages of their political influence, in part by settling the population in distinct settlement clusters, called *douars,* and assigning rights to land in terms of membership in the settlement cluster rather than by virtue of tribal membership. Most *douars* came to contain sections from quite different tribes, thus atomizing the tribes and, with it, the power of the great lords. "The government does not lose from view," said Government Commissioner General Allard, "that the general tendency of the policy should be to reduce the influence of the chiefs and to break up the tribes" (quoted in Nouschi, 1961, 309–310).

An example of how the tribes were fragmented and relocated is furnished by the history of the Arab-speaking Ouled Kosseir of the Shelif (Yacono, 1955, II, fig. 40, 289), one of the two most powerful tribes in the region before the advent of the French. They had numbered 9,000 and held lands amounting close to 38,500 hectares. Thirty years after the conquest, they had lost 18,800 hectares to the state and two individual *colons* through outright expropriation, and another 2,000 hectares through individual land sales after the establishment of private titles in land.

When the French created the settlement of Malakoff, they peopled it with four segments of Ouled Kosseir. By 1884, these four segments had been joined with six new segments drawn from four different tribes, as well as one additional segment of their own tribe. Two of the four original Kosseir segments were then reassigned to other French communes, leaving only three Kosseir segments in Malakoff. In 1887, these were joined by a fourth, but by this time the six non-Kosseir segments drawn from four different tribes had been reinforced by the arrival of four more segments, belonging to four distinct tribes. By 1892, one of the original Kosseir segments had moved elsewhere, and another had split, sending the members of the fissioning group off to join another commune. There had been added two further segments of Sbeah. In 1911, another Kosseir segment joined the settlement, but so did eleven new sections, belonging to eleven different tribal groups. One other Kosseir segment had broken up, and the migrants had gone elsewhere. By the time France became involved in World War II this scrambling had proved so successful that the tribe had ceased to exist as a relevant social and political unit within the Algerian polity. When, in 1941, the French caretaker government at Vichy took steps to reconstitute the tribes in the interests of improved control, French administrators concurred sadly that the steps taken in 1863 had done their job all too well in ending tribal power once and for all (Nouschi, 1961, 306; see also fn. 1, same page).

The *douars* inhabited by segments of former tribes were not made independent entities in their own right, but organized into larger communes on the French model. These communes were of three kinds: (1) communities dominated by Europeans, where the municipal council and mayor were elected by French citizens, and where Muslims were allowed to chose only a fourth of the delegates, even though the Muslim population might constitute the majority; (2) mixed communities of Europeans and Muslims headed by a civil administrator and backed by an appointed council of Frenchmen and native chiefs (*caids*); and (3) indigenous communities commanded by a French officer, assisted by a native chief. All Muslims were permitted use of their own customary or Quranic law, but special laws against nonpayment of taxes, political activity against France, public reunions—including pilgrimages and public feasts—without permits, travel without permits, refusal to register births or deaths—singled out the Muslims as a population with special disabilities. The entire edifice of control was capped by making Algeria administratively part of metropolitan France. Assimilation to French cultural norms was set up as an ideal, but separation—under conditions of economic, social, political, and legal inequality—became the established fact.

The breakup of tribal units and the chiefly power associated with them, however, produced several unforeseen consequences. It made it impossible for the chiefs to carry out free distributions of grain in time of famine from stores accumulated through gifts and levies paid by their tribal dependents. The law of 1863 also put an end to the distribution of charity by local religious lodges (*zaouias*), drawing supplies from their *habus* properties. These properties had become private lands and were thrown upon the market. Moreover, the new *douars* only rarely renewed the traditional custom of maintaining food reserves in communal silos, which had been supplied by traditional payments. Thus disappeared a set of vital economic defenses, leaving the rural population dependent wholly upon the activities of moneylenders and credit merchants in time of need.

A further paradoxical consequence of tribal fragmentation was the accentuated growth within the *douars* of the councils of tribal notables (*djemaa*). The French recognized these councils in both the mixed and indigenous communes, either granting them considerable autonomy or using them in a consultative capacity, especially in matters of Muslim law. *Douars* of Muslims had, however, also been attached to the communities dominated by Europeans where theory made no provision for native participation. In such settlement clusters, however, there also developed a honeycomb of what one French legal expert has called "djemaas-occultes," hidden councils (Charnay, 1965, 228). Both open and hidden councils maintained thus a tradition of decision-making on the local level, despite the fact that the tribal structure had been dismantled. They thus maintained also a tradition of local self-management which was to prove of capital importance in aiding the rebel cause in 1954.

The native population thus saw itself increasingly deprived of land and pushed back by the advancing colonists upon ever more unproductive terrain. Its traditional mechanisms of ensuring economic security had been abrogated, lineages and tribes had been scattered, the familiar political structure dismantled. The response to such deprivation was in part wholesale migration, in part open revolt. Migrations eastward to Tunisia, both of country people and town dwellers, took place in 1830, 1832, 1854, 1860, 1870, 1875, 1888, 1898, 1910, and 1911 (Lacheraf, 1965, 179). The sentiment prompting these population movements was reported by General Devaux in 1861 when he quoted chiefs advocating migration because

> one could live more easily, more freely in the Regency [of Tunis], and there is no lack of land, for agriculture or for herds. Without doubt, one will also benefit by not living any more in contact with Christians (quoted in Nouschi, 1961, 290).

As late as 1911, people departed from Tlemcen in western Algeria for Syria, because they felt "cursed by God" (Nouschi, 1962, 22).

But the French encroachment also produced revolts. The first of these, lasting from 1832 to 1847, was led by Abd el Kader.

This revolt is significant not only for its duration, but also for the social organization developed by the rebels. Abd el Kader was not merely a sworn enemy of the French, but also of the Turks from whom France had conquered the colony. He therefore refused to draw to his side any of the big chiefs who had been the collaborators and beneficiaries of the Turkish regime. Instead of the Turkish "checkerboard pattern" of checks and balances, setting group against group to the ultimate benefit of the Turkish elite, he envisaged a pyramid of tribal leaders, in which the *sheikhs* of tribes would be led by a *sheikh of sheikhs*, the *sheikhs of sheikhs* in turn by a *caid*, a number of *caids* by an *aga*, a number of *agas* by a *khalifa*, and a number of *khalifas* by the *emir*, Abd el Kader himself. On each level of organization the power of the secular leader was to be balanced by a religious judge. The entire structure would be held together by an appeal to Islam in which the emir would appear as the instrument of God, gathering the community of the faithful in a holy war against Christianity. The concept resembles nothing as much as the Wahabi State of the Nedj (Boyer, 1960, 85), with its tribal organization fitted into the apparatus of a fundamentalist theocratic state. In reality the structure remained theoretical and Abd el Kader, as other rulers in the Maghreb before him, had to face the basic problem of uncertain allegiance and dissidence. He also found ranged against him the big and powerful religious confraternities which distrusted any centralizing force, and thus turned for support to the more localized lodges built up around local saints and religious teachers (Boyer, 1960, 92). His distrust of the great families, combined with support of Islam, has caused Algerian nationalists to see in Abd el Kader a forerunner of the populist revolt of the twentieth century.

In their fight with Abd el Kader the French received aid from the military chiefs of the Turkish government. They saw in the French allies capable of protecting their privileged position in the country. The French, in turn, during the opening years of their occupation of the country, were quite willing to make use of these chiefs in administering the Muslim population, taking care, however, to divide power carefully among several of these notables, "vassals rather than officials" (Bernard, 1930, 187). Yet, as French administration of the country took hold, it became increasingly clear that it would be necessary to weaken the great chiefs and their hold over the tribes. Circumstances played into their hands. During the period between 1866 and 1870 severe famine and epidemics caused the government of Napoleon III to request the most powerful of the chiefs to take out bank loans to buy food for the starving populace. The collapse of the Second Empire, under the hammer blows of the Prussian military machine, however, caused the banks to ask for immediate repayment of the loans. A big chief like Moqrani was thus caught in the typical dilemma of a power holder of the traditional type, confronted with the financial and political mechanism of a new kind of social order:

> The peasants cannot pay back the advances he has granted them; humanly, a Moqrani cannot chase them from their lands to recover the advances in grain or in silver to which he consented in time of crisis: custom does not permit this. On the other hand, the creditors, themselves pressed by the banks, want their money back (Nouschi, 1961, 399).

Deserted by his French allies, pressed by his creditors, he rose in desperate revolt (1871–1872). His was the last revolt of a native feudatory. Yet his revolt was also marked in the rural communities by the formation of rebel committees, numbering between ten and twelve elected members (so-called *shartia*, from *sharata*, to impose conditions on someone). These committees acted against despotic native officials, supervised the process of justice, and exercised sanctions against dissidents. Many native officials were faced with a choice between joining the revolt or losing their authority. The revolt proved useless. At the same time the prospect of a rebellion in the countryside seems to have haunted numerous Muslim chiefs and merchants sufficiently to cause them to throw in their lot with the French against the rebels. Thus the notables of Constantine on April 21, 1871, addressed themselves to the French authorities in a letter in which

> they asked the governor not to confuse them, educated, enlightened people . . . who appreciate with gratitude the protection

and justice of France, with the "bedouins" or people of the tribes. . . . [We are] sedentary and literate citizens, who love quiet, peace, tranquility and comfort. . . . Desirous of acquiring resources, they dedicate themselves to manual occupations, to trade, to agriculture, to all kinds of industry; they respect authority, they are friends of order. . . . They want to live at ease with their wives and children. One must conclude from this . . . that the "bedouin" will not renounce their traditional conduct, the customs of their mountains, unless they are subjected to severe and energetic repression which fills them with a dread and terror that causes them to fear for their lives. Only force and violence can conquer their nature (L. Rinn, quoted in Lacheraf, 1965, 60–61).

Force and violence were not long in coming. They took the form of punitive expropriations in favor of European colonists, carried out to make the native population pay for the costs of the rebellion. The expropriations were justified by the Superior Government Council in the following words:

The expropriation is a punishment capable of leaving a permanent trace; a seizure of property well justified by persistent and repeated return to crime will smite the spirit of the guilty sufficiently by subjecting them to an effective repression with consequences which cannot be wiped out. The real employment of expropriation, that is peace; that is blood and ruins avoided in the future . . . political interest, the security of the colony, the civilizing of races who will not come to us until the hope of shaking our domination has disappeared from their minds, a clairvoyant humanity which avoids the disasters of the future by the severity of the present command the maintenance of expropriation and its consequences (Nouschi, 1961, 406).

In addition, special punitive levies eight times larger than the annual tax charges, were imposed on the rebellious areas, and collected through the agency of the chiefs who had remained faithful to the French. The chiefs, said the peasants, "have taken our skin and bones and now they break our bones to eat the marrow" (Nouschi, 1961, 420, fn. 59). The terrible memory of these years when "justice and truth disappeared," "brother was set against brother," and the chiefs "grew rich through treason" has remained green in Kabyle chants recorded half a century later. It reinforced a permanent ambivalence toward the traditional chiefs which was to be of moment in the turmoil leading up to the war of independence.

Under French aegis, there thus survived a native aristocracy which would make common cause with the French and which the French co-opted as administrators of the rural population on behalf of the French state. French rule served at one and the same time as their guarantee against the claims of their own Muslim subjects, and against unlimited encroachment on their lands and power by the *colons*. Deprived of the tribal structure to which they owed their indigenous power before the conquest, they nevertheless exercised political functions of sufficient scope on behalf of the conquerors to interpose themselves between the natives and France. These large Muslim landowners, said French ethnologist Jean Servier, hide

> France from the Algerian people. Generally, they are the descendants of the aristocracy established by the Turks, maintained through the ignorance of the first French governments and then maintained by habit. Controlling wealth they control men: the starved cohort of their workers—their slaves—who, promoted to the rank of voters, have enabled their sovereigns to attain the dignities of the Republic, the responsibilities of representatives of the people. . . . They have obtained for years the electoral charges, rendered sacred as lords of veritable fiefs by the Republic (quoted in Aron, 1962, 202).

Thus, at first, selective enfranchisement merely underwrote, in a new way, the dominance of powerful families in support of French rule. One such kinship group, for example, furnished in 1951 a senator, a deputy, and two representatives to the Algerian assembly, as well as two representatives to the General Council (Boyer, 1960, 230). Such a policy served to "break the contact between conquerors and indigenous mass," while that mass becomes "without effective recourse the prey of the avid clientele which surrounds the local chiefs" (E. Mercie, quoted in Aron, 1962, 293). The continued presence of such an "aristocracy of the big tents" thus

Q

became a further obstacle to any major effort to adapt the native population to French-sponsored administrative schemes, conservative or aiming at reform. The size of this class of power holders can be estimated by noting that at the time of the outbreak of the revolt of 1954 there were five hundred Muslim landholders each controlling landed property in excess of five hundred hectares (Aron, 1962, 292).

While the Muslims were thus expropriated and forced to witness the dismemberment of their social framework, Algeria was thrown wide open to European immigration and settlement. The new *colons* were all Frenchmen in name, but only half of them were of direct French origin, drawn mainly from the poor south-center of France and—after the French defeat of 1871—from Alsace. The other half was made up primarily of Spaniards and Italians, of Corsicans and Maltese. It was the mixed character of this population which caused the French writer Anatole France to say in 1905 that France had during seventy years fleeced, chased, and run to ground the Arabs in order to people Algiers with Italians and Spaniards. At first segregated residentially into separate settlements, they quickly came to make common cause through intermarriage and through common hatred of Arabs. Louis de Baudicour, writing in 1856, compared their attitude toward the Arabs with that of the Southern planters toward their Negro slaves:

> they never departed from the sentiment of hierarchy: they dominate and must dominate, for if the master loses face, the servant despises him and cuts him down. They thus undergo this test of strength without flinching. But, with the years, a double doubt weakens their faith: they see the Arabs whom they refuse passionately to regard as equals, multiply and organize themselves; this people will submerge them; they are unable to understand that this is because they have not known how to establish contacts while there was still time (quoted in Favrod, 1962, 81).

It is this fear which creeps miasma-like through the early novels of Albert Camus, himself born and raised in Algeria; and it was this fear which caused the *colons* first to resist any and every effort at reform initiated in metropolitan France, and later to embrace one or another variety of fascism, culminating in their support of the terroristic OAS at the end of the war of independence.

Initial settlement often had the character of a pioneer enterprise in hostile lands and among hostile people. Michel Launay, a rural sociologist working in a section of the department of Oran, quotes a *colon* father talking to his son about this early period:

> Your grandfather labored with four oxen; during the night, the oxen were chained down and guarded so they would not be stolen; one chain per oxen. Threshing was done by driving oxen over the grain, then one got 5 or 6 *colons* together to transport 15 or 20 hundredweights of wheat per cart: a convoy was necessary to go to Oran, or one would be attacked near Misserghin. Native laborers were not used, only *colons* with very large amounts of land made use of them; the natives were only shepherds. One did not dare to employ them at the farm so they could not look over the place and mount their attack at night. On their side, the natives did not want to work with the Europeans. It is only around 1900 that one began to employ natives. When I began to work, in 1888, we did not yet have natives. To clear and harvest there were only work teams of Spanish laborers. Young Spanish girls worked during harvest, and the daughters of the owners themselves helped: *colons* helped each other. The natives began to work in the harvest during the war of 1914, when the farmers were mobilized (1963, 137).

The mainstay of *colon* economy, and the mainstay of the Algerian economy as a whole, came to be vineyard cultivation and the production of wine, especially after 1880 when the phylloxera louse destroyed much of French viticulture and France was forced to import much of her wine. Wine exports from Algeria came to form 50 percent of all Algerian exports. The acreage in vineyards more than doubled between 1900 and 1954 at the expense of food crops and pasture.

> The result is that the vine has displaced and polluted all else: it has chased away the wheat, it has chased away the sheep, it has chased away the forest and the dwarf palm. It has polluted the river where the skins and pips, lees, and refuse are thrown (Launay, 1963, 18).

This was especially true in western Algeria where low rainfall favored the extension of vineyards up to the very limits of the steppe. This area became the center of European rural settlement; nine-tenths of all Algerian vineyards—and thus most of the main cash crop—were in the hands of Europeans. At the same time, vineyard cultivation greatly contributed to social and economic differentiation among the *colons* themselves. Wine production and transport demands considerable capital outlays in pressing cellars, vats, and other plant, and thus favored the ascendancy of the large *colon* over the small who had to rely on him for credit and access to processing plant. It also placed in the hands of a powerful oligarchy of wine merchants, shippers, and bankers, much of the political control of the colony. In general, Algerian agriculture was marked by a heavy trend toward concentration. By 1950, 85 percent of the European-held lands were held by some 30 percent of the 22,000 European landowners; while 70 percent held the remaining 15 percent of the land. Many *colons* lost their land and moved to town. By 1954, over three-quarters of a million Europeans or more than 80 percent of the entire European population lived in urban centers. Here their occupations mirrored the skewed character of an agrarian country, dependent on one major cash crop, in its relation to an industrial metropolis. Of a total work force of some 300,000 Europeans, 35,000 were skilled workers and 55,000 were listed as unskilled; the remainder worked either in administration or management (close to 50,000) or in services of one kind or another (about 160,000). Most of these were "office employees, small traders, caterers and mechanics" (Murray and Wengraf, 1963, 19). Despite these differences, they were at one in defense of their privileges which made the lowest French *colon* the superior of any Arab. Their unity was the product of their common fear of the Muslim majority.

How did that majority react to the changes imposed on it? The revolt of El Moqrani was to be the last major effort at armed resistance until some eighty years later. It was also to be the last major effort, until 1954, of the rural population to take the political initiative. There set in a long period of political inactivity, which only gave way to new political efforts around the time of World War I. Moreover, renewed political activity would be first a matter of the cities, including the cities of France with their newly generated proletariat, before it would spread once again into the rural hinterland. Frantz Fanon, who has analyzed in overly Manichaean terms the conflict between conquerors and conquered, has portrayed their relations as one of continuous and endemic violence. That opposition was certainly present during the eighty-three years between Moqrani's revolt and 1954, but it remained covert rather than overt, quiescent rather than emphatic. This was a period not so much of incubation of the revolution-to-be, but rather of muted changes and adjustments, experiments in social and cultural relations, with attendant advances and retreats. At the same time it was a period marked by shifts in the cognitive and emotional evaluation of different possibilities, rather than by a single-minded ideological rehearsal of things to come. Those Algerians who took any interest in politics and expressed a concern about the relation of Algeria to France oscillated between two main positions; sometimes they held both positions simultaneously, sometimes in quick succession. The political parties of the period, to the extent that they expressed these concerns, were epiphenomena of this internal struggle, rather than causative agents in their own right. The defendants of one position called for increased contact with French cultural norms and assimilation to them. Socially, this assimilationism was most congruent with the interests of middle-class professionals of whom there were about 450 in the higher ranks, whose social standing depended on their French education, and who saw in their French degrees a passport to mobility. The other tendency was anti-assimilationist and directed toward an effort to define an Algerian nationality, different from the French and opposed to it. On a behavioral level this tendency manifested itself—even among assimilationists—in an attitude of reserve against foreign encroachment upon the intimate spheres of family life and religion. This attitude of reserve bears the Arabic name of *kitman*, a Quranic term signifying hiding place, hence a tendency to turn inward. In adapting themselves to the French, says Jacques Berque, the Muslim population stands guard over absolutely inviolable zones. It turns in on itself. This is the internal aspect of these societies which thus comes to the fore. The religious side for instance. It is almost certain that the Islamic faith, or more exactly said, Islamic devotion, is very much more alive since the advent of the Europeans than before, after thirty years of the protectorate than after ten (1956, 532–533).

Bourdieu has made the same point in stating that for the Algerians adherence to traditional forms came to fulfill "essentially a symbolic function; it played the role, objectively, of a language of refusal"; and illustrated this point with reference to the traditional custom of veiling of which Frenchmen were especially critical: the veil worn by Muslim women

> is above all a defense of intimacy and a protection against intrusion. And, confusedly, the Europeans have always perceived it as such. By wearing the veil, the Algerian woman creates a situation of non-reciprocity; like a disloyal player, she sees without being seen, without allowing herself to be seen. And it is the entire dominated society which, by means of the veil, refuses reciprocity, which sees, which penetrates, without allowing itself to be seen, regarded, penetrated (1960, 27).

Islam would thus prove to be one of the roots of Algerian nationalism. In the course of the 1920's and 1930's, the attitude of refusal and withdrawal would issue in a new and active movement, founded in an attempt to return to the purity of the Quran. The centers of this Islamic revival lay not in the new French towns of the Mediterranean littoral, but in the old Islamic towns of the hinterland, once the seats of active and well-to-do Islamic traders and entrepreneurs, such as Tlemcen, Nedroma, Constantine, Mila, Tebessa, Sidi Okba, Biskra, and Ghardaïa. With the advent of French rule, many of them receded into the background; Constantine and Tlemcen, for instance, once possessed of a thriving textile industry, declined under the impact of French competition. It is no accident, as Morizot has pointed out (1962, 81), that Tlemcen—pivot of the religious exodus of 1911—produced Messali Hadj, the first organizer of a nationalist Algerian party, while

Constantine gave rise to Ben Badis, the Algerian protagonist of a revived and militant Islam.

Islam had strong roots in Constantine. Its native merchants and aristocratic landholders had survived the revolt of Abd el Kader which had brought in its wake the sack and de-urbanization of so many other towns, such as Blida and Médéa. This elite had also survived the revolt of Moqrani, by assuring the French of their loyalty and innocuousness. Thus Constantine, in contrast to other Algerian cities, was able also to maintain itself as a major center of Islamic traditional learning. Taught by the Islamic schoolmen of Constantine, Sheikh Abd-el-Hamid Ben Badis was to fuse Algerian religious tradition with the innovating influence of the Islamic reform movement of the early twentieth century. In the context of North Africa, this brought the reformers into direct conflict with local forms of Islam, as practiced in numerous religious lodges.

Orthodox Islam, as laid down by the Prophet Muhammad in the Quran, knows no saints or organizations intermediate between men and God: all Muslims are theoretically equal members of the community of the faithful, the *umma*. But nearly everywhere in the Islamic world—and especially so in the Maghreb—religious practice, as opposed to religious dogma, has centered on local shrines and local holy men. "There is a sharp contrast between the Muslim southern shore of the Mediterranean, and the non-Islamic northern shore," says the anthropologist Ernest Gellner.

> The dominant form of official Christianity incorporates rural shrines, etc., in its system, and provides specialized religious personnel. Protestantism, an egalitarian and literate cult of the Book, is a *deviant* and segmented tradition. In Islam, all this is reversed: "Protestantism," i.e. rigorous impersonal urban religion, respectful of the Book, has remained at the centre of orthodoxy, and the hierarchical and personal religion of the shrine, on the other hand, is the local, regional, segmented deviant heterodoxy (1963, 147).

This segmented localized form of Islam has served to connect points in the rural hinterland, with their local rural traditions, with the body of Islam in general; but it has done so at the expense of great religious differentiation, with each lodge, each holy man, entertaining a variant form of the universal religion. These lodges, and the popular religious fraternities built upon them, had acted strongly in support of Abd el Kader during his resistance against the French and remained anti-French until the turn of the century. Thereafter, however, they had come into accommodation with the French authorities who supported them consciously as convenient means for keeping the body social of Algeria as divided as possible.

The Badissia, as the reform movement came to be known after the name of its principal figure, was antagonistic to the traditional holy men. Instead it asserted the authority of the reformist school-men, the *ulema,* and furthered the creation of numerous orthodox schools (*medersas*) in the hinterland. Beginning in the cities, they nevertheless seeded the hinterland with associations of all kinds, including Islamic boy scouts, under the aegis of their slogan: "Arabic is my language, Algeria is my country, Islam is my religion." Their social support in the countryside was provided in the main by the middle-class peasantry and among the small merchants, entrepreneurs, and teachers of the rural towns (Launay, 1963, 175–177). Such an affiliation of independent peasantry with the new urban world by means of religious associations—new organizational forms within the traditional religious matrix—is known from other parts of the world. Finally, it may have received reinforcement through the stimulus of economic interests. The Badissia strongly opposed the heterodox religious feasts carried on by the holy men and the expenditures associated with them. Such expenditures constitute a major drain on a peasantry and their abolition by a religious reform movement is again a common feature in many parts of the world. In many parts of the Andes and Middle America, for instance, it has underwritten conversions to Protestantism in otherwise traditionally Catholic Indian communities. The Badissia also demanded the restoration of the properties of religious foundations, seized by the French. As a notable of Aoubelli said to Michel Launay: "Since at the conquest many Muslims gave their property to the habus to save them from annexation by the French, the claim to a return [of these properties] challenged the whole picture of colonial property" (1963,

149). In the words of Jacques Berque, the Badissia created a new and *Jacobin* Islam.

This Jacobin Islam would have especially strong appeal not only to Islamic traders and entrepreneurs of declining towns in the hinterland, but also to the rural class of middling landowners, as shown in Michel Launay's investigation of the area of Ain-Temuchent, in Oran Province. In this district, Europeans had come into ownership of 65 percent of the land used in agriculture, while Muslims retained 35 percent. Since this is an area of profitable viticulture introduced by the Europeans, the relative distribution of vineyard land is important: Europeans owned 89 percent of land in vineyards, Muslims only 11 percent (1963, 68). Among the Muslims there were some rich *fellahin*, with holdings ranging between 200 and 600 hectares in wheat or 21 to 50 hectares in vineyards; they made up 1 percent of all Muslim landowners. The "peasants who could make ends meet," however, with between 50 and 200 hectares in wheat or 1 to 20 hectares in vines, composed roughly one-third of the Muslim population. Closely related to this middle range of landholders were numerous small traders. This middle peasantry was also socially the main bulwark of rural society. The middle peasant, says Launay,

> retains his dignity, he remains—through his link with the land—attached to his ancestors, and he is not a "slave," he is lord of his land; the agricultural worker receives no "esteem," he is totally dependent upon someone else's will (1963, 203).

The Badissia was carried into the district from Oran, principally by merchants, in turn influenced by Muslim merchants in Oran (1963, 150–151). In 1937 a *medersa* or Islamic school was established in the town of Temuchent, to be followed by the construction of the reformist school in the rural *douar* of Messaada, among a tribal section which had lost much of its good land when the French expropriated more than 500 hectares to found the community center of Rio Salado (1963, 146–147). From here, the ideas of the Badissia spread throughout the district, principally among the middle peasantry (1963, 148). The agricultural workers and the poor peasants in general clung to their traditional holy men and resisted the reformers (1963, no. 1, 113; 150–151; 371). It was this same stratum, the middle peasants; in Ain-Temuchent which furnished support for the uprising of 1954:

> The organizers of the insurrection were the small holders, not the little proletarianized small holders but the small holders almost able to make ends meet, well-off in comparison with agricultural workers (1963, 175–176).

> The egalitarian preaching of the Ulema, of the "Badissia," reflected the ideal of the peasant and the absence of precision in an agrarian reformist dream willed by God which gives to each man an equal share of sunshine, corresponds to the first undifferentiated phase of the national revolution (1963, 371).

René Delisle is thus quite correct when he says that

> the insurrection of 1954 and the independence of 1962 are thus, in this respect, only the necessary conclusion of the action initiated in 1930 by the reformist Ulemas, restorers of Islam and of Arab tradition (1962–63, 24).

If reformist Islam provided one of the sources of Algerian nationalism, the other source lay in the increasing development of an Algerian semi-proletariat. This, in turn, was the product of two major causes: the decay of the traditional pattern of Algerian sharecropping, the *khammesat* (from *khammes,* a fifth), coupled with the need—especially strong in Central Algeria, among the Berber-speaking Kabyles—to supplement a meager agriculture with some other form of employment.

Under the *khammesat,* the sharecropper received not only tools and seed, but also money advances and food, sums which were then subtracted from the final produce. The new French legal codes, however, allowed sharecroppers to abandon their landlords without previous reimbursement of these costs. While the law thus freed the sharecroppers from a form of traditional bondage, it also hastened the decline of sharecropping and the advent of day labor. Previous conditions of servitude had canceled out the variable effects of good and poor years, by standardizing sharecropper duties and rights. Now workers sought positions as sharecroppers during bad years, in order to guarantee their livelihood, but abandoned their owners with the advent of a promising year. Shortly after the passage of the law the *qaid* of Heumis testified that

> French law having emancipated the sharecropper, the owners in large numbers preferred not to give them work, for fear of losing their advances. The sharecropper no longer finds work because one does not want to engage him in ways other than by the day (quoted in Yacono, 1955, II, 310–311).

The result was both an increased number of men looking for work, and a reduction in the area previously cultivated (1955, fn. 1, 311).

In the vineyard areas there was a wholesale exodus from sharecropping into wage labor. Whereas a hectare of wheat requires merely ten workdays per worker per year, a hectare of vineyard requires fifty such workdays. Given an increasing shift toward the use of cash in a money economy, a man could earn roughly five times as much in the vineyards as he could in cereal production. With rapid population increases, therefore, increasing numbers of sharecroppers became wage laborers. This shift, however, had its own built-in limits in that work in the vineyards, as in Mediterranean agriculture in general, is unevenly distributed, falling mainly in September when grapes are picked and in December when the vines are pruned. At the same time the rush of workers into the vineyards produced an oversupply of workers, with seasonal workers outnumbering permanent workers two to one. They had thus forsaken the traditional security of the sharecropper who yielded up a large part of the crop he produced in return for a guaranteed plot of land and money advances from his patron for unstable and unpredictable employment. Now, said an old Muslim teacher to Launay, "the agricultural worker cannot be sure of anything" (1963, 119). One effect of growing wage labor was therefore the creation of a large floating semi-proletariat, which was to bear all the stigmata of a growing economic insecurity.

Yet the growing trend toward wage labor possessed still another face. Increasingly many areas—but most notably the mountains of Kabylia—began to experience the pressures of population growth on available food resources. French colonization had driven the natives into the barren hinterland, often producing compact and dense settlements in terrain which could not support such numbers. Military pacification and the spread of modern health care further curtailed the Malthusian checks on the population growth. As a result, many Kabyles were forced to seek alternative sources of livelihood outside their mountains; yet in the search for new employment they tended to follow an old pattern. Already, before the advent of the French, certain village clusters had been noted for their special contributions to town life. Thus men from Biskra had served in the towns as porters, water carriers, tanners, and auctioneers; men from the region of Laghouat had sold oil; Mozabites functioned as carriers, vendors of food and charcoal, petty traders, and employees in the baths. Kabylia had furnished construction workers and gardeners (Morizot, 1962, 21). With the advent of the French, these external activities began to mushroom:

> while internal local activities began progressively to atrophy, the activities oriented towards the outside, already well developed among some groups, would undergo extraordinary growth, becoming essential even where they had once been only supplementary. Today, the disequilibrium between one and the other is especially marked in Kabylia (1962, 75).

After the turn of the centuries, Kabyles were to move into towns everywhere in Algeria as traders, storekeepers, transportation workers, police, government agents, bank employees, porters, and miners. In the interior, too, they frequently became minor government officials, tax collectors, medical aides, gendarmes, teachers. This development was further aided by the French who hoped to turn traditional Kabyle dissidence from the Arab-dominated centers of the littoral to their own political advantage. Their readiness to occupy positions opened up by the French gave them an advantage over other Algerians less driven by necessity to serve the conquerors. In French eyes they seemed "as enterprising" as Protestants, "as democratic" as Americans. Schools were established in the

Berber-speaking zones earlier than elsewhere in Algeria, and during the period of French occupation nearly all teacher-training institutes were manned by Kabyles (Favret, 1967, 91–92).

At the same time, Algerians—and again most especially the Berber-speakers from Kabylia—began to be recruited into the labor force of metropolitan France. World War I witnessed the first massive employment of Algerians in France itself, to replace French laborers called to the colors and now at the front. Between 1915 and 1918 some 76,000 Algerians left to work in French factories. This trend has continued steadily over the years, until in 1950 there were some 600,000 Algerians in the metropolis. This large-scale movement caught up great numbers of Algerians in the forced draft of acculturation. They received their education, as Germaine Tillion has put it, in the "school of the cities." As a result, there developed, on French soil, a fully fledged Algerian proletariat with strong and enduring ties to the rural Algerian hinterland. This working-class milieu had two immediate effects. First, it incubated the first modern nationalist Algerian movement, in the formation of the Étoile Nord Africaine in Paris in 1925, in which Messali Hadj became the dominant personality. Left-wing party and trade-union activity associated with this experience in urban France provided the migrant workers both with models of organization and with fragments of socialist ideology which they found of use in interpreting the condition of their homeland (see Bromberger, 1958, 80). It proved doubly significant, moreover, that—upon their return to Algeria—they could do little to give substance to their aspirations through the colon-dominated socialist and Communist unions and parties of the colony. From the first, the logic of the colonial situation forced them to give their support to nationalist parties, first to the Messalist Partie Populaire Algérien, and later to its more militant successors.

The second consequence of the French experience was that it produced among the Algerian workers in France the realization that an adequate French education constituted a passport to entry into the modern technical civilization. "Twenty-five years later," says Germaine Tillion, one meets certain doctors, certain lawyers, certain professors, certain mathematicians or chemists whose brilliant studies have been paid for during these already long distant years by a father or an elder brother out of his laborer's salary. To achieve this result, the illiterate émigré must have had to deprive himself daily of what in France we call the "vital minimum," and even before he could do that he had to grasp the mechanisms and the values of an alien world, indoctrinate his family, separate his little boy from his mother, and then push him—ardently, patiently, proudly—to the fore (1961, 119–120).

Both of these trends—the growth of reformist Islam on the one hand, the city-ward migration of Algerian workers on the other—were to contribute decisively to the outbreak of the Algerian revolt of 1954. Reformist Islam provided the cultural form for the construction of a new network of social relations between clusters of middle peasants in the countryside and the sons of the urban elite of the hinterland towns. The city-ward migration of the Algerian peasantry—most especially that of the Kabyles—not only brought them into contact with industrial and urban patterns of life, but produced a professional class in the course of that migratory experience. Once again networks were forged which linked clusters of peasants in the countryside with spokesmen and representatives in the cities. In studies of prominent Moslems involved in the revolution and its sequel four features stood out: most were young men, whose formative political experience lay in the years of indecision of the 1930's and 1940's; a disproportionate number compared to their role in the total population of Algeria were of Berber origin; many were French-educated; many had served in the French army during World War II (Gordon, 1966, 87–88). Jean Morizot, a French administrator in Algeria, even went so far as to say that

when the rebellion passed its local or regional stage, it would show itself to us under Kabyle leadership (1962, 128).

Wholly against the expectations of the French who had always pursued a policy of keeping the Berbers culturally and politically separate from the Arab population, in order to better divide and rule, the forces generated by a common involvement in processes set up by the French impact itself would bring these disparate groups into fusion.

Undoubtedly this fusion was speeded up by the events of the period preceding World War II, and the world war itself. As long as there was hope that reform in France could produce greater liberty and autonomy for Muslim Algerians, there also remained some hope that the expectations of both assimilationists and nationalists could be met without the use of force and violence. Even Ben Badis put great hope in the advent of the Popular Front government in the French metropolis in the years between 1936 and 1938. But as it became increasingly clear—during long years of political prevarication and failure—that no French government capable of instituting reform was likely to emerge, the militant nationalists gained ground. As French unwillingness and inability to make concessions hardened, the tendency toward clandestine operations also gained momentum. To this must be added the impact of domestic trends. Between 1930 and 1954 the number of small Muslim owners decreased by a fifth, the number of day laborers rose by more than a quarter. During World War II and after, harvests were poor, wine production was down, and livestock was lost in large numbers. Even more significant, undoubtedly, were the more proximate causes of a political nature: France suffered a crushing defeat in 1940, revealing her weakness to all who had eyes to see. German propaganda reinforced the impression of French weakness. At the same time, half of the French nation was engaged in fighting the other half in underground operations, sharply raising the level of all-round uncertainty and illegality. The advent of fascism in France strongly supported violence on the part of fascist *colons* against the Algerian population. Algerians were mobilized in considerable numbers to fight for France, thus both undergoing military training and achieving a level of significant equality with French fellow-combatants. All of this came to a head in the events which took place at Sétif, on May 1, 1945. Some 8,000 to 10,000 Muslims had gathered to celebrate the Allied victories in Europe; many came with placards calling for the release from prison of Messali Hadj and for equality between Muslims and Christians. Shots were fired and a riot ensued which spread to other towns. The riot was fiercely repressed by French air and ground forces. Estimates of Muslims killed vary between 8,000 and 45,000, with 15,000 a not unlikely number. There is little doubt, says the Swiss journalist Charles-Henri Favrod, that "it was these events of 1945 which decided the revolution of 1954." French inability and unwillingness to grant concessions in time spelled the end of the assimilationist cause. This is most clearly exemplified in the person of Ferhat Abbas, long a leader of the assimilationists, who decided in April of 1954 that a party which "fights in favor of a 'revolution by law' can no longer advance . . ." (quoted in Murray and Wengraf, 1963, 63).

On the other hand, militant and subversive movements increasingly developed among the proletarian nationalists. The Parti Populaire Algérien (PPA), driven underground in 1939, developed in 1947 a paramilitary arm in the MTLD—the Mouvement pour le Triomphe des Libertés Democratiques. Within the MTLD, in turn, there grew up a secret terrorist society called Organisation Spéciale (OS); by 1949 it had 1,900 members. The founder members of the OS became the members of the Comité Revolutionnaire d'Unité et d'Action (CRUA) which unleashed the revolt of 1954. Not all the members of the PPA, however, were to join in the revolt. On the contrary, the struggle for independence against the French was to be accompanied throughout by a bloody struggle between partisans of the revolt and units derived from Messali Hadj's original PPA. This struggle was to prove especially bloody in metropolitan France where close to a thousand Muslims died in internecine warfare.

The insurrection broke out on the night of October 31 to November 1, 1954, with some three score incidents of attacks on French garrisons and police stations, ambushes, and arson. These incidents were widely scattered, but most of them erupted in eastern Algeria, most especially in the mountains of the Aurès. The insurgents were few in number, probably no more than five hundred, with three hundred of them concentrated in the Aurès; they possessed less than fifty obsolete shotguns (Humbaraci, 1966, 33–34).

The Aurès was a logical first base for the revolt. Occupied by Berber-speakers, it has long been a zone of dissidence from any central government. Jacques Soustelle, anthropologist and governor-general of Algeria in 1955, was to say:

> one sees clearly that the Romans erred in limiting their occupation to the approaches to the mountain, since it remained for centuries the reservoir of uncontrolled forces ready to overflow. Our penetration in the Aurès and Nemenchas has been very weak: we have committed the same error as the Romans, with the same results (1956, 14–15).

Berber social and political organization resembles an "ordered anarchy"; anthropologists speak of it as unilineal and segmentary. Nuclear families form part of family lines, related through males. These, in turn, form segments or fractions (Arab *ferqa*, Berber *harfiqth*); segments and fractions form tribes. Any one settlement is made up of members of several fractions, each of which is affiliated, in turn, with a more widespread tribe. These fractions oppose each other if their interests diverge, but unite if threatened, especially by a third party stronger than themselves. In theory this works as a system of checks and balances as long as the units are more or less stable. Under French rule, however, this ideal balance had been upset. Improved health services had removed the checks on population growth, and served to increase the pressure of population against available resources. The spread of money economy and the introduction of new needs—for coffee, sugar, ground grain—undermined traditional patterns of self-sufficiency. Land became a commodity, to be bought and sold. After World War I the migration of men to France initiated a system of monetary remissions in which work in the metropolis underwrote the economy of the mountains. All these trends accentuated competition among men and exacerbated opposition between tribal fractions. The rebels adroitly exploited these local feuds, finding allies among one or another local fractions in the mountain area and helping them against their enemies. They also formed bandit groups. In the

R

Aurès they established their first military district (Wilaya I); it remained a rebel bastion throughout the war. At the same time, between November 1954 and mid-March 1956, small determined groups of fighters began hit-and-run raids in other parts of Algeria.

With the advent of the revolt, CRUA became the executive committee of the National Liberation Front (Front de Libération Nationale or NLF). It was to consist of an External Delegation, based in Cairo, and an Internal Delegation, consisting of the military leaders of the revolt in Algiers. These military leaders were to head up six military districts or *wilayas;* a seventh district would comprise metropolitan France. The total organization headed by the military leaders was to be known as the Army of National Liberation (Armée de Libération Nationale or ALN). At the core of the army were to be the *mujahidin,* fighters for the faith, who were to be the regulars, surrounded by a fringe of civilian guerrillas, *mussabilin,* "those whom the caravan abandons by the road," death squads over whom the prayer of the dead was said (Tillion, 1961, n. 6, 145), and *fidayin,* non-uniformed terrorists and saboteurs. The formal table of organization of the army could not hide the fact, however, that the organizational structure of the NLF represented a compromise solution between the interests of civilian and military leaders, a strain that was to be compounded during the war by further conflicts between various military leaders, and between those carrying on the guerrilla war inside the country and those who organized armed units outside. Jean Daniel has said that there existed in the NLF not one organizational pyramid, but a multitude of pyramids, and that "the unity of the NLF was never realized except in situations which forced the multiplicity of pyramids to move in the same direction" (1962–63, 128). Ideologically, too, what held the movement together was a common nationalism. Socialist phraseology appeared occasionally in NLF pronouncements, but remained vague enough not to become the rallying cry of any one fraction against another, until after the advent of Algerian independence. By April 1956, French sources estimated rebel strength at 8,500 fighters and some 21,000 auxiliaries. Possessed of insufficient troop strength, the French were unable to prevent the westward spread of rebel units along the parallel mountain chains of the Atlas, despite repeated commando raids into the hostile interior.

By April 1956, however, French units brought to Algeria from France, Germany, and French West Africa augmented French forces to about 250,000 men; conscription was soon to add another 200,000. This increased force permitted a change in French tactics from the use of occasional flying columns to the *quadrillage* or grid system in which towns and centers of communication were held in strength, while mobile units of paratroopers, volunteers, and Foreign Legionnaires probed the hinterland. This new tactic did not eliminate the ALN, but it did check its activity in the back country. Toward the end of 1956, the ALN therefore mounted an offensive in the urban centers. Terrorist attacks increased in all cities, but especially in Algiers where 120 acts took place in December alone. The ALN had successfully infiltrated the Muslim quarter of the city, the Casbah, with its population of 80,000. Here it had recruited some 4,000 men to its ranks, around a core of *Lumpenproletariat*, "hooligans with a pure heart," who were given an opportunity to wash themselves clean of past sins (Ouzegane, 1962, 252, 253). While the shift to urban terrorism had important psychological effects on the urban population, especially among Muslims who were won to the cause of the ALN in proportion to the inability of the French to protect them, it proved ineffective militarily. Between February and October 1957, the 10th Paratroop Division commanded by General Massu effectively destroyed the terrorist organization in Algiers.

Checked within the country itself, the ALN was thus forced to seek alternative sources of support, which it found in neighboring Tunisia and Morocco. These two neighboring states, which had achieved independence from France in 1956, permitted the establishment of training centers on their soil and recruitment to these new forces among Algerians both within and without Algeria. By the end of 1957, there were more than 60,000 Algerian refugees in Tunis, and 40,000 in Morocco. Recruitment by the ALN for this new "external" army grew apace. By the end of 1957, again, it numbered 25,000 troops, while the "internal" forces amounted to only 15,000.

Yet this shift in ALN tactics also produced a comparable response from the French. By mid-September 1957 the French completed construction, along the Moroccan frontier, of an elaborate barrier of electrified wire, alarm systems, strong points, mine fields, and observation posts. A similar barrier was completed on the Tunisian side, thus effectively sealing off the external armies from the internal zone of operations. In 1958 the French also expanded their military effort inside Algeria. Each of the known ALN bases was cordoned off by a "pacified" zone, and attacks were mounted in turn on each of the separate military districts of the ALN. Communication between the districts was effectively destroyed, while all attempts of the ALN to mount battalion-size counterthrusts proved ineffective. Thus the rebels were forced back once again upon the small-group tactics with which they had begun the insurrection. French military activity was, moreover, supported by a vast effort at relocating the civilian population, thus separating the rebels from possible sources of support. More than 1.8 million people were moved from their homes between 1955 and 1961, while others fled from the zones of military operation into the already overcrowded cities. Finally, the French counterthrust was capped by the employment of psychological warfare, ranging from mass persuasion and the provision of social services by army personnel to forcible indoctrination and torture.

The French effort had several consequences for the nationalist camp. It accentuated feuds among the leadership, especially between the leaders of the revolt outside Algeria and the military chieftains in the field. It isolated the military districts from each other and from outside sources of arms and support, curtailing their fighting capacity, and reducing them ultimately to the level of petty principalities, at loggerheads with one another over resources, tactics, and strategy. At the same time it left untouched the growing "external army" which grew more important for the nationalist leadership as a bargaining point in any final negotiations for peace in direct proportion to the decline of the internal army in both strength and effectiveness. Thus the end of the war was to find the external army intact as the only organized body of Algerians under the leadership of Houari Boumedienne.

At the same time, the French effort dialectically produced the forces of its own undoing. It has been said that as the French proved victorious, the hold of the nationalist cause over the minds of Algerians paradoxically grew apace. Some of the reasons for this were internal. The experience of forcible relocation, flight of refugees to the cities, the destruction of agricultural resources, the annihilation of nomadic groups who could no longer mount their migrations—all these pulverized the social relations of traditional society and produced a fearsome ideological vacuum. The conflict itself further polarized French settlers and Muslims, reinforcing their separate identities, which French efforts at psychological warfare exacerbated rather than reduced. At the same time the costs of the conflict became ever more burdensome. In addition to loss of life and the stresses attendant upon war, the financial cost of the war to France proved huge: 50 billion new francs and 1.7 million dollars in foreign currency spent on arms and attempts to close budgetary deficits (Humbaraci, 1966, 55). But the social and political costs of the war were even higher, for it brought into the open a series of hidden conflicts which severely curtailed France's ability to continue the fight. France had not only gone through the defeat and dislocation of World War II; it had just witnessed defeat at the hands of the Viet Minh in Viet Nam. People were weary of war, a fact that came into prominence as soon as conscripts were drafted in metropolitan France to fight in Algeria. At the same time, a new financial and technocratic elite hoped for an expansion of French participation in a European common market, in place of continuing the expensive and fruitless colonial wars. On the other hand, there were ranged the intransigent French *colons* in Algeria, who could countenance no peaceable accommodation with the Muslim majority, and a professional army which had returned from Viet Nam grimly determined to install military dominance in Algeria and metropolitan France rather than to accept defeat in another guerrilla war. These segmental conflicts, in turn, were but symptoms of a larger long-standing conflict between metropolitan and overseas France.

> The truth of the matter is that the history of the French republic and that of the French colonial empire were impelled by different forces, went their different ways, and seldom met. . . . The empire was something with which the French people had nothing whatever to do, and its story was that of machinations of high finance, the Church, and the military caste, which tirelessly re-erected overseas the Bastilles which had been overthrown in France (Luethy, 1957, 205).

In the course of the Algerian war, these conflicts became manifest in three major episodes. During the first of these de Gaulle came to power to end the Fourth Republic on the shoulders of a threatened army *coup d'état* in Algiers and *colon* demonstrations (May 1958). The second was an abortive insurrection against de Gaulle, staged by settlers and army leaders in Algiers in January 1960. The third was a revolt of army leaders in Algeria in April 1961, a revolt which was put down and which fizzled out in a wave of *colon* terrorism. The government in Paris successfully coped with the threat of instability which emanated from the colony; but it also decided to end that threat in the future by ridding itself of a colony that had become an economic, military, and political liability. The peace negotiations between the French government and the representatives of the Algerian rebels produced a tacit alliance calculated to put an end to the threat to metropolitan France through the sacrifice of the volatile French *colons* and their proto-fascist military allies. Thus, victory came to the ALN less through its own brave and desperate struggle during seven and one-half years of war than through the strains which the war had produced in the foundations of the French polity.

The Algerian events are important not only because a small force of guerrillas challenged a large modern army and deprived it of victory, but because it gives rise to two influential theories on warfare involving peasant populations. One is the "theory of revolutionary war," developed and advocated by officers of the French army that fought in Algeria. The other is the theory of colonial revolutions put forward by Frantz Fanon, doctor, propagandist, and diplomat for the Algerian liberation movement.

The "theory of revolutionary war" grew out of the bitter experience of the French army in Viet Nam. In the wake of that defeat General Lionel-Max Chassin discovered in the writings of Mao Tse-tung the secret of Communist successes: "It is impossible to win a war, especially a civil war, if the people are not on your side." From now on, according to the new theorists, wars would be fought among the masses, for control of the masses, by a mixture of organizational and psychological techniques. The organizational techniques, which they hoped to borrow from Mao, relied on the famous "hièrarchies parallèles," the combination of organizations based on territoriality with functional organizations. In such a system "the individual caught in the fine mesh of such a net has no chance whatever of preserving his independence" (Jean Hoggard, in *Revue Militaire d'Information*, 1957, quoted in Fall, 1967, 134). The psychological techniques were derived, at least in part, from *The Rape of the Masses*, by Serge Chakotin, a book written on the eve of World War II, purporting to show democratic Germans how they could defend democracy against Hitler by means of a "violent propaganda" based on the supposed lessons of Pavlovian conditioning. The processes of organization and psychological conditioning were to go forward simultaneously through army action in *quadrillage*, forcible relocation, interrogation, the occasional use of torture, and through military-sponsored social work and psychological persuasion. Such an approach has enormous appeal to military technicians and social scientists who think of their findings primarily as techniques for human control. The great flaw of this new vision of war—which attained the status of a religion among many French officers involved in the war—lies in its omission of the human middle term in its multiple cultural aspects—economic, social, political, and ideological. Assuming Algerians to be like Frenchmen, possessed of identical culture patterns and interests, the military technicians visualized their task simply as one in which organization reproduces the experimental design of the laboratory and simple conditioning provides the experimental subject with a new set of habits, without the simultaneous creation of a new cultural order for which these new habits could be relevant. Certainly one may also question whether simple conditioning suffices to restructure human responses in the desired way; but it does not seem impossible, at least in the future, that some forms of complex conditioning can in fact achieve such a result. It is clear, however, that what was missing from "the theory of revolutionary war" was any vision of real revolution, of a transformation of the environment congruent with new patterns of habit. Under the conditions of colonial warfare, in Algeria as later in Viet Nam under American auspices, the theory was emptied of any cultural content to produce simply obedience to naked power imposed from without.

Frantz Fanon's theory, in contrast, preaches the need for colonial peoples to shake off foreign oppression by force and violence, not merely as a military technique, but as an essential psychological precondition to independence. The colony was established by force and is perpetuated by force. The exercise of force against the native strips him of his essential manhood; he can recover his manhood only when he himself uses violence against his oppressor. The use of violence

> frees the native from his inferiority complex and from his despair and inaction; it makes him fearless and restores his self-respect (1963, 73).

But the use of violence also has its social aspect. It unifies the people—the

> practice of violence binds them together as a whole, since each individual forms a violent link in the great chain, a part of the great organism of violence which has surged upwards in reaction to the settler's violence in the beginning (1963, 73).

Thus violence is a "cleansing force"; and Fanon argues that it is not the nationalist middle class and the proletariat that are likely to wield this instrument of cleansing violence, because they "have begun to profit—at a discount to be sure—from the colonial set-up, have special interests at heart" (1963, 47), but the peasantry, who "are rebels by instinct" (1963, 102). Moreover,

> in their spontaneous movements the country people as a whole remain disciplined and altruistic. The individual stands aside in favour of the community (1963, 90).

In the towns, the likely recruits to the rebellion will not be the proletariat, organized into trade-unions which already have particular individual interests to defend, but the *Lumpenproletariat*, derived from the landless peasants who have streamed to the cities, to become "the gangrene ever present at the heart of colonial domination." The leaders of the revolt, finally, will be

> men who have worked their way up from the bottom . . . often unskilled workers, seasonal laborers or even sometimes chronically unemployed. For them the fact of militating in a national party is not simply taking part in politics: it is choosing the only means whereby they can pass from the status of an animal to that of a human being (1963, 100).

No one can read Fanon without being gripped both by his moral passion and by his insight into the mechanisms of aggression and repression which find their expression in personal and group violence. Yet, in an immediate sense, Fanon's thesis is but the antithesis of the position defended by the French coronels. Against their insistence that men can be captured and rendered impotent by organization, he preaches upheaval, dissolution, disorder. Against their use of psychological violence against the native, he preaches violence against the oppressor. But just like the coronels, Fanon pays no attention to the cultural realities of past history, of group relationships, of the shifting and changing alliances and schisms of concrete human beings, caught up in concrete experiences of past and present. His Manichaean world—like the technocratic pseudo-revolutionary order of the coronels—is devoid of economy, society, polity, and ideology and their determinants. In Fanon, violence is not "politics by other means," in Clausewitz's mundane phrase, violence used as a rational technique calculated in terms of particular human interrelationships; it becomes instead a cosmic force needed to cleanse the universe in order to achieve salvation. Violence there certainly was, and the rural population certainly responded to it. But the appeal to violence was most successful in Kabylia, where it permitted the hostile tribal sections to compose their segmental conflicts in a common confrontation with an external enemy. The escalation of violence thus permitted the "massing effect" so characteristic of segmentary societies, in which the autonomous segments form ever larger coalitions proportional to the magnitude of the external threat. Violence in this setting was both cause and effect of a certain social order, not merely a psychologically motivated act in which men took back their manhood from the oppressor who had robbed them of it. Moreover, the French counterthrusts were often singularly undiscriminating in their brutality: violence was frequently a response to military violence visited alike upon men, women, and children. This is not to gainsay Fanon's penetrating insights into the psychological mechanisms of colonial oppression and submission; but it is necessary to indicate that psychology needs to operate within a social matrix; it is not an independent force. We can well understand why the Algerian conflict would have produced such ideologists of counterrevolutionary and revolutionary violence; yet neither the ideology of the coronels nor the ideology of Frantz Fanon could provide us with a guide to an understanding of what happened in Algeria, during the war and after.

The Turkish writer Arslan Humbaraci subtitled his book on Algeria "A Revolution That Failed." The most significant facts about postwar Algeria stem from the defeat of the internal rebellion and the survival of the external army. When the French departed, the external army entered Algeria. The exhausted Kabyle rebels were no match for its military and political might. The departure of 900,000 Frenchmen at the same time vacated numerous positions in government and services, which adherents of the rebellion regarded as rightfully their own. Whatever tenuous bonds between professionals, peasantry, and workers survived the crushing of the internal rebellion now became further attenuated as the fortified Algerian middle class reaped the rewards of ten years of effort and joined the Algerian elite. Socialist experiments, initiated by Ahmed Ben Bella, involving self-management of nationalized French agricultural holdings and shops, resulted in overbureaucratization and a grave decline of production. At the same time, Algeria remained dependent for credits on France, granted in return for continuing rights to oil and gas discovered in the Sahara. Ben Bella's attempt to stem the decline by organizing the NLF into a monolithic party of the Communist type proved unable—on any level—to contain the centrifugal forces created by economic decline, continued dependence on France, and the rapid "bourgeoisification" of the new Algerian power holders. In 1965, the army stepped in in order to stabilize the situation. Under Houari Boumedienne it continues to proclaim for "socialism," but emphasizes that its socialism is "Algerian" and not "imported," and relies for much of its definitions of socialism on the Islamic *ulema*. Nationalized shops have been returned to their owners; banks, foreign trade, and heavy industry—never nationalized—continue in private hands; and the regime has expressed itself in favor of foreign private investment. Algeria continues to be strongly dependent on French aid, becoming in effect France's closest "client-state" (Humbaraci, 1966, 271). At the core of the society stands a strong army, officered by a strongly nationalist staff. The mood is nationalist Islamic Algerian. It is the Jacobin Islam of Ben Badis which has ultimately proved victorious.

SIX

CUBA

¡Con lo que un yanqui ha gastado
no más que en comprar botellas
se hubiera Juana curado!

With what a Yankee spends
just buying bottles,
Juana could have been cured!

Nicolas Guillén: Visita á un Solar

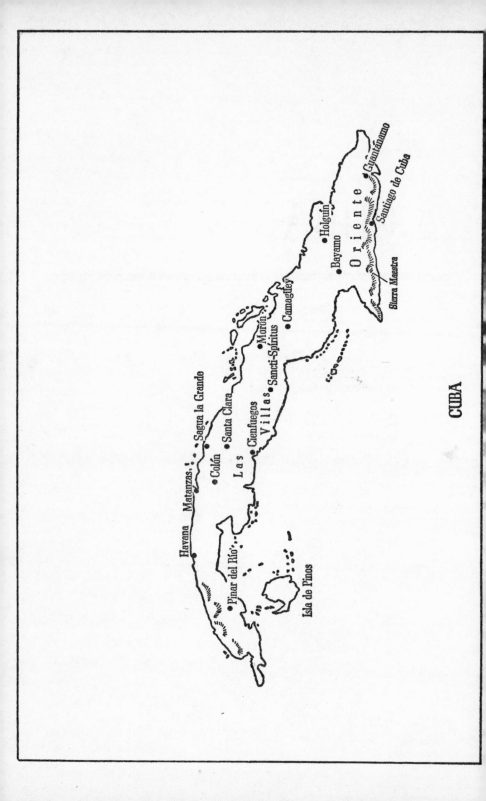

CUBA

The sixth revolution with which we shall concern ourselves took place only ten years ago and only ninety miles off the shores of the United States. The country is Cuba. On December 2, 1956, Fidel Castro and his guerrilla band landed in Cuba in their boat *Granma* which had taken them from Mexico to shore in Cuba at Las Coloradas. Met with force, they suffered a severe defeat; only a handful of survivors escaped into the mountains of the Sierra Maestra. Yet, two years later, on January 1, 1958, Castro's guerrilla movement took formal political power in Havana. What was the setting for these events, and what is their explanation?

A number of characteristics set off Cuba from the cases we have been discussing to date. First, it is relatively small in scale, certainly when compared to Russia or China; its population amounted to 5,829,000 in 1953, its land area to 44,000 square miles. Second, the island's culture lacks temporal depth in Cuba: Cuban society is a product of the Spanish conquest of the Western Hemisphere, beginning with its discovery by Christopher Columbus in 1492. The original Arawak-speaking Indians were wiped out or absorbed; the ecological successors of the Arawak-speaking population were the incoming Spaniards and an African population imported under conditions of slavery. Thus where Russia, China, Viet Nam, Algiers, and Mexico have immemorial roots in an autochthonous neolithic past, Cuba was created to answer the needs of the expanding European commercial system of the modern period. Within Europe, the hegemony of Spain proved short-lived, but Spanish expansion was nevertheless a significant phase in "the creation of the world as a social system."

Third, although we now think of Cuba's economy as dominated by the production of sugar cane, the victory of sugar cane over other crops is a relatively late development in the history of the island. During the first centuries of Spanish occupation, the island served primarily as a strategic base, guarding the sea-lanes which connected the port of Cadiz in Spain with the American ports in Panama and Mexico. Havana grew up in direct response to the organizational requirements of the Spanish silver fleet and of the Spanish effort to supply the American colonies with European goods: from the start, Havana had its face set toward the sea, and toward contacts with the world beyond the confines of the island. The remainder of the island grew some tobacco and coffee, and also devoted itself to livestock keeping, to provide meat for the home market and hides and tallow for export. Yet until the turn of the eighteenth to the nineteenth century, agriculture and ranching were small in scale. There follows from this that

> for over two centuries, Cuba was able to build its society slowly, without protracted disturbance from the outside, and to avoid the plantation mode of development. One can justly refer to the growth of a "creole adaptation" in the Cuban setting (Mintz, 1964, xxii).

Just as agriculture and ranching were small-scale until the turn to the nineteenth century, so African slavery was relatively less significant in Cuba before 1800 than in the other islands and littorals of the Caribbean. This, then, constitutes a fourth peculiarity of Cuban development. At the end of the seventeenth century, the total colored population of Cuba numbered no more than 40,000, as compared with tiny Barbados with its 60,000 slaves, Haiti with 450,000 slaves, and Virginia with 300,000 slaves (Guerra y Sánchez, 1964, 46). Even when sugar production expanded and slavery on plantations was intensified, after 1800, the bulk of Negroes in Cuba lived on small farms and cattle ranches, or worked in urban employment. Alexander von Humboldt, visiting the island around the turn of the eighteenth to the nineteenth century, estimated that only 60,000 slaves were employed in sugar production, 74,000 in other staple crops, and 45,000 in diversified crops. Over 73,000 worked in urban occupations. Where the Caribbean and mainland colonies of other powers

> were, for the most part, populated by masses of slaves without any hope of improving their condition, and the only Europeans who

inhabited these plantation settlements were overseers, government officials, and adventurers (Mintz, 1964, xxiii),

slave labor in Cuba on small farms and in artisan trades provided a base for an easier transition from slavery to freedom.

> In the atmosphere of urban, small farm, and skilled slavery that prevailed in Cuba, there was no sharp break between slave and free, or between colored and white freedmen. All three groups performed the same work and often shared the same social existence in the urban centers, and in the rural areas they worked side by side in truck farming, cattle raising, tobacco growing, and a host of other rural industries (Klein, 1967, 195).

Intermarriage was common, and the right of a slave to have his price publicly announced in a court of law and to buy himself free by installment was recognized. It is estimated that as late as the mid-nineteenth century, roughly two thousand slaves annually availed themselves of these rights, and entered upon the road to manumission.

Yet, while slavery was relatively small-scale and minor in the first three centuries of Cuban existence, the importation of slaves was intensified after the rich French slave colonies of the Caribbean of Haiti and Santo Domingo fell prey to the ravages of war and rebellion, and capital wedded to sugar production migrated from the declining French colonies into the relatively untouched Spanish holdings. Between 1792 and 1821, some 250,000 Negro slaves passed through Havana customs, and an estimated additional 60,000 were brought in through other unauthorized ports. Once in Cuba, these slaves were subjected to an increasingly harsh regime of labor. Three things must, however, be said about the role of Negroes in the Cuba of the nineteenth century. First, the intensification of slave labor—coming after a period of relative mildness—also intensified the sentiment of opposition to the institution. Second, there remained a large group of free Negroes on the island who provided important leadership in the slave rebellions of 1810, 1812, and 1844. Third, the relative autonomy of slave groups during the preceding centuries combined with the recency of massive slave imports to preserve significant African cultural pat-

S

terns on Cuban soil. This was not only evident in the growth of Afro-Cuban religious organizations which represented an autonomous fusion of African and Christian beliefs and rituals, but also in Negro secret societies, such as the mafia-like Abakuá society which governed the docks of Havana (López Valdés, 1966). Both cult and extralegal organization provided foci for a continuing self-conscious Negro social and political life. Such religious and political factors played a significant part in Negro opposition to slavery as well as in the formation of a Negro consciousness among the Cuban lower class.

The increased sentiment of national solidarity, sustained by a continuing sense of a common "Creole" heritage, and of opposition to slavery crested in the wars against Spain. The wars, in turn, reinforced them when early plots led to the Cuban war of independence in 1868. A negotiated peace was signed at El Zanjón in 1878, but a few Cuban leaders like the folk-hero Antonio Maceo and Calixto García kept the flames of rebellion alive until full-scale warfare broke out again in 1895.

From 1896 on the war was fought, on the Spanish side, under the leadership of General Valeriano Weyler with the full panoply of anti-guerrilla tactics later to become popular in Algeria and Viet Nam, such as the use of fortified barriers to seal off one region from another, the employment of armed sweeps through the countryside, the forcible relocation of population, and the concentration camp. Casualties in this bloody war are estimated at 400,000 Cubans and 80,000 Spaniards. In 1898, when the Cuban rebels had succeeded in depriving the Spaniards of control in most of the rural areas of the island, the United States entered the fray. United States participation effectively broke the Spanish hold on the remaining cities, but it also laid the basis for acrimonious disputes between the rebels and the new allies. The revolutionary assembly of Jimagayú had, in 1895, regarded the war as a continuation of earlier efforts to oust the Spaniards, and considered itself the representative body of the Cuban Republic in Arms. The United States neither recognized the assembly nor the right of its general, Calixto García, to participate in the Spanish surrender of Havana. This action served effectively to turn Cuban nationalism—with all of the momentum gained during the prolonged struggle for independence—against the United States. Further seeds of dissension were sown during the American occupation of the island until 1909, and as a result of limitations on Cuban sovereignty stipulated in the so-called Platt Amendment to the Cuban constitution of 1901 which stipulated that Cuba would make no treaties impairing her sovereignty; contract no foreign debt without guarantees that the interest could be served from ordinary revenues; granted the United States the right to intervene in order to protect Cuban sovereignty and a government capable of protecting life, liberty, and property; and allowed the United States to buy or lease land for coaling or naval stations. Following acceptance of the amendment, the United States ratified a tariff pact which gave Cuban sugar preference in the American market and protection to selected American products in the Cuban market. As a result of American action, sugar production came into complete domination of the Cuban economy, while Cuban domestic consumption was integrated into the larger market of the United States. It is no wonder that Cuban nationalists came to view the United States with bitterness and hatred. The Cuban historian Herminio Portell Vilá has written that

> the Cuban revolution of 1868–1898 accomplished its goal of destroying the bases of the political, economic, and social structure of the country, in order to reconstruct them to the national advantage. The incendiary torch, the struggle, the reconcentration camps, the defeat of the Spanish party, were preparing the future for a new Cuba when North American intervention re-established and consolidated the economic and social aspects of the destroyed regime, with all their political implications (1966, 72–73).

In this perspective, Cuban intellectuals long spoke of a "frustrated revolution," frustrated by the United States.

If in the last decades before American occupation the Cuban sugar industry had already begun to eliminate the traditional small-scale plantation and the small-scale grinding mill, it was "under the aegis of North American power that the earlier changes were extended throughout the sugar industry and the whole industry vastly enlarged" (Mintz, 1964, xxix). The result was the growth of the land-factory combine, unifying in one and the same organizational entity "masses of land, masses of machinery, masses of men, and masses of money" (Ortiz, 1947, 52). As the sugar mills or *centrals* increased their capacity to handle larger quantities of cane, the number of mills decreased from 1,190 in 1877 to 207 in 1899, and again to 161 in 1956 (Guerra y Sánchez, 1964, 77; Villarejo, 1960, 81). At the same time the mills expanded their holdings in cane. By 1959, the twenty-eight largest producers of cane owned 1,400,000 hectares and rented an additional 617,000 hectares, thus holding more than 20 percent of Cuba's land in farms and nearly a fifth of Cuba's soil (Seers, 1964, 76). United States–owned companies controlled nine of the ten largest *centrals,* and twelve out of twenty in the next size class; *centrals* under U.S. control produced about 40 percent of the island crop, and controlled 54 percent of the island's grinding capacity. It was not difficult, therefore, to see the grinding mills as foreign redoubts "where an executive proconsul holds sway as the representative of a distant and imperial power" (Ortiz, 1947, 63), exercising control through an extensive vertical structure.

> There are not merely the decisions of policy taken by the sugar companies in the United States, from that radiating center of moneyed power known as Wall Street, but the legal ownership of the central is also foreign. The bank that underwrites the cutting of the cane is foreign, the consumer's market is foreign, the administrative staff set up in Cuba, the machinery that is installed, the capital that is invested, the very land of Cuba held by foreign ownership and enfeoffed to the central, all are foreign, as are, logically enough, the profits that flow out of the country to enrich others (1947, 63).

As large-scale farming grew, moreover, independent small-scale farming necessarily declined. Instead, the growing *centrals* furthered the development of a class of dependent cultivators, the *colonos,* who—operating 85 percent of all farm units on only one-fifth of farm land—needed the mill to grind their cane and to finance their crop. Most of the sugar, plantation and *colono* cane alike, was sold to the United States where its entry was governed by a quota system, apportioning sugar sales between domestic and foreign producers. Sugar cane came to account for 80 to 90 percent of all of Cuba's exports, and for a third of the island's total income. Geared so narrowly to the requirements of the American market, it also suffered the booms and vicissitudes of that market, as prices rose or fell, with enormous repercussions on the skewed distribution of income within the island.

To man the mills and to cut the cane, the sugar industry also created a massive labor force, composed of the descendants of former slaves, of pauperized smallholders, and of Haitian and Jamaican migrants. The result was the growth of a large rural proletariat, severed from any ownership of the land and forced to sell its labor power in an open labor market. It consisted of some 500,000 cane cutters and of about 50,000 mill workers. The presence of this labor force in Cuba makes the Cuban case radically different from the other cases considered in this study. A rural proletariat is *not* a peasantry. As the anthropologist Sidney Mintz has written,

A rural proletariat working on modern plantations inevitably becomes culturally and behaviorally distinct from the peasantry. Its members neither have nor (eventually) want land. Their special economic and social circumstances lead them in another direction. They prefer standardized wage minimums, maximum work weeks, adequate medical and educational services, increased buying power, and similar benefits and protections. In these ways, they differ both from the peasantry—who are often conservative, suspicious, frugal, traditionalistic—and from the farmers, who are the agricultural businessmen, the forward-looking, cash-oriented, rural middle class. Such differentiation does not exhaust the sociology of the Cuban countryside; but at least they indicate that to talk of Cuba's "peasantry" as if the rural population were an undifferentiated mass of impoverished landowners is to miss entirely the complexity of rural Latin America. Peasants who, by a swift process of plantation development, have been transformed into rural proletarians, are no longer the same people (Mintz, 1964, xxxvii).

Tied to the rhythm of the sugar industry, this Cuban proletariat—as sugar-cane workers in other areas of the Caribbean—suffered severely from severe seasonal variations in employment within the industry. The sugar harvest is concentrated within a restricted period of three to four months; after the harvest only a handful of workers are needed to plant new cane and weed the fields, and only a few are required to service the processing mills. The dramatic and all-important period of the harvest, the *zafra*, contrasts with the extended "dead" time or *tiempo muerto*, when two-thirds of all mill workers and nineteen-twentieths of all field workers were laid off altogether (Zeitlin, 1967, 51). The Cuban sugar industry thus not only established the regime of a single dominant crop on the island; it also harnessed a large and concentrated labor force to an economic cycle alternating between prolonged periods of hunger and short periods of intense activity. The desire of the Cuban sugar workers to break out of this cycle was to constitute one of the major sources of support for the revolutionary government after its advent to power (Zeitlin, 1967).

In return for an assured sugar quota within the United States market, Cuba—in turn—permitted the importation into the island of both American capital and products. United States entrepreneurs on the island came to own

> over 90 percent of the telephone and electric services, one-half of the public railways service, one-fourth of all bank deposits . . . and much of the mining, oil production and cattle ranching. . . . The major American companies were closely knit, both by interlocking directorates and by common interest; business was conducted and decisions made with reference to their mutual interest (MacGaffey and Barnett, 1962, 177).

At the same time, Cuba could not protect its own nascent industries through appropriate tariffs on U.S. imports. "Cuban tariff concessions," observed the economist Henry Wallich, "limiting the possibilities of domestic industry, have served more or less as the price for a reasonable sugar quota in the United States market" (1950, 12).

During the first quarter of the twentieth century, plantation monoculture, operated under the new auspices, provided a motor for relatively rapid growth in the Cuban economy; during this period the purchasing power of Cuban sugar more than doubled. Thereafter, however, the economy began to show signs of stagnation. In 1951 the Truslow mission of the International Bank for Reconstuction and Development (Economic and Technical Mission, 1951, 57) summarized its impressions of Cuba by saying that

> since 1924–25, the Cuban economy has been both unstable and undynamic. It has been barely holding its own in long-term trends of real income per capita. It has been characterized by large amounts of unemployment, underemployment, and general insecurity for independent producers and commercial people as well as for wage earners.

It characterized the economy as one "which has lost its pre-1925 'dynamic' and has not yet found a new dynamic." Similarly, Dudley Seers characterized the picture as

> one of chronic stagnation from the 1920's onward in real per capita income. The upward trend in income barely kept pace with the rise of population (Seers, 1964, 12).

While the economy did not keep pace with population, it was not, however, a poor economy in the absolute terms used by many students of development economics to measure the performance of a developing economy. Among the twenty Latin American republics Cuba ranked fifth in annual income per capita, third in persons not employed in agriculture, third or fourth in life expectancy, first in railroad construction and possession of television sets, second in energy consumption, fourth in the production of doctors per thousand inhabitants (Goldenberg, 1965, 120–121). Moreover, there had been some crop diversification after World War II: for instance, where before the war almost all maize and beans had been imported into Cuba, toward the end of the 1950's Cuba produced nearly what it consumed. Similarly, there had been some diversified industrial development. But "what inhibited the island's economic growth was not the absolute supplies of factors of production, but the way in which they were organized" (O'Connor, 1964a, 247).

Cuba provides an excellent example of a "skewed" economy and society. Linked to the American market, it was made subject to the powerful updraft created by the American economic system; yet the very mechanisms which bound Cuba to the United States also placed limits on her capacity to make autonomous decisions about the employment of her resources.

Thus, for example, Cuba did not develop a

> sizable, indigenous, Cuban capitalist class. In practice as well as in definition, a capitalist must have the power and the freedom to develop and choose between significant entrepreneurial alternatives, and this range of choices must include the sources and terms of capital accumulation. To cite one illustration from American history, capitalists rely in certain phases of their development on a running national debt as a means of accumulating capital, yet this crucial device was denied to the Cubans by American leaders. Cuban capitalists lacked other similar freedoms because of the power of various Americans who made such decisions formally or informally (Williams, 1966, 191–192).

The Cuban upper class, therefore, was incapable of developing an independent economic or political role. Its greatest source of security lay in investment in real estate and speculative construction, often in connection with the demands of the tourist trade. Much of its income was secured through tax evasion, usury, and corruption. Its capital investments were mainly made under the guardianship of American businessmen, in North American institutions. Unable to be an independent bourgeoisie, it was also unable to act as a *national* bourgeoisie. Many of its members were former Spanish or American nationals. Nor could they forge an effective tie to a landed Creole aristocracy of the kind existent in the hinterland of other Latin American countries, since this group had been effectively replaced by corporate managers operating under U.S. auspices. The Cuban upper class thus also lacked "the typical protective carapace of oligarchic power" (Blackburn, 1963, 64, fn. 40). Centered upon Havana, its "traditions, ideas, and ideals underwent continuing and skewed mutation in the direction of American culture" (Williams, 1966, 190), without any concomitant increase in its capacity for autonomous management of that culture. Fidel Castro, in his speech of December 1 to 2, 1961, characterized this stratum and its members *tout court* as a "lumpen bourgeoisie." Similar processes also affected the growth of the so-called middle classes. Commerce was generally in the hands of Spaniards and Chinese. Cubans were mainly represented in the free professions and in the government apparatus. American enterprises employed some 160,000 persons (Harbron, 1965, 48). A hypertrophied government apparatus absorbed, in 1950, 186,000 officials or about 11 percent of the total working population, allocating to them 80 percent of public revenues (Goldenberg, 1965, 130). The remainder was made up of *colonos*, professionals, army personnel, and artisans not displaced by the encroachment of American industry. The limits of this heterogeneous "class" were uncertain. Some of its members were successful, over the years, in rising into the upper class (Carvajal, 1950, 35); others were "still linked to the lower class sectors from which they proceeded" (Álvarez, 1965, 628). Among them were the more privileged workers employed in light industry and utilities. Among them also were persons connected with that great "proliferating, parasitic mass," 250,000 strong, of servants, petty waiters, petty traders, entertainers, and procurers, "created by the combination of unemployment with the luxury life styles of the local rich and the tourists" (Blackburn, 1963, 83). Nor can the total size of this segment be estimated correctly. Some observers (e.g., Draper, 1965, 105; and Raggi, 1950, 79) assign one-third of the Cuban population to this uncertain category; others (e.g., Nelson, 1966, 196) felt "not at all certain that a middle class exists." There is general agreement, however, that the personnel of this middle class was exposed to great economic pressures which frequently blocked their mobility or endangered their gains. There is general agreement also that the middle class lacked coherence and any common ability to defend their common interests. Rather, they constituted "a sharply divided aggregate of self-seeking factions" (MacGaffey and Barnett, 1962, 39).

Like the upper class, so the members of the middle class were polarized around the great urban center of Havana, which—with its population of 790,000—came to include one out of every seven Cubans. Havana was both the point of entry of American influence and the chief link between the island and the society and economy of the American continent. Showing great contrasts between its middle and upper classes, geared to American-style ideals of mobility and consumption, and the urban poor, it nevertheless demonstrated in its ambience and life styles the magnetism of the American "way of life." Yet just as much of Cuban society was "to a certain extent parasitical," with its large population of unemployed that had to be supported by the working part of the population and its display of nonproductive activities (Goldenberg, 1965, 134), so Havana was parasitical upon the wider Cuban society. It exemplified, *par excellence*, the contrast between a "hinterland that lagged further and further behind, and a middle-class sector almost too large for the economy to sustain" (Draper, 1965, 105). No wonder that Che Guevara (1968a, 31) was to compare an underdeveloped country to "a dwarf with enormous head and swollen chest" whose "weak legs or short arms do not match the rest of his anatomy"; and George Blanksten put his finger on one of the major sources of Castro's power when he said that "Castro's rise to power was the triumph of rural Cuba over Havana" (1962, 123).

Between the great mass of sugar-cane cutters and the middle classes there also intervened an urban proletariat, some 400,000 strong. We have already seen that its more privileged ranks—workers in light industry and in utilities—merged imperceptibly with the middle-class category; they were, in fact, organized into craft unions which functioned to defend their particular privileges. The poorer strata of the working class, on the other hand, merged imperceptibly with the great mass of urban unemployed and underemployed, estimated at some 700,000. The Cuban union movement claimed a membership of some one million, but as the International Bank for Reconstruction and Development reported in 1950,

> membership is too frequently more nominal than real (in the sense of active, informed participation). The standard of educa-

tion of the members is generally low. Cuban unions, for the most part, lack a really strong democratic base, and they are not firmly founded in legitimate collective bargaining relations at the factory and shop level. They tend, therefore, to become sounding-boards for ambitious political leaders who seek to advance some doctrine or party in the name of organized labor or to promote their personal fortunes and positions in politics (quoted in Smith, 1966, 131).

Within such a structure in a state of continuous imbalance, what was the nature of the political field? Here again we may note the powerful influence of the American presence. It made itself manifest partly in direct intervention, partly in placing limits on the kind of political activity permitted to the Cuban population. In the early days of the new republic, the United States intervened twice with troops, putting marines on the island from 1906 to 1908 and again from 1912 to 1922. Yet it also used its ability to grant recognition to Cuban political leaders whom it favored, and withheld it from leaders of whom it disapproved. Thus the United States readily recognized and supported the military strongman regimes of General Gerardo Machado (1925–1933) and of General Fulgencio Batista (1934–1944, 1952–1958). On the other hand it refused recognition to the reformist regime, in 1933–1934, of Ramón Grau San Martín, who advocated nationalization of utilities and agrarian reform, and who might have steered a course different from that of his predecessor Machado and his successor Batista. Says the political scientist Federico G. Gil:

> The refusal of the United States to recognize Grau San Martín was an important factor in the fall of his government. Concerned with the dangers inherent in social revolution and its impact on U.S. vested interests in the island, American policy was aimed at preservation of the status quo. . . . One cannot help but wonder whether or not events in Cuba would have taken a different course, if the United States at that time had favored needed social and economic changes. . . . It is valid to pose such a question, for in some respects the Cuban phenomenon of the 1950's was simply the reincarnation of the revolutionary process interrupted in the 1930's (1966, 150).

The unwillingness of the United States to countenance any substantive change, both within Cuba and in Cuba's relation to United States interests, created grave and realistic doubts regarding the capacity of any Cuban government to further the interests of the island as a whole. Instead, Cuban politics, deprived of national goals, became a kind of charade in which the only gains possible were those wrested by individual factions from the treasury of the neo-colonial client state, an option which, moreover,

> perpetuated the Spanish legacy that public office should be made a source of private profits. Politics thus became the key to social advancement, and so little more than a squabble between factions for the ownership of the government. Parties cut across group interests, and *personalismo* rather than principle determined party alignments. . . . Government was, in fact, like the lottery which used to play such an important part in Cuban politics. Public life was permeated by a boom psychosis, with the middle sectors bidding against each other for government sinecures (Hennessy, 1966, 23–24).

These competitive bids were often accompanied by gang warfare and other types of violence (Stokes, 1953; Suárez, 1967, 11–15); the pay-off was more often than not access to public and private funds, with corruption accepted as a kind of public capitalization of the victorious group. Critics of Cuban politics, in turn, often called for a "moralization" of government, rather than for a structural alteration in the conditions of immorality. In this respect, too, the present Castro regime finds its antecedents in a number of political figures—such as Antonio Guiteras, Grau San Martín's minister of the interior, who launched the slogan "Verguenza contra dinero" (Shame against money); and Eduardo Chibás of the Ortodoxo party, who committed suicide in the days preceding Batista's second take-over. The Castro-led Movement of the Twenty-Sixth of July, with its strongly puritanical attitude toward public morality, has built upon this strongly felt need for "a change in public customs" (Gil, 1962, 386).

Most observers have interpreted the dictatorial regimes of

Fulgencio Batista as just two more instances of the Hispanic or Latin American penchant for personal leadership or *personalismo*. Personal leadership is certainly an important pattern in Latin American politics, but an analysis couched in personalistic terms misses three aspects of the Cuban situation which require further explication. First, it is obvious that the various political forces in Cuba were too weak for any one group or class to transcend the political stalemate. As James O'Connor has phrased it, "the balance of class forces—taking into account size, organization, and morale—created a political nexus in which no class had political initiative" (1964b, 107). Such a situation gave advantages to a dictator who could play off the various relevant groups against each other. Second, it is not often noted that the Batista regimes actually represent efforts to give representation—in non-electoral form—to various important interest groups. It drew on all classes and "representatives of all classes could be located in key decision-making positions in all governments since 1935. This included labor" (1964b, 107). In this context one should recall that labor was represented in the first Batista regime by two Communists in ministerial positions and by Communist trade-union leaders. When power passed from the Communist leadership to anti-Communist trade-union leaders in 1950, these new leaders were included in the second Batista government. At the same time, the Communist party did nothing to challenge the regime politically, relying entirely on trade-union tactics. Nor did they support the Castro rebels. They denounced the Moncada rising of 1953 as "adventuristic putschism," criticized the rebels in the sierra as terrorists and conspirators, and opposed the strikes called in 1958. It was only in July 1958 that a Communist leader, Carlos Rafael Rodríguez, who had been a minister in Batista's government in 1940, went to the sierra to make contacts with the Fidelistas.

This quasi-syndicalist organization of the Batista regime produced the third aspect which requires comment. On the one hand, it tied a segment of each significant class to the apparatus of the government, thus at once giving them a firm stake in its maintenance, while at the same time weakening it by setting it off against possible competitors. James O'Connor has characterized the situation as follows:

> Far more important, by the 1950's representatives of each class had firmly entrenched themselves in the state bureaucracy. Thus the character of Castro's struggle was determined in part by the outcome of the earlier upheaval which removed a solid class base for political rule and laid the groundwork for each class to establish some kind of stake in the national political economy. These vested interests profited both from the network of market controls and redistributive national economic policies. In this way the paradoxical situation developed that segments of each class enjoyed a large stake in the system, while others stood to gain from its annihilation (1964b, 108).

With some members of each social category in and some out, there could develop only multiple conflicts between ins and ins, and ins and outs, but no radical opposition—in sociological terms— between defenders and antagonists of the social system as a whole. The sociologist Lewis Coser has pointed out that "conflict, rather than being disruptive and disassociating, may indeed be a means of balancing and hence maintaining a society as a going concern" (1956, 137). Thus in the Cuban case conflict merely led to deadlock, and deadlock produced conflict, without any group being able to develop sufficient leverage to raise the system from its moorings. Yet, as James O'Connor has written,

> economic development [after 1950] required total national autonomy; political stability (the precondition for foreign investments) in the absence of a strong, stable class for bourgeois rule, required dependence on Washington. Economic development required an independent monetary system and monetary autonomy; political stability required that the island be secured against inflation, and that the peso be kept on a par with the dollar by retaining the island as a monetary colony of the United States. Economic development required that Cuba be able to postpone, adjust, modify its international payments; political stability required prompt, full payments (in 1957–58, 70 per cent of United States credit collections were termed "prompt," and 90 per cent were paid within thirty days). Economic development required

that Cuba be able to seize the advantages of common instruments of national economic policy—multiple exchange rates, import quotas, and so on; political stability required that Cuba's international commercial arrangements be arranged in the interests of United States traders. Economic development required that Cuba liberate itself from the sugar quota system; political stability required that Cuba's fate be linked to the interests and mood of the United States Congress (1964b, 106).

Maintenance of the political deadlock thus contributed directly to inhibit economic development and to guarantee that political stability which made it impossible to transcend the imbalances of the social system. Under these conditions, only the injection of a new force from "outside" the system could provide the additional impetus required to shake up the ongoing structure of conflict and conflict-resolution, and the resulting condition of political impotence.

That "outside" force proved to be the rebel band of Fidel Castro. Twice in the past thirty years "internal" politics had proved insufficient in effecting a major structural change in Cuban society. During the period of opposition against the bloody butcher Machado and during the short-lived radical nationalist regime of Grau San Martín, university students had seized control of the University of Havana and workers had occupied railroad stations, public utilities, and sugar *centrals*, to set up short-lived "soviets" or councils of workers, peasants, and soldiers on the Russian model. The movement had been especially strong in Oriente Province, the later hearth of the rebel effort. The seizures had been sponsored by the youthful Communist party, organized in 1926; the Communists had also proved effective in organizing the first national sugar workers union (SNOIA) and "peasant leagues" among rural workers. Despite its considerable prestige and power, however, the Communist party proved ineffective in going any further. There is evidence that it held back from the fight against Machado for fear of provoking imperialist intervention (Zeitlin and Scheer, 1963, 112); did not support the Grau regime which it regarded as "bourgeois landlord"; came out in open support of the first Batista regime; and focused on trade-union goals rather than political goals after that. It thus came to represent the prototype of the "party machine that must be fed," against which Régis Debray has been inveighing. It thus remained essentially passive during the first two years of the guerrilla effort.

The Movement of the Twenty-Sixth of July, led by Castro, thus represents both a continuity with past radical action and a departure from it. Castro himself had won his political spurs in the violent gang fights of the so-called action groups of the late forties which were opposed to the coalition of the Communist party with Batista and which favored insurrectional tactics. During a brief interlude of electoral politics in 1952 he himself ran as a candidate of the Ortodoxo party in elections which, however, never took place as a result of Batista's second seizure of power. On July 26, 1953, he organized an attack of 125 men on the Moncada army barracks in Santiago de Cuba. The attack gave the movement its distinctive name, but proved abortive. Castro was imprisoned, to be released two years later. In exile in Mexico, he broke with the Ortodoxo party to organize a new insurrection. A landing by Cuban forces from Mexico was to be coordinated with another uprising in Santiago; eighty-two men under Castro's leadership landed in Cuba, but the uprising failed and Castro's party was nearly wiped out between December 2 and 5, 1956. The dozen survivors of the event fled into the Sierra Maestra where they reorganized themselves to continue the battle against Batista, this time with guerrilla tactics.

From then on, there was a widening gulf in Cuba between organizations which hoped to mobilize the urban and rural masses for a revolutionary effort, and the Castroites who relied on military action by a small group, using the mountains of Oriente Province as their privileged sanctuary. This conflict has come to be known as the opposition of the *llano* or lowlands and the mountains or *sierra* (see Guevara, 1968a, 196–197). From the point of view of the Communist party, the rebel band followed a Blanquist strategy, so named after the French revolutionary Auguste Blanqui. Blanquism has been described by Engels as the view that a relatively small number of resolute, well-organized men would be able, at a given favorable moment, not only to seize the helm of the State, but also to keep power, by energetic and unrelenting action, until they had succeeded in drawing the mass of the people into the revolution by marshalling them around a small band of leaders.

This view was anathema to most Communists. Lenin had written that "the uprising must be based on the revolutionary upsurge of the people"; yet here was a movement which hoped to produce the upsurge of the people by "parachuting" a rebel group into the Cuban situation.

How did the rebel group galvanize the masses? The original core of the rebel force was composed primarily of what have been called "revolutionary intellectuals," mostly middle-class origins. Some were students (Raúl Castro, Fauré Chomón), some lawyers (Castro, Dorticós), some doctors (Faustino Pérez, René Vallejo), some teachers (Frank País), a few urban unemployed (Camilo Cienfuegos, Ephigenio Almejeiras). "None of us," writes Che Guevara (quoted in Draper, 1965, 68),

> none of the first group who came in the "Granma," who established ourselves in the Sierra Maestra, and learned to respect the peasant and worker while living with them, had worker's or peasant's backgrounds.

The first man with connections among the rural population to join the rebellion was Guillermo García, a cattle dealer in the area in which the rebels made their stand; on May 6, 1957, he was promoted to captain and "took charge of all the peasants who joined the column" (Guevara, 1968a, 102). Yet peasant recruitment was slow.

> The fundamental problem was: if they saw us they had to denounce us. If the Army learned of our presence through other sources, they were lost. Denouncing us did violence to their own conscience and, in any case, put them in danger, since revolutionary justice was speedy. In spite of a terrorized or at least neutralized and insecure peasantry which chose to avoid this serious dilemma by leaving the Sierra, our army was entrenching itself more and more (Guevara, 1968a, 197).

T

In the face of slow recruitment among the peasantry, reinforcements sent into the sierra from the plains—especially by Frank
País, operating out of Santiago de Cuba—proved crucial. Fifty men
with weapons joined the column between debarkation on December 2, 1956, and the attack on the army post at Uvero on May 28,
1957; we may surmise that most of these were industrial workers or
rural proletarians from Oriente Province (see Arnault, 1966, 147,
fn. 13). Peasant recruitment speeded up thereafter.

> Little by little, as the peasants came to recognize the invincibility
> of the guerillas and the long duration of the struggle, they began
> responding more logically, joining our army as fighters. From that
> moment on, not only did they join our ranks but they provided
> supportive action. After that the guerilla army was strongly en-
> trenched in the countryside, especially since it is usual for peasants
> to have relatives throughout the zone. This is what we call "dress-
> ing the guerillas in palm leaves" (Guevara, 1968a, 197).

Two factors in this recruitment seem of importance. First, the rural
population surrounding the Sierra Maestra was quite different in
character from the rural proletariat characteristic of most of Cuba.
Guevara has commented on this in his discussion of "Cuban
exceptionalism" (1968a, 29):

> the first area where the Rebel Army—made up of survivors of the
> defeated band that had made the voyage on the *Granma*—oper-
> ated, was an area inhabited by peasants whose social and cultural
> roots were different from those of the peasants found in the areas
> of large-scale semi-mechanized agriculture. In fact, the Sierra
> Maestra, locale of the first revolutionary beehive, is a place where
> peasants struggling barehanded against latifundism took refuge.
> They went there seeking a new piece of land—somehow over-
> looked by the state or the voracious latifundists—on which to
> create a modest fortune! They constantly had to struggle against
> the exactions of the soldiers, who were always allied to the
> latifundists; and their ambition extended no farther than a prop-
> erty deed. Concretely, the soldiers who belonged to our first
> peasant-type guerilla armies came from the section of this social
> class which shows most strongly love for the land and the posses-
> sion of it; that is to say, which shows most perfectly what we can
> define as the petty-bourgeois spirit. The peasant fought because he

wanted land for himself, for his children, to manage it, sell it, and get rich by his work.

Thus the social matrix into which the rebellion inserted itself was unusual for Cuba. While squatters existed in other parts of Cuba, their number was especially high in Oriente Province (Seers, 1964, 79), where they lived very much on the margin of the law. There is also reference to the zone of the Sierra Maestra as one of the chief zones for growing and smuggling marijuana (Goldenberg, 1965, 155), an activity which must have reinforced the extralegal orientation of the area and thus rendered it a haven for the slowly growing guerrilla band who gained peasant sympathies as a kind of Robin Hoods or social bandits. A second factor of some importance seems to have been that the rebel band itself became an ongoing part of the local economy, thus tying peasant interests to their continuing presence and success. "The sierra peasant," says Guevara,

> did not have cattle and generally theirs was a subsistence diet. They depended on the sale of their coffee to buy indispensable processed items, such as salt. As an initial step we arranged with certain peasants that they should plant specific crops—beans, corn, rice, etc.—which we guaranteed to purchase. At the same time we came to terms with certain merchants in nearby towns for the supplying of foodstuffs and equipment (1968a, 203).

The growing strength of the rebel band in the mountains contrasted with various failures to stage uprisings in the plains. These included a student attack on the presidential palace in Havana on March 13, 1957; a general strike set for August 1957; a rising of naval officers at Cienfuegos on September 5, 1957; and another strike set for April 9, 1958. Yet by spring of 1958 a second rebel front had been opened in the Sierra Cristal, to the north of Oriente Province; by May two rebel columns moved east into the provinces of Camagüey and Las Villas. In November and December of 1958 the rebels cut the communications with urban centers in Oriente and began to take command posts and small towns in the plains. Guevara took Santa Clara on December 31, 1958. Batista fled the country on January 1, 1959, and on January 8 the rebels entered Havana. It is estimated that the rebel army as such never exceeded more than two thousand armed men.

James O'Connor's view that Batista's regime was an effective coalition of class segments who were given a stake in the ongoing structure while other segments were left out, is supported by the way in which various groups of "outs" began to throw their support to the rebels, while some "ins" withdrew from participation in the regime. There is certainly evidence for middle-class support for the rebels, despite later disclaimers by Castro himself. In his discussion of "Cuban exceptionalism," Guevara made clear reference to such support (1968a, 28):

> We don't believe that it could be considered exceptional that the bourgeoisie, or at least a good part of it, showed itself favorable to the revolutionary war against the tyranny at the same time that it was supporting and promoting movements seeking for negotiated solutions which would permit them to substitute for the Batista regime elements disposed to curb the revolution. Considering the conditions in which the revolutionary war took place and the complexity of the political tendencies which opposed the tyranny, it was not at all exceptional that some latifundist elements adopted a neutral, or at least non-belligerent, attitude toward the insurrectionary forces. It is understandable that the national bourgeoisie, struck down by imperialism and the tyranny, whose troops sacked small properties and made extortion a daily way of life, felt a certain sympathy when they saw those young rebels from the mountains punish the military arm of imperialism, which is what the mercenary army was. So non-revolutionary forces indeed helped smooth the road for the advent of revolutionary power.

It was obviously this middle sector which provided the supplies for the rebels in the mountains. Two Cuban writers, Torres and Aronde (1968, 49) have put it simply: "Money was needed: it was the bourgeoisie who had it. . . ." Guevara also makes reference to "a large underground movement among the armed forces, led by a group of so-called pure military men" (Guevara, 1968a, 201). One such movement produced the abortive uprising at the Cienfuegos Naval Base on September 5, 1957. The same kind of support was furnished by the non-revolutionary Communist party which took until mid-1958 to make active contact with the rebels in the mountains. While it never encouraged the armed movement directly, through participation with its mass organizations, it is evident that it contributed to the final destruction of the Batista regime by its very nonparticipation and passivity.

What the insurrection in the mountains thus accomplished was a gradual swing-over of anti-Batista elements and groups that had lived in symbiosis with the regime. Through its tactics it had provided the extra "push" required to break the deadlock of existing political forces. Just as Batista had been able to stand above all class forces, because no given force was strong enough to dominate the others, so also the rebel government was able to create an effective national center which proved immune to challenge once relations between Cuba and the United States were broken off. From this point of view it is perhaps immaterial whether Castro was driven into active opposition by the attitude of the United States government, or whether he had always envisaged a point in his operation when a rupture in ongoing relations with the United States would become a necessity. If Cuba was to gain autonomous decision-making power over its own internal processes, it required an independent center of power to effect these decisions. Such an independent center of power, however, could not persist if any of the contending interest groups within Cuba could form an effective alliance with power groups on the American mainland. The break with the United States may from this point of view have been indispensable to the victors, if they hoped to reap the fruits of their victory.

CONCLUSION

It is not communism that is
radical, it is capitalism.

Bertolt Brecht

The revolutions and rebellions which have furnished the raw material for our six case histories all belong to the twentieth century; yet the tensions which gave rise to them all had their roots in the past; and we have tried to present, in each case, an outline of that past. We have striven to do so not in terms of abstract categories—such as the retention of "tradition" or the advent of "modernity"—but in terms of a concrete historical experience which lives on in the present and continues to determine its shape and meaning. Everywhere, this historical experience bears the stigmata of trauma and strife, of interference and rupture with the past, as well as the boon of continuity, of successful adaptation and adjustment—engrams of events not easily erased and often only latent in the cultural memory until some greater event serves to draw them forth again. In all our six cases this historical experience constitutes, in turn, the precipitate in the present of a great overriding cultural phenomenon, the world-wide spread and diffusion of a particular cultural system, that of North Atlantic capitalism. This cultural system—with its distinctive economics—possesses its own distinctive history of development within a distinctive geographical area. Not only were its characteristic features different from those of other cultural systems both before it and after; it was profoundly alien to many of the areas which it engulfed in its spread.

Its hallmark is its possession of a social organization "in which labor is sold, land is rented, capital is freely invested" (Heilbroner, 1962, 63). These

> do not exist as eternal categories of social organization. Admittedly, they are categories of *nature*, but these eternal aspects of the productive process—the soil, human effort, and the artifacts which can be applied to production—do not take on, in every society, the specific separation which distinguishes them in a market society. . . . Modern economics thus describes the manner in which a certain kind of society, with a specific history of acculturation and

institutional evolution, solves its economic problems. It may well be that in another era there will no longer be "land," "labor," and capital (1962, 63).

The guiding fiction of this kind of society—one of the key tenets of its ideology—is that land, labor, and wealth are commodities, that is, goods produced not for use, but for sale. Land, labor, and money could,

> of course, not be really transformed into commodities as actually they were not produced for sale on the market. But the fiction of their being so produced became the organizing principle of society. Of the three, one stands out: labor is the technical term used for human beings, in so far as they are not employers but employed; it follows that henceforth the organization of labor would change concurrently with the organization of the market system. But as the organization of labor is only another word for the forms of life of the common people, this means that the development of the market system would be accompanied by a change in the organization of society itself. All along the line, human society had become an accessory of the economic system (Polanyi, 1957, 75).

Land, also, is not a commodity in nature; it only becomes such when defined as such by a new cultural system intent on creating a new kind of economics. Land is part of the natural landscape not created to be bought and sold, and it is not regarded as a commodity in most other kinds of societies where rights to land are aspects of specific social groups and its utilization the ingredient of specific social relationships. To the Mexican Indian, to the Russian or Vietnamese peasant, land was an attribute of his community. Before the advent of the French, the Algerian peasant had access to land by virtue of his specific membership in a tribe or through political relationships with the *bey* as head of state. Even the Chinese peasant, long used to buying and selling land, regards land as more of a family heirloom than as a commodity. Possession of land guaranteed family continuity, selling it offended "the ethical sense" (Fei, 1939, 182). Only in Cuba, already established as a plantation colony under capitalist auspices, was land relatively unencumbered by social ties and requirements. In all of the other cases, if land was to become a commodity in a capitalist market, it had first to be stripped of these social obligations. This was accomplished either by force which deprived the original inhabitants of their resources in land—as happened notably in Mexico and Algeria; or through the colonization of new land, unencumbered by customary social ties, as in Cochin China; or it could be accomplished indirectly by furthering the rise of "the strong and sober" entrepreneurs within the peasant communities, who could abandon their ties to neighbors and kin and use their surpluses in culturally novel ways to further their own standing in the market. Thus capitalism necessarily produces a revolution of its own.

This revolution from the beginning, however, takes the form of an unequal encounter between the societies which first incubated it and societies which were engulfed by it in the course of its spread. The contact between the capitalist center, the metropolis, and the pre-capitalist or non-capitalist periphery is a large-scale cultural encounter, not merely an economic one. It is not often realized to what extent European capitalism owes its growth to special historical and geographical circumstances in which the barbarians of northwest Europe took over the technological repertoire of Rome without its constraining organizational framework.

> The actual experience of the European peoples was that of a frontier community endowed with a full complement of tools and materials derived from a parent culture and then almost completely severed from the institutional power system of its parent. The result was unique. It is doubtful if history affords another instance of any comparable area and population so richly endowed and so completely severed (Ayres, 1944, 137).

Europe emerged as an area technologically well endowed for overseas commerce and raiding, yet relatively unrestrained by entrenched institutions and their "ceremonial" overhead. Oriented toward overseas conquest, it could benefit both from the plunder of archaic states located along its transoceanic paths of exploration, and from the slave trade, prerequisites for "primary accumulation," unique opportunities unlikely to repeat themselves after the nineteenth century. Finally, success in plundering the world offset the internal dislocations occasioned by conversion of men, land, and money into commodities within the homeland and gave citizens a stake in overseas expansion. Although this development was essentially predatory in character, it is not so much its use of force and its penchant for exploitation which is at stake in this discussion, but the character of its specific mode of operation. Capitalism surely did not invent exploitation. Everywhere it spread in the world, it encountered social and cultural systems already long dependent upon the fruits of peasant labor. Nor can it be supposed that the peasantry did not revolt repeatedly against the transfer of its surpluses to superior power holders; the historical record is replete with peasant rebellions. It is significant, however, that before the advent of capitalism and the new economic order based on it, social equilibrium depended in both the long and short run on a balance of transfers of peasant surpluses to the rulers and the provision of a minimal security for the cultivator. Sharing of resources within communal organizations and reliance on ties with powerful patrons were recurrent ways in which peasants strove to reduce risks and to improve their stability, and both were condoned and frequently supported by the state. Indeed, "many superficially odd village practices make sense as disguised forms of insurance" (Lipton, 1968, 341). What is significant is that capitalism cut through the integument of custom, severing people from their accustomed social matrix in order to transform them into economic actors, independent of prior social commitments to kin and neighbors. They had to learn how to maximize returns and how to minimize expenditures, to buy cheap and to sell dear, regardless of social obligations and social costs.

> The market society had not, of course, invented this drive. Perhaps it did not even intensify it. But it did make it a *ubiquitous* and *necessitous* aspect of social behavior. . . . With the monetization of labor, land, and capital, transactions became *universal* and *critical* activities (Heilbroner, 1962, 64).

Where previously market behavior had been subsidiary to the existential problems of subsistence, now existence and its problems became subsidiary to marketing behavior. Yet this could only function if labor, land, and wealth were turned into commodities, and this, in turn, is only a short-hand formula for the liquidation of encumbering social and cultural institutions. Capitalism "liberated" man as an economic agent, but the concrete process of liberation entailed the accumulation of human suffering against which anti-capitalist critics, conservatives *and* radicals alike, would direct their social and moral criticism. This liberation from accustomed social ties and the separation which it entailed constituted the historical experience which Karl Marx would describe in terms of "alienation." The alienation of men from the process of production which had previously guaranteed their existence; their alienation from the product of their work which disappeared into the market only to return to them in the form of money; their alienation from themselves to the extent to which they now had to look upon their own capabilities as marketable commodities; their alienation from their fellow men who had become actual or potential competitors in the market: these are not only philosophical concepts; they depict real tendencies in the growth and spread of capitalism. At work everywhere, they were most starkly in evidence in the new colonies, regarded by the colonists as outright supply depots for the metropolitan market. There the racial and cultural prejudices of the new conquerors allowed them a latitude in treating the native population as "pure" labor which they had not enjoyed in the home country.

Everywhere the dance of commodities brought on an ecological crisis. Where in the past the peasant had worked out a stable combination of resources to underwrite a minimal livelihood, the separate and differential mobilization of these resources as objects to be bought and sold endangered that minimal nexus. Thus in Russia land reform and commercialization together threatened the peasant's continued access to pasture, forest, and plowland. In Mexico, Algeria, and Viet Nam commercialization menaced peasant access to communal land; in Mexico and Cuba it barred the peasant from claiming unclaimed public land. In Algeria and China, it liquidated the institution of public granaries. In Algeria, it ruptured the balance between pastoral and settled populations. In

Mexico, Viet Nam, Algeria, and Cuba, finally, outright seizures of land by foreign colonists and enterprises drove the peasants back upon a land area no longer sufficient for their needs.

Paradoxically, these processes of containment, subversion, and forced withdrawal of the peasantry coincided with a rapid acceleration of population growth. This acceleration was in large part a side effect of the very process of commercial expansion which threatened the stability of the peasant equilibrium. American food crops hitherto confined to the New World—like maize, manioc, beans, peanuts, and sweet potatoes—began a world-wide diffusion in the wake of the transoceanic conquests, and took root in many parts of the world where they furnished an expanded existential minimum for growing populations. Improved communication permitted the transport and sale of food surpluses into deficit areas. Colonization frequently opened up new areas, providing hitherto unavailable niches for developing populations. Somewhat later, incipient industrialization began to offer new alternatives for support, and improved health care cut into mortality rates. Yet, the new generations often found themselves in situations where many resources, and especially land, were already spoken for and where existing social structures often failed to absorb the added burden of supernumerary claimants. Some of the magnitude of the pressures generated can be gauged from figures showing total population increases. At the beginning of the nineteenth century Mexico had a population of 5.8 million; in 1910—at the time of the outbreak of the revolution—it had 16.5 million. European Russia had a population of 36 million in 1796; at the beginning of the present century it had 129 million. China numbered 265 million in 1775, 430 million in 1850, and close to 600 million at the time of the Revolution. Viet Nam is estimated to have sustained a population between 6 million and 14 million in 1820; it counted 30.5 million inhabitants in 1962. Algeria had an indigenous population of 3 million in 1830, of 10.5 million in 1963. Cuba's population rose from 550,000 inhabitants in 1800 to 5.8 million in 1953. The peasant thus confronted a growing imbalance between population and resources. In such a situation the peasant's risks multiplied, and the mechanisms for the alleviation of these risks grew ever more unreliable. Such an imbalance could not, in the long run, endure; the fiction that men, land, and wealth were *nothing but* commodities entailed its own ruin. For the complete application of this ideology could not but

> result in the demolition of society. For the alleged commodity "labor power" cannot be shoved about, used indiscriminately, or even left unused, without affecting also the human individual who happens to be the bearer of this particular commodity. In disposing of a man's labor power the system would, incidentally, dispose of the physical, psychological, and moral entity "man" attached to that tag. Robbed of the protective covering of cultural institutions, human beings would perish from the effects of social exposure (Polanyi, 1957, 73).

Thus, paradoxically, the very spread of the capitalist market-principle also forced men to seek defenses against it. They could meet this end either by cleaving to their traditional institutions, increasingly subverted by the forces which they were trying to neutralize; or they could commit themselves to the search for new social forms which would grant them shelter. In a sense all our six cases can be seen as the outcome of such defensive reactions, coupled with a search for a new and more humane social order.

Yet the advent of capitalism produced still another—and equally serious—repercussion. It initiated a crisis in the exercise of power.

Tribal chief, mandarin, landed nobleman—the beneficiaries and agents of an older social order—yield to the entrepreneur, the credit merchant, the political broker, the intellectual, the professional. The social weight of peasantry and artisans decreases, as other groups—miners, railroad workers, industrial workers, agricultural laborers, commercial agricultural producers—gain in relative importance. The managers of fixed social resources yield to the managers of "free-floating" resources. Groups oriented toward subsistence production diminish, and groups committed to commodity production or to the sale of labor power grow in size and social density. Such a circulation of elites and social groups is characteristic of all culture change in a complex society: the new processes at work evoke positive responses in some groups, defensive reactions in others. Yet capitalism is unusual both in the speed and intensity of its operation, as it creates "free-floating" resources previously held fast by a tissue of social and political connections. It mobilizes economic resources and renders them amenable to new forms of allocation and use; yet in so doing it also cuts the tie between these resources and any connection they may have had with traditional social prerogatives and political privileges. It proves a powerful solvent of the integument of power, exacerbating tension not only through its own action, but freeing also tensions and contradictions previously contained by the traditional system of power. As the economic resources of chiefs, mandarins, and landed nobles become subject to the movement of the market, their claims to social and political command are increasingly called into question. Many of their inherited titles end up on the auction block.

These processes do not, of course, proceed at an even pace in all realms of society and in all of its regions. For some time, the power holders of the older order coexist with the power holders of the new; social groups which once controlled the foundation of the society retreat only slowly before groups harnessed to novel processes. Some regions of the country involved remain anchored in tradition, while others are caught up completely in the grip of change. This coexistence of old and new strata, of regions dominated by the past and regions in the grip of the future, spells trouble for the society as a whole.

Commitments and goals point in different directions: the old is not yet overcome and remains to challenge the new; the new is not yet victorious. The dislocations caused by rapid change are still visible to all; the wounds caused by them, raw and open. New wealth does not yet have legitimacy, and old power no longer commands respect. Traditional groups have been weakened, but not yet defeated, and new groups are not yet strong enough to wield decisive power. This is especially marked in colonial situations, where capitalism has been imported from abroad by force of arms. The conquerors drive a wide wedge into the body of the conquered society, but only rarely can they be certain of the ramifications of their actions, of the ways in which cultural shock waves propagate themselves through the traditional strata of society, of the ultimate repercussions in the hinterland and in the nether regions of the social order. Moreover, both cultural barriers and the logistic difficulties of sustained dominance tend to leave uncontrolled wide areas of society which become sanctuaries for groups that seek refuge in time of stress. Finally, abdication of ultimate decisions to the "invisible hand" of the market affects both the willingness and the capacity to take responsibility for local consequences. Inherited control mechanisms fail, but the new mechanisms engage only rarely, with considerable slippage.

Such a situation of weak contenders, unable to neutralize each other's power, seems to invite the rise or perpetuation of a dominant central executive, attempting to stand "above" the contending parties and interest groups, and to consolidate the state by playing off one group against the other. All our cases show such a phenomenon before the revolution: Díaz ruled over Mexico; tsarist autocracy held Russia in its grip; Chiang Kai-shek strove to install such a dictatorship in China; France exercised autocratic rule in Viet Nam and Algiers through her governor general, vastly more authoritative than the head of the government at home; and Cuba was dominated by Batista. Yet because the dictatorship is predicated on the relative debility of the class groups and political forces which constitute society, its seeming strength derives from weakness, and its weakness ultimately becomes evident in its impotent struggle against challengers from within, unless it can find allies strong enough to sustain it against the challenge.

Two examples show that this is possible, but that the conditions for such consolidation are apt to be unique. In both Germany and Japan the executive allied itself not with new groups, but with a section of the traditional feudal aristocracy which provided the backbone of an efficient centralized bureaucracy. The commercial and professional groups, rather than striving for independent ends, accepted the feudal values as their own, thus consenting to guidance by the aristocrats. The peasantry was similarly held fast to the inherited cultural ceremonial of obligations between social superiors and inferiors, and by the development of a national ideology of kinship or kinship-based *Gemeinschaft*. The entire structure received further cohesion through its integration with a military machine, and projection of tension within the society outward against real and putative enemies. Such an effective mobilization of feudal relationships and values served as a check on the social dislocations produced by the widening market, but did so at the cost of increased militarism and final military defeat (see Moore, 1966, 313).

Where the social dislocations produced by the market go unchecked, however, the crisis of power also deranges the networks which link the peasant population to the larger society, the all-important structure of mediation intervening between center and hinterland. Increased commercialization and capitalization of rent produce dislocations and tensions which often weaken the agents of the process themselves. A good example is furnished by the condition of Ch'uhsien, a market town in Anhwei, studied by anthropologist Morton Fried shortly before the Communist take-over in 1949. The landlords of Ch'uhsien relied largely on a system in which tenants paid in rent 40 percent of the staple crops at harvest time. This allowed for some flexibility in determining the amount to be paid, and arguments between landlord and tenant over the disputed margin were mediated by a culturally standardized form of "good will," called *kan-ch'ing*. By extending "good will" to his tenant, the landlord essentially granted a discount on the rent in return for the tenant's reliable performance in paying rent; the tenant traded the promise of his reliability for the protection by the landlord in case of some untoward event, like a poor harvest or sickness in the family. In the unsettled conditions of Chinese Anhwei, the landlord was thus passing on to the tenant the margin of gain which he would otherwise have had to pay out to agents or to political power holders in order to attach the rent by force. Yet even this flexible system soon encountered limitations. Not all tenants can have good *kan-ch'ing* with their landlords; when landlords are hard-pressed, *kan-ch'ing* was abrogated; and tenants in some rural areas

U

away from the police power of the county seat, defied the land-lords and paid no rent. In such instances the rents were frequently collected by an armed squad of the local militia, or even, on special occasion, by a unit of the Nationalist Army, which accompanied the agent or landlord (Fried, 1953, 196).

The best the gentry can do under these circumstances "is to establish good *kan-ch'ing* with a few persons while relationships with others deteriorate" (Fried, 1953, 224). In response to this situation, the landlords of Ch'uhsien had, over the last fifty years, begun to move away to town. Elsewhere in China the process had already run its course. In much of Southeast China, landlords had interposed between themselves and the dependent peasantry a corps of agents who collect rent or interest, and hire or remunerate labor on an impersonal basis. They were thus able to respond to the promptings of the market, but at the cost of insulating themselves completely from the populace and from any noneconomic cues regarding its condition.

The Chinese case is but a paradigm for a general process, at work in all six cases we have encountered. The economic mediators are bearers of the process of monetization and the agents of social dissolution; at the same time their obedience to the market demands that they maximize returns, regardless of the immediate consequences of their actions. By rendering the process of commodity-formation bureaucratic and impersonal, they remove themselves physically from these consequences; at the same time they lose their ability to respond to social cues from the affected population. Instead, they couple economic callousness with a particular kind of structurally induced stupidity, the kind of stupidity which ascribes to the people themselves responsibility for the evils to which they are subject. Defensive stereotypes take the place of analytical intelligence, in one of those classical cases of blindness with which the gods strike those whom they wish to destroy.

At the very same time, the political mediators who man the relays of power connecting state and village also face increased uncertainty. The traditional power holders—be they mandarins or aristocrats—have had their power curtailed, unless they enter into collusion with economic agents to their mutual advantage and to the disadvantage of the state. In either case, however, they can no longer shield the local populations against encroachment from outside, a role which in the past often redounded to their own interests. The new power holders, on the other hand, find their exercise of power already shorn of effectiveness by the axiom that economic transformation takes precedence over social order. If they are aware of social dislocations caused by the spread of the market, they may be able to raise their voice in protest, but they cannot—at the cost of losing their position—stop them of their own accord. They thus lack control over the decisive processes which affect society; this would involve the mobilization of dissatisfied populations against a state of which they are the primary beneficiaries. They are thus caught up in the characteristic conflict between "formal" and "substantive" bureaucracy, between the operations of a bureaucracy which merely administers rules, and operations which answer to the strategic issues of social coordination and conflict. Like the economic power holders they retreat from participation in the existential problems of the population into the protective carapace provided by the administrative machinery. At best they can keep their ear "to the ground" through the use of police spies and informants, not to cope with the causes of unrest, but to curtail its symptoms. In a situation in which they have abdicated the power to formulate new goals and to marshal resources as means to these goals, they retreat into administration. Their social hallmark becomes *attentisme*, their slogan, as in the Vietnamese, to withdraw, "to wrap themselves in their blankets" (*trum men*).

Yet they are soon faced with competition from new social groups which begin to emphasize substantive problems against purely administrative ones. Some of these are geared to the service of the new economic arrangements: comprador merchants, "financial experts," labor bosses, foremen. But in addition to these junior executives of the capitalist market in the dependent country, there also appear other groups, similarly sponsored by culture contact and answering to its new requirements: the petty officials of the state bureaucracy, the professionals, the schoolteachers. These share certain characteristics. For one thing, they are not involved in the transmission and sale of goods; they are purveyors of skills. These skills are only in the rarest of cases traditional within the society; they are much more likely to have been learned from the West or from Western-type educational institutions established within the dependency. Moreover, these skills are based on literacy, of specialized acquaintance with a corpus of literature which departs from the traditions of the country and suggests new alternatives. Within the traditional society literacy was in most cases a hallmark of high status. The new literati partake of the reflected glory of this traditional evaluation of literacy, but at the same time their acquaintance with nontraditional sources makes them participants in a communication process which far outstrips the inherited canons of knowledge. They operate in a communication field vastly larger than that of the past, and full of new learning which suggests powerful visions not dreamed of in the inherited ideology.

At the same time, they are caught up in professional predicaments. Many of them do not find employment, or must supplement their professional work with other sources of endeavor. Yet if they do they find themselves in direct communication with clients whose problems they must to some extent make their own; they are caught up in the strain between the demands placed upon them and their limited ability "to do anything" about them. The petty official is limited in his freedom of action by bureaucratic restraints; the professional, the teacher, and the lawyer soon become aware that they are limited to coping with symptoms, but do not have a handle on the conditions which produce these symptoms. Moreover, their clients are drawn from society at large, rather than being confined to any particular group to which they might be tied by heredity or tradition. They thus confront a situation in which they answer to a much larger social field and communication network than the traditional power holder, and yet experience every day the very real limitations on their power. Finally, they suffer directly from the crisis of power and authority. A member of such a group is apt to evince a deep preoccupation with authority. Even though he seeks and seems actually to break away from the authority of the powerful traditions in which he was brought up, the intellectual of under-developed countries, still more than his confrere in more advanced countries, retains the need for incorporation into some self-transcending, authoritative entity. Indeed, the greater his struggle for emancipation from the traditional collectivity, the greater his need for incorporation into a new, alternative collectivity. Intense politicization meets this need (Shils, 1962, 205).

For such "marginal men" political movements often provide a "home," of which they are otherwise deprived by their own skill, their social positions, and their divorce from traditional sources of power. Increasingly, these "intellectuals" of the new order press their claims against both economic and political power holders. What they need is a constituency; and that constituency is ulti-mately provided by the industrial workers and dissatisfied peasants whom the market created, but for whom society made no adequate social provision. In all of our six cases we witness such a fusion between the "rootless" intellectuals and their rural supporters.

Yet this fusion is not effected easily (see Hindley, 1965). The peasant is especially handicapped in passing from passive recogni-tion of wrongs to political participation as a means for setting them right. First, a peasant's work is most often done alone, on his own land, than in conjunction with his fellows. Moreover, all peasants are to some extent competitors, for available resources within the community as well as for sources of credit from without. Second, the tyranny of work weighs heavily upon a peasant: his life is geared to an annual routine and to planning for the year to come. Momentary alterations of routine threaten his ability to take up the routine later. Third, control of land enables him, more often than not, to retreat into subsistence production should adverse conditions affect his market crop. Fourth, ties of extended kinship and mutual aid within the community may cushion the shocks of dislocation. Fifth, peasant interests—especially among poor peasants—often crosscut class alignments. Rich and poor peasants may be kinfolk, or a peasant may be at one and the same time owner, renter, sharecropper, laborer for his neighbors and seasonal hand on a nearby plantation. Each different involvement aligns him differently with his fellows and with the outside world. Finally, past exclusion of the peasant from participation in decision-making beyond the bamboo hedge of his village deprives him all too often of the knowledge needed to articulate his interests with appropriate forms of action. Hence, peasants are often merely passive spectators of political struggles or long for the sudden advent of a millennium, without specifying for themselves and their neighbors the many rungs on the staircase to heaven. But, ultimately, the decisive factor in making a peasant rebellion possible lies in the relation of the peasantry to the field of power which surrounds it. A rebellion cannot start from a situation of complete impotence; the powerless are easy victims. Power, as Richard Adams has said (1966, 3–4),

> refers to the control that one party holds over the environment of another party . . . power ultimately refers to an actual physical control that one party may have with respect to another. The reason that most relationships are not reduced to physical struggles is that parties to them can make rational decisions based on their estimates of tactical power and other factors. Power is usually exercised, therefore, through the common recognition by two parties of the tactical control each has, and through rational decision by one to do what the other wants. Each estimates his own tactical control, compares it to the other, and decides he may or may not be superior.

The poor peasant or the landless laborer who depends on a landlord for the largest part of his livelihood, or the totality of it, has no tactical power: he is completely within the power domain of his employer, without sufficient resources of his own to serve him as resources in the power struggle. Poor peasants and landless laborers, therefore, are unlikely to pursue the course of rebellion, *unless* they are able to rely on some external power to challenge the power which constrains them. Such external power is represented in the Mexican case by the Constitutionalist army in Yucatán which liberated the peons from debt bondage by action "from above"; by the collapse of the Russian Army in 1917 and the reflux of the peasant soldiery, weapons in hand, into the villages; by the creation of the Chinese Red Army as an instrument designed to break up landlord power in the villages. Where such external power is present, the poor peasant and landless laborer have latitude of movement; where it is absent, they are under near-complete constraint. The rich peasant, in turn, is unlikely to embark on the course of rebellion. As employer of the labor of others, as money lender, as notable co-opted by the state machine, he exercises local power in alliance with external power holders. His power domain within the village is derivative: it depends on the maintenance of their domains outside the village. Only when an external force, such as the Chinese Red Army, proves capable of destroying these other superior power domains, will the rich peasant lend his support to an uprising. The only component of the peasantry which does have some internal leverage is either landowning "middle peasantry" or a peasantry located in a peripheral area outside the domains of landlord control. Middle peasantry refers to a peasant population which has secure access to land of its own and cultivates it with family labor. Where these middle peasant holdings lie within the power domain of a superior, possession of their own resources provides their holders with the minimal tactical freedom required to challenge their overlord (see Alavi, 1965). The same, however, holds for a peasantry, poor or "middle," whose settlements are only under marginal control from the outside. Here landholdings may be insufficient for the support of the peasant household; but subsidiary activities such as casual labor, smuggling, livestock raising—not under the direct constraint of an external power domain—supplement land in sufficient quantity to grant the peasantry some latitude of movement. We have marked the existence of such a tactically mobile peasantry in the villages of Morelos, in the communes of the Central Agricultural Region of Russia; in the northern bastion established by the Chinese Communists after the Long March; as a basis for rebellion in Viet Nam; among the fellahin of Algeria; and among the squatters of Oriente in Cuba.

Yet this recruitment of a "tactically mobile peasantry" among the middle peasants and the "free" peasants of peripheral areas poses a curious paradox. This is also the peasantry in whom anthropologists and rural sociologists have tended to see the main bearers of peasant tradition. If our account is correct, then—strange to say—it is precisely this culturally conservative stratum which is the most instrumental in dynamiting the peasant social order. This paradox dissolves, however, when we consider that it is also the middle peasant who is relatively the most vulnerable to economic changes wrought by commercialism, while his social relations remain encased within the traditional design. His is a balancing act in which his balance is continuously threatened by population growth; by the encroachment of rival landlords; by the loss of rights to grazing, forest, and water; by falling prices and unfavorable conditions of the market; by interest payments and foreclosures. Moreover, it is precisely this stratum which most depends on traditional social relations of kin and mutual aid between neighbors; middle peasants suffer most when these are abrogated, just as they are least able to withstand the depredations of tax collectors or landlords.

Finally—and this is again paradoxical—middle peasants are also the most exposed to influences from the developing proletariat. The poor peasant or landless laborer, in going to the city or factory, also usually cuts his tie with the land. The middle peasant, however, stays on the land and sends his children to work in town; he is caught in a situation in which one part of the family retains a footing in agriculture, while the other undergoes "the training of the cities" (Germaine Tillion). This makes the middle peasant a transmitter also of urban unrest and political ideas. The point bears elaboration. It is probably not so much the growth of an industrial proletariat as such which produces revolutionary activity, as the development of an industrial work force still closely geared to life in the villages.

Thus it is the very attempt of the middle and free peasant to remain traditional which makes him revolutionary.

If we now follow out the hypothesis that it is middle peasants and poor but "free" peasants, not constrained by any power domain, which constitute the pivotal groupings for peasant uprisings, then it follows that any factor which serves to increase the latitude granted by that tactical mobility reinforces their revolutionary potential. One of these factors is peripheral location with regard to the center of state control. In fact, frontier areas quite often show a tendency to rebel against the central authorities, regardless of whether they are inhabited by peasants or not. South China has constituted a hearth of rebellion within the Chinese state, partly because it was first a frontier area in the southward march of the Han people, and later because it provided the main zone of contact between Western and Chinese civilization. The Mexican north has similarly been a zone of dissidence from the center in Mexico City, partly because its economy was based on mining and cattle raising rather than maize agriculture, partly because it was open to influences from the United States to the north. In the Chinese south it was dissident gentry with a peasant following which frequently made trouble for the center; in the Mexican north it was incipient businessmen, ranchers, and cowboys. Yet where you have a poor peasantry located in such a peripheral area beyond the normal control of the central power, the tactical mobility of such a peasantry is added to by its location. This has been the case with Morelos, in Mexico; Nghe An Province in Viet Nam; Kabylia in Algeria; and Oriente in Cuba. The tactical effectiveness of such areas is strengthened still further if they contain defensible mountainous redoubts: this has been true of Morelos, Kabylia, and Oriente. The effect is reinforced where the population of these redoubts differs ethnically or linguistically from the surrounding population. Thus we find that the villagers of Morelos were Nahuatl-speakers, the inhabitants of Kabylia, Berber-speakers. Oriente Province showed no linguistic differences from the Spanish spoken in Cuba, but it did contain a significant Afro-Cuban element. Ethnic distinctions enhance the solidarity of the rebels; possession of a special linguistic code provides for an autonomous system of communication.

It is important, however, to recognize that separation from the state or the surrounding populace need not be only physical or cultural. The Russian and the Mexican cases both demonstrate that it is possible to develop a solid enclave population of peasantry through state reliance on a combination of communal autonomy with the provision of community services to the state. The organization of the peasantry into self-administering communes with stipulated responsibilities to state and landlords created in both cases veritable fortresses of peasant tradition within the body of the country itself. Held fast by the surrounding structure, they acted as sizzling pressure cookers of unrest which, at the moment of explosion, vented their force outward to secure more living space for their customary corporate way of life. Thus we can add an additional multiplier effect to the others just cited. The presence of any one of these will raise the peasant potential for rebellion.

But what of the transition from peasant rebellion to revolution, from a movement aimed at the redress of wrongs, to the attempted overthrow of society itself? Marxists have long argued that peasants without outside leadership cannot make a revolution; and our case material would bear them out. Where the peasantry has successfully rebelled against the established order—under its own banner and with its own leaders—it was sometimes able to reshape the social structure of the countryside closer to its heart's desires; but it did not lay hold of the state, of the cities which house the centers of control, of the strategic nonagricultural resources of the society. Zapata stayed in his Morelos; the "folk migration" of Pancho Villa receded after the defeat at Torreón; Nestor Makhno stopped short of the cities; and the Russian peasants of the Central Agricultural Region simply burrowed more deeply into their local communes. Thus a peasant rebellion which takes place in a complex society already caught up in commercialization and industrialization tends to be self-limiting, and, hence, anachronistic.

The peasant utopia is the free village, untrammeled by tax collectors, labor recruiters, large landowners, officials. Ruled over, but never ruling, they also lack acquaintance with the operation of the state as a complex machinery, experiencing it only as a "cold monster." Against this hostile force, they had learned, even their traditional power holders provided but a weak shield, even though they were on occasion willing to defend them if it proved to their own interest. Thus, for the peasant, the state is a negative quantity, an evil, to be replaced in short shrift by their own "homemade" social order. That order, they believe, can run without the state; hence, peasants in rebellion are natural anarchists.

Often this political perspective is reinforced still further by a wider ideological vision. The peasant experience tends to be dualistic, in that he is caught between his understanding of how the world ought to be properly ordered and the realities of a mundane existence, beset by disorder. Against this disorder, the peasant has always set his dreams of deliverance, the vision of a Mahdi who would deliver the world from tyranny, of a Son of Heaven who would truly embody the mandate of heaven, of a "white tsar" as against the "black tsar" of the disordered present (Sarkisyanz, 1955). Under conditions of modern dislocation, the disordered present is all too frequently experienced as world order reversed, and hence evil. The dualism of the past easily fuses with the dualism of the present. The true order is yet to come, whether through miraculous intervention, through rebellion, or both. Peasant anarchism and an apocalyptic vision of the world, together, provide the ideological fuel that drives the rebellious peasantry.

But the peasant rebellions of the twentieth century are no longer simple responses to local problems, if indeed they ever were. They are but the parochial reactions to major social dislocations, set in motion by overwhelming societal change. The spread of the market has torn men up by their roots, and shaken them loose from the social relationships into which they were born. Industrialization and expanded communication have given rise to new social clusters, as yet unsure of their own social positions and interests, but forced by the imbalance of their lives to seek a new adjustment. Traditional political authority has eroded or collapsed; new contenders for power are seeking new constituencies for entry into the vacant political arena. Thus when the peasant protagonist lights the torch of rebellion, the edifice of society is already smoldering and ready to take fire. When the battle is over, the structure will not be the same.

No cultural system—no complex of economy, society, polity,

and ideology—is ever static; all of its component parts are in constant change. Yet as long as these changes remain within tolerable limits, the over-all system persists. If they begin to exceed these limits, however, or if other components are suddenly introduced from outside, the system is thrown out of kilter. The parts of the system are rendered inconsistent with each other; the system grows incoherent. Men in such a situation are caught painfully between various old solutions to problems which have suddenly shifted shape and meaning, and new solutions to problems they often cannot comprehend. Since incoherence rarely appears all at once, in all parts of the system, they may for some time follow now one alternative, now another and contradictory one; but in the end a breach, a major disjuncture will make its appearance somewhere in the system (Wilson and Wilson, 1945, 125–129). A peasant uprising under such circumstances, for any of the reasons we have sketched, can, without conscious intent, bring the entire society to the state of collapse.

But in the cases which we have analyzed, we have encountered not only the peasant rebels, rising for "land and liberty." On the battlefield, the peasants also encounter other groups, most often the intelligentsia-in-arms, ready to benefit from the prevailing disorder in order to impose on it a new order of their own. Two organizational phenomena, over and above the armed peasant band, make their appearance in our case histories; one is the military organization; the other is the para-military party organized around a certain vision of what the new society is to be. Yet our cases also show marked differences in the way these two organizational forms are conjugated with each other.

In the Mexican case, final victory was won neither by Zapata's guerrillas nor by Villa's cowboy *dorados*. The palm of success went to a civilian-military leadership in control of a specialized army— separate and distinct from any *levée en masse* of the peasantry; equipped with a rudimentary experience in bureaucratic management; and in possession of the strategic resources of Mexico's export trade. As a result this "revolutionary family" of civilians-turned-generals proved able to construct a new apparatus of central control which transformed itself over time from a coalition of military commanders into a unitary official party. This party, in turn, used the state to give support to rising clusters of entrepreneurs and professionals, while at the same time allocating a share of the proceeds from capitalist development to previously unrepresented agricultural and industrial groups in the interests of "social justice." A somewhat similar course was followed in Algeria. Although the Algerian nationalists began the war as a guerrilla operation closely linked to the villages of the hinterland, French success in reducing the guerrilla threat within the country finally placed the external army in Tunis and Morocco in command of the country, as the only remaining organized body in the new independent polity. Efforts to organize the wartime coalition of nationalists against the French into a monolithic party "after the fact" met with failure. Thus it fell to the army to stabilize the society. While a socialist rhetoric was used to promise a measure of reward to peasants and workers, as in Mexico, the state has placed its reliance on a guided maximization of private enterprise. In both these cases, then, the peasant rebellions of the hinterland set fire to the pre-existing structure; but it fell to the army and its leadership to forge the organizational balance wheel which would enable the post-revolutionary society to continue on its course.

In Russia, China, and Viet Nam, however, we must note that the roles of army and party were reversed. In these three cases, it was the political parties of middle-class revolutionaries who engineered the seizure of power and created the social and military instruments which conquered the state, and ensured transition to a new social order. It is probably not an accident that these are also three countries which were characterized by patterns of conspiratorial and secret societies before the advent of revolution. Furthermore, a common Marxist ideology—and especially the Leninist concept of the revolutionary leadership, leading the masses in the interest of the masses—furnished a ready-made idiom in which to cast their own experience of fusion between rebel soldiery and revolutionary leadership. Such common denominators also facilitated rapid learning and transfer of successful patterns from one situation to another. It is here—and only here—that the party as a separate body comes to dominate the other organizations thrown up by the revolution.

Yet there are also important distinctions between the Russian experience on the one hand, and the Chinese and Vietnamese experience on the other. In Russia the Communist party seized power on the crest of worker uprisings in the cities and organized the state for a war in defense of the revolution. The peasantry, in the meantime, staged its own uprisings in the countryside, parallel with the industrial insurrection in the cities, but in essential independence of them. Linking their village councils as village soviets to the soviet structure in name, they in fact simply expanded their living space and traditional organizations over the countryside. The war in defense of the revolution then followed the seizure of power; it did not accompany it. In marked contrast to China and Viet Nam, the Red Army—by putting a military shield around the central peasant regions, in defense against the periphery—reinforced still further the "settling-in" process of the rebellious peasants.

In China and Viet Nam, however, we not only find warfare directed by the party, but a kind of warfare which organizes the peasant population as it proceeds. Again special cultural predispositions appear to have been at work: these are areas in which manifold village associations have always been traditional in the villages. Under Communist control these came to serve as a template for welding army and peasantry into a common body. This common organizational grid—connecting the centralized army mainly recruited from the peasantry, the part-time guerrilla forces stationed in the villages, and the village population—both obviated the development of uncoordinated peasant revolts and the autonomous entrenchment of the peasantry which had occurred in Russia. It proved to be a system capable not only of withstanding prolonged warfare, but of even thriving upon it. It can be argued that this organizational grid gains in strength as it is engaged in combat, as evidenced both by Chinese Communist resistance to the Japanese invasion and by the Vietnamese experience over the last twenty years.

Finally, in the Cuban case, we find an island not populated primarily by peasants, but by a wage-working sugar proletariat. Organized into trade-unions by Communists—and under their continuing influence—the sugar proletariat, however, did little to assist the rebellion. The Communist party and allied organizations were, together with other groups, caught in a political deadlock in which no one group possessed sufficient independent leverage to break out of the governmental spoils system. This leverage was provided instead by a small group of armed rebels who, very much by accident, had established themselves in the one part of the island inhabited by a tactically mobile peasantry. Once in power, this rebel group could make use of the Communist party apparatus to provide a new organizational grid for the country and to carry through a social revolution in an unusual symbiosis of rebel army and party organization.

The question of why in some cases it is the army which generates the new political controls, while in other situations this task falls to the party, has no easy answer. We found army controls to have been important in Mexico and Algeria. Perhaps it is no coincidence that these two societies continue to operate on the basis of the market: controls must fall upon society rather than upon the economy. The army furnishes the organizational pivot for the social order, but the economy is left unencumbered to develop according to the dictates of the market. Where both society and economy rest upon command, however, as in Russia, China, Viet Nam, and Cuba, the market is abrogated, and ideological considerations and appeals take the place of the "invisible hand" in moving men to action. For a long time Russia remained the model case of party dominance over the means and ends of command; yet recently China has moved in a quite different direction. In Russia, the party remained clearly dominant over the army; it even proved successful in checking the growth of a new quasi-army within its own ranks, when it curtailed the powers of the secret police. In China, after a period of initial fusion of party and army during the years of protracted war and in the initial years of consolidation after the revolution, party and army appear to have come into conflict during the Great Cultural Revolution, and party dominance has been curtailed. We may hazard a guess that this divergence is a function of the different development of the two revolutions, including their very different bases of social support (see Lowenthal, 1967, 387–388; Schram, 1967, 325, 341–342).

The Russian Revolution drew its main support from industrial workers in key industrial regions, and not from the peasantry. To the Russian Communists, control of the strategic heights of the economy remained a primary goal; and the rapid expansion of the scale and scope of these strategic heights through rapid industrialization, the main guarantee of Soviet continuity. To the extent that industrialization also aided effectiveness in warfare, the ends of party and army clearly coincided. Industry and school were seen as the two templates upon which Soviet Man was to be forged, and ideology was used primarily to fan the flames of forced-draft industrial progress. Industrialization went hand in hand with the growth of an effective managerial class and a population of skilled industrial workers. Emphasis was on differential reward for skill and labor. The outcome was a strongly hierarchical society, operated by technocrats, "experts and Red," but above all experts. China, too, embarked on a program of rapid industrialization, but from the beginning there seem to have been tensions between groups in the party which favored the Russian model of development, and those who, during the years of protracted war, had learned to put their faith in a peasant army with an egalitarian ideology. The experience of war in the hinterland had taken them far from cities and industrial areas; it had taught them the advantages of dispersal, of a wide distribution of basic skills rather than a dense concentration of advanced skills. The citizen-soldiers of the guerrilla army had, in fact, lived lives in which the roles of peasant, worker, soldier, and intellectual intermingled to the point of fusion. Moreover, army experience—rather than industry and school—had provided the inspiration to discipline and initiative, sacrifice and commitment. Where in Russia the peasant could become an effective member of the new order only by passing through the fiery ovens of industrialization, in China the relation of the peasant to the citizen-army was immediate and concrete. Perhaps it is for this reason that it was the People's Liberation Army which increasingly emerged as an effective counterforce to the ever more managerial and bureaucratic party. While any interpretations of the Great Cultural Revolution from the outside remain guesswork, it is at least clear that the role of the party in China has been greatly reduced in favor of a coalition of armed forces with local nonparty committees. Nor is this trend confined to China. A similar trend is evident in Cuba where Castro has studiously avoided the installation of a permanent managerial apparatus, pivoted upon the Communist party, and relied instead on the ongoing mobilization of a citizenry-in-arms. As in China, it is the rural area which furnishes the energy for this army-as-party, while the traditional urban center, Havana, loses in organizational importance. In both cases, it is too early to know whether this represents a relapse into rural romanticism, or whether such politicized militarization of the populace can lead—with the aid of modern means of communication—to new and viable forms of popular organization.

These considerations have taken us a long way from the parochial rebellions of the peasantry with which we began our study. Yet it has been the argument of these chapters that the peasant is an agent of forces larger than himself, forces produced by a disordered past as much as by a disordered present. There is no evidence for the view that if it were not for "outside agitators," the peasant would be at rest. On the contrary, the peasants rise to redress wrong; but the inequities against which they rebel are but, in turn, parochial manifestations of great social dislocations. Thus rebellion issues easily into revolution, massive movements to transform the social structure as a whole. The battlefield becomes society itself, and when the war is over, society will have changed and the peasantry with it. The peasant's role is thus essentially tragic: his efforts to undo a grievous present only usher in a vaster, more uncertain future. Yet if it is tragic, it is also full of hope. For the first time in millennia, human kind is moving toward a solution of the age-old problem of hunger and disease, and everywhere ancient monopolies of power and received wisdom are yielding to human effort to widen participation and knowledge. In such efforts—

however uncertain, however beset with difficulties, however ill-understood—there lies the prospect for increased life, for increased humanity. If the peasant rebels partake of tragedy, they also partake of hope, and to that extent theirs is the party of humanity. Arrayed against them, however, are now not merely the defenders of ancient privileges, but the Holy Alliance of those who—with superior technology and superior organization—would bury that hope under an avalanche of power. These new engineers of power call themselves realists, but it is a hallmark of their realism that it admits no evidence and interpretation other than that which serves their purposes. The peasantry confronts tragedy, but hope is on its side; doubly tragic are their adversaries who would deny that hope to both peasantry and to themselves. This also is America's dilemma in the world today: to act in aid of human hope or to crush it, not only for the world's sake but for her own.

BIBLIOGRAPHY

MEXICO

Barrera Fuentes, Florencio, 1955, *Historia de la Revolución Mexicana: la etapa precursora*, Biblioteca del Instituto Nacional de Estudios históricos de la Revolución Mexicana, Talleres Gráficos de la Nación, Mexico.

Berzunza Pinto, Ramón, 1956, "Las vísperas yucatecas de la Revolución," *Historia Mexicana*, Vol. 6, pp. 75–88.

——, 1962, "El constitucionalismo en Yucatán," *Historia Mexicana*, Vol. 12, pp. 274–295.

Bulnes, Francisco, 1904, *Las grandes mentiras de nuestra historia: la nación y el ejército en las guerras extranjeras*, Librería de la Vda. de Ch. Bouret, Paris.

——, 1920, *El Verdadero Díaz y la Revolución*, Editorial Hispano-Mexicana, Mexico.

Chevalier, François, 1959, "Survivances seigneuriales et présages de la révolution agraire dans le Nord du Mexique," *Revue Historique*, Vol. 122, pp. 1–18.

——, 1961, "Le soulèvement de Zapata (1911–1919)," *Annales*, Vol. 16, pp. 66–82.

Cué Cánovas, Agustín, 1947, *Historia social y económica de México: la Revolución de Independencia y México Independiente hasta 1854*, Editorial América, Mexico.

Cumberland, Charles C., 1952, *Mexican Revolution: Genesis under Madero*, University of Texas Press, Austin.

——, 1960, "Sonora Chinese and the Mexican Revolution," *Hispanic American Historical Review*, Vol. 40, pp. 191–211.

——, 1968, *Mexico: The Struggle for Modernity*, Oxford University Press, New York and London.

Diez, Domingo, 1967, *Bosquejo Histórico Geográfico de Morelos*, Editorial Tlahuica, Cuernavaca.

Dillon, Richard H., 1956, "Del rancho a la presidencia," *Historia Mexicana*, Vol. 6, pp. 256–269.

Figueroa Domenech, J., 1899, *Guía general descriptiva de la Republica Mexicana: Historia, Geografía, Estadística*, 2 vols., Ramón de S.N. Araluce, Mexico.

Friedrich, Paul, 1966, "Revolutionary Politics and Communal Ritual," in Marc J. Swartz, Victor W. Turner, and Arthur Tuden, eds., *Political Anthropology*, Aldine Publishing Co., Chicago, pp. 191–220.

González Navarro, Moises, 1957, *El Porfiriato: La Vida Social*, Vol. 4 of Daniel Cosío Villegas, ed., *Historia Moderna de México*, Editorial Hermes, Mexico.

Iturriaga, José E., 1951, *La Estructura Social y Cultural de México*, Fondo de Cultura Económica, Mexico.

Katz, Friedrich, 1964, *Deutschland, Díaz, und die mexikanische Revolution*, VEB Deutscher Verlag der Wissenschaften, Berlin.

Lewis, Oscar, 1951, *Life in a Mexican Village: Tepoztlan Restudied*, University of Illinois Press, Urbana.

Lister, Florence C., and Robert H. Lister, 1966, *Chihuahua: Storehouse of Storms*, University of New Mexico Press, Albuquerque.

McBride, George McCutchen, 1923, *The Land Systems of Mexico*, American Geographical Society Research Series No. 12, American Geographical Society, New York.

Meyer, Michael C., 1967, *Mexican Rebel: Pascual Orozco and the Mexican Revolution 1910–1915*, University of Nebraska Press, Lincoln.

Molina, Enríquez, Renato, 1932, "La Revolución y los ferrocarriles en México," *El Economista*, Vol. 9, No. 113 (Dec. 8), pp. 291–292.

Mora, José M. L., 1837, *Obras sueltas*, 2 vols., Librería de Rosa, Paris.

Nava Otero, Guadalupe, 1965, "La Minería," in Daniel Cosío Villegas, ed., *Historia Moderna de México*, Vol. 7, Part 1: *El Porfiriato, La Vida Económica*, Editorial Hermes, Mexico, pp. 179–310.

Paz, Octavio, 1961, *The Labyrinth of Solitude*, Grove Press, New York.

Pfeifer, Gottfried, 1939, "Sinaloa und Sonora," *Mitteilungen der Geographischen Gesellschaft in Hamburg*, Vol. 46, pp. 289–460.

Phipps, Helen, 1925, *Some Aspects of the Agrarian Revolution in Mexico: A Historical Study*, University of Texas, Austin.

Pimentel, Francisco, 1866, *La economía política aplicada á la propriedad territorial en México*, Imprenta de Ignacio Cumplido, Mexico.

Pinchon, Edgcumb, 1941, *Zapata, the Unconquerable*, Doubleday, Doran and Co., New York.

Quirk, Robert E., 1953, "Liberales y Radicales en la Revolución Mexicana," *Historia Mexicana*, Vol. 2, pp. 503–528.

———, 1960. *The Mexican Revolution, 1914–1915: The Convention of Aguascalientes*, Indiana University Press, Bloomington.

Sierra, Justo, 1950, *Evolución política del pueblo Mexicano*, Fondo de Cultura Económica, Mexico.

Simpson, Eyler, 1937, *The Ejido*, University of North Carolina Press, Chapel Hill.

Sotelo Inclán, Jesús, 1943, *Raíz y razón de Zapata*, Editorial Etnos, Mexico.

Southworth, John R., 1910, *El Directorio oficial de las minas y haciendas de Mexico*, Mexico.

Tannenbaum, Frank, 1937, *Peace by Revolution: An Interpretation of Mexico*, Columbia University Press, New York.

Whetten, Nathan L., 1948, *Rural Mexico*, University of Chicago Press, Chicago.

Wolf, Eric R., 1958, "The Virgin of Guadalupe: A Mexican National Symbol," *Journal of American Folklore*, Vol. 71, pp. 34–39.

———, 1959, *Sons of the Shaking Earth*, University of Chicago Press, Chicago and London.

Zavala, Silvio, 1940–41, "México. La Revolución. La Independencia. La Constitución de 1824," in Ricardo Levene, ed., *Historia de América*, Jackson, Buenos Aires, Vol. 7, pp. 3–96.

RUSSIA

Anweiler, Oscar, 1958, *Die Rätebewegung in Russland 1905–1921*, Studien zur Geschichte Osteuropas V, Brill, Leiden.

Avrich, Paul, 1967, *The Russian Anarchists*, Princeton University Press, Princeton; Oxford University Press, London.

Berdiaiev, Nikolai A., 1937, *The Origin of Russian Communism*, Centenary Press, London.

Bill, Valentine T., 1959, *The Forgotten Class: The Russian Bourgeoisie from the Beginnings to 1900*, Praeger, New York.

Chamberlin, William H., 1957, *The Russian Revolution 1917–1921*, 2 vols., Macmillan, New York.

Confino, Michael, 1963, *Domaines et seigneurs en Russie vers la fin du XVIIIᵉ siècle: Etude de structures agraires et de mentalité économique*, Institut d'Etudes Slaves de l'Université de Paris, Collection Historique, Vol. 18, Paris.

Deutscher, Isaac, 1954, *The Prophet Armed: Trotsky 1879–1921*, Oxford University Press, New York and London.

Dunn, Stephen P., and Ethel Dunn, 1963, "The Great Russian Peasant: Culture Change or Cultural Development," *Ethnology*, Vol. 2, No. 3, pp. 320–338.

———, 1967, *The Peasants of Central Russia*, Holt, Rinehart and Winston, New York and London.

Elisséeff, Serge, 1956, "The Orthodox Church and the Russian Merchant Class," *Harvard Theological Review*, Vol. 49, pp. 185–205.

Fainsod, Merle, 1958, *Smolensk Under Soviet Rule*, Harvard University Press, Cambridge, Mass.; Macmillan, London.

Fischer, George, 1960, "The Intelligentsia and Russia," in Cyril E. Black, ed., *The Transformation of Russian Society*, Harvard University Press, Cambridge, pp. 253–274.

Footman, David, 1962, *Civil War in Russia*, Faber and Faber, London.

Gordon, Manya, 1941, *Workers Before and After Lenin*, Dutton, New York.

Gorer, Geoffrey, and John Rickman, 1951, *The People of Great Russia*, Chanticleer, New York; Cresset Press, London.

Harcave, Sidney S., 1964, *First Blood: The Russian Revolution of 1905*, Macmillan, New York; Bodley Head, London.

Hobsbawm, Eric J., 1962, *The Age of Revolution 1789–1848*, Weidenfeld and Nicolson, London.

Inkeles, Alex, 1960, "Summary and Review: Social Stratification in the Modernization of Russia," in Cyril E. Black, ed., *The Transformation of Russian Society*, Harvard University Press, Cambridge, Mass. and London. pp. 338–350.

Leroy-Beaulieu, Anatole, 1962 [selections from writings 1881–1889], *The Russian Peasant*, Coronado Press, Sandoval, N. Mexico.

Lukacs, John, 1967, "A Dissenting View of the Day That Shook the World," *The New York Times Magazine*, Oct. 22, pp. 32–33, 70–79, 82–89.

Luxemburg, Rosa, 1940, *The Russian Revolution*, Workers Age Publishers, New York.

Lyashchenko, Peter I., 1949, *History of the National Economy of Russia to the 1917 Revolution*, Macmillan, New York.

Male, D. J., 1963, "The Village Community 1924–1930," *Soviet Studies*, Vol. 15, pp. 225–246.

Malia, Martin, 1961, "What Is the Intelligentsia?" in Richard Pipes, ed., *The Russian Intelligentsia*, Columbia University Press, New York, pp. 1–18.

Maynard, Sir John, 1962, *The Russian Peasant and Other Studies*, Collier, New York and London.

Miliukov, Paul, 1962, *Russia and Its Crisis*, Collier, New York.

Mitrany, David, 1961, *Marx Against the Peasant: A Study in Social Dogmatism*, Collier, New York.

Owen, Launcelot A., 1963, *The Russian Peasant Movement 1906–1917*, King, London.

Prawdin, Michael, 1961, *The Unmentionable Nechaev: A Key to Bolshevism*, Allen and Unwin, London.

Radkey, Oliver H., 1958, *The Agrarian Foes of Bolshevism: Promise and Default of the Russian Socialist Revolutionaries February to October 1917*, Columbia University Press, New York & London.

———, 1963, *The Sickle under the Hammer: The Russian Socialist Revolutionaries in the Early Months of Soviet Rule*, Columbia University Press, New York and London.

Raeff, Marc, 1966, *Origins of the Russian Intelligentsia: The Eighteenth-Century Nobility*, Harcourt-Brace and World, New York.

Robinson, Geroid T., 1949, *Rural Russia under the Old Regime: A History of the Landlord-Peasant World and a Prologue to the Peasant Revolution of 1917*, Longmans, Green and Co., New York.

Tompkins, Stuart R., 1957, *The Russian Intelligentsia: Makers of the Revolutionary State*, University of Oklahoma Press, Norman.

Treadgold, Donald W., 1957, *The Great Siberian Migration: Government and Peasant in Resettlement from Emancipation to the First World War*, Princeton University Press, Princeton, N.J.

Trotsky, Leon, 1932, *The History of the Russian Revolution*, The University of Michigan Press, Ann Arbor; Gollancz, London.

Ungern-Sternberg, R. von, 1956, "Die Struktur der russischen Gesellschaft zu Beginn des XX Jahrhunderts," *Schmollers Jahrbuch*, Vol. 76, pp. 169–197.

Vakar, Nicholas P., 1962, *The Taproot of Soviet Society: The impact of Russia's culture upon the Soviet State*, Harper and Row, New York and London.

Volin, Lazar, 1940, "The Peasant Household under the Mir and the Kolkhoz in Modern Russian History," in Caroline Ware, ed., *The Cultural Approach to History*, Columbia University Press, New York, pp. 125–139.

———, 1960, "The Russian Peasant from Emancipation to Kolkhoz," in Cyril E. Black, ed., *The Transformation of Russian Society*, Harvard University Press, Cambridge, Mass. and London. pp. 292–310.

Wallace, Sir Donald Mackenzie, 1908, *Russia*, Holt, New York.

Wesson, Robert G., 1963, *Soviet Communes*, Rutgers University Press, New Brunswick.

Yaresh, Leo, 1957, "The 'Peasant Wars' in Soviet Historiography," *American Slavic and East European Review*, Vol. 16, pp. 241–259.

CHINA

Balazs, Etienne, 1964, *Chinese Civilization and Bureaucracy*, Yale University Press, New Haven and London.

Buck, John Lossing, 1930, *Chinese Farm Economy*, University of Chicago Press, Chicago.

———, 1937, *Land Utilization in China*, University of Nanking, Nanking.

Chesneaux, Jean, 1962, *Le Mouvement Ouvrier Chinois de 1919 à 1927*, Mouton, The Hague.

Chow, Yung-Teh, 1966, *Social Mobility in China: Status Careers Among the Gentry in a Chinese Community*, Atherton Press, New York.

Crook, Isabel, and David Crook, 1959, *Revolution in a Chinese Village: Ten Mile Inn*, Routledge and Kegan Paul, London.

Eberhard, Wolfram, 1965, *Conquerors and Rulers: Social Forces in Medieval China*, Brill, Leiden.

Elegant, Robert S., 1963, *The Centre of the World: Communism and the Mind of China*, Methuen, London.

Fei, Hsiao-Tung, 1939, *Peasant Life in China: A Field Study of Country Life in the Yangtze Valley*, Kegan Paul, Trench, Trubner and Co., London.

Fei, Hsiao-Tung, and Chang Chih-I, 1945, *Earthbound China: A Study of Rural Economy in Yunnan*, University of Chicago Press, Chicago.

Feuerwerker, Albert, 1958, *China's Early Industrialization: Sheng Hsuan-huai (1844–1916) and Mandarin Enterprise*, Harvard University Press, Cambridge, Mass. and London.

———, 1968, *The Chinese Economy, 1912–1949*, Michigan Papers in Chinese Studies No. 1, Center for Chinese Studies, University of Michigan, Ann Arbor.

Fried, Morton H., 1952, "Chinese Society: Class as Subculture," *Transactions of the New York Academy of Sciences*, ser. II, Vol. 14, pp. 331–336.

———, 1953, *Fabric of Chinese Society: A Study of the Social Life of a Chinese County Seat*, Praeger, New York.

———, 1964, "Ideology, Social Organization and Economic Development in China: A Living Test of Theories," in Robert A. Manners, ed., *Process and Pattern in Culture, Essays in Honor of Julian H. Steward*, Aldine Publishing Co., Chicago, pp. 47–62.

Gamble, Sidney D., 1963, *North China Villages: social, political, and economic activities before 1933*, University of California Press, Berkeley.

Hofheinz Jr., Roy Mark, 1966, *The Peasant Movement and Rural Revolution: Chinese Communists in the Countryside (1923–7)*, Ph.D. Thesis, Department of Government, Harvard University.

Institute of Pacific Relations, 1939, *Agrarian China: Selected Source Materials from Chinese Authors*, George Allen and Unwin, London.

Isaacs, Harold R., 1966, *The Tragedy of the Chinese Revolution*, Atheneum, New York; Oxford University Press, London.

Israel, John, 1966, *Student Nationalism in China 1927–1937*, Stanford University Press, Stanford and London.

Johnson, Chalmers A., 1962, *Peasant Nationalism and Communist Power*, Stanford University Press, Stanford and London.

Karol, K. S., 1967, "Why the Cultural Revolution?" *Monthly Review*, Vol. 19, No. 4, pp. 22–34.

Laai Yi-faai, Franz Michael, and John C. Sherman, 1962, "The Use of Maps in Social Research: A Case Study in South China," *The Geographical Review*, Vol. 52, No. 1, pp. 92–111.

Landis, Richard B., 1964, "The Origins of Whampoa Graduates Who Served in the Northern Expedition," in Robert K. Sakai, ed., *Studies on Asia*, University of Nebraska Press, Lincoln, Vol. 5, pp. 149–163.

Lang, Olga, 1946, *Chinese Family and Society*, Yale University Press, New Haven.

Lattimore, Owen, and Eleanor Lattimore, 1944, "The Making of Modern China," *The Infantry Journal*, Washington, D.C.

Levenson, Joseph R., 1964, *Modern China and Its Confucian Past*, Anchor Books, Doubleday and Co., Garden City, N.Y.

Lindbeck, J. M. H., 1967, "Transformations in the Chinese Communist Party," in Donald W. Treadgold, *Soviet and Chinese Communism: Similarities and Differences*, University of Washington Press, Seattle, and London. pp. 73–104.

Loh, Pichon P. Y., ed., 1965, *The Kuomintang Debacle of 1949: Collapse or Conquest?* D. C. Heath, Boston; Harrap, London.

McColl, Robert W., 1964, *The Rise of Territorial Communism in China in 1921–1934: The Geography Behind Politics*, Ph.D. Thesis, Department of Geography, University of Washington, Seattle.

——, 1967, "The Oyüwan Soviet Area, 1927–1932," *Journal of Asian Studies*, Vol. 27, pp. 41–60.

Mao Tse-tung, 1965, *Selected Works*, Vol. 1, Foreign Languages Press, Peking.

Michael, Franz, 1964, "State and Society in Nineteenth-Century China," in Albert Feuerwerker, ed., *Modern China*, Prentice-Hall, Englewood Cliffs, N.J., pp. 57–69.

——, 1966, *The Taiping Rebellion: History and Documents*, Vol. 1, University of Washington Press, Seattle and London.

Miyakazi, Ichisada, 1963, "The Reforms of Wang An-Shih," in John Meskill, ed., *Wang An-shih—Practical Reformer?* D. C. Heath and Co., Boston, pp. 82–90.

Moise, Edwin, 1967, *The Economic Basis of Chinese Communism*, research paper written for Dr. Norma Diamond, Anthropology 458, University of Michigan, typescript.

Murphey, Rhoads, 1962, "The City as a Center of Change: Western Europe and China," in Philip L. Wagner and Marvin W. Mikesell, eds., *Readings in Cultural Geography*, University of Chicago Press, Chicago and London. pp. 330–341.

North, Robert C., with the collaboration of Ithiel de Sola Pool, 1965, "Kuomintang and Chinese Communist Elites," in Harold D. Lasswell and Daniel Lerner, eds., *World Revolutionary Elites*, M.I.T. Press, Cambridge, Mass. and London. pp. 317–455.

Rowntree, Joshua, 1905, *The Imperial Drug Trade*, Methuen, London.

Rue, John E., 1966, *Mao Tse-tung in Opposition, 1927–1935*, Stanford University Press, Stanford and London.

Schurmann, Franz, 1966, *Ideology and Organization in Communist China*, University of California Press, Berkeley and Los Angeles; Cambridge University Press, London.

Shih, Vincent Y. C., 1967, *The Taiping Ideology: Its Sources, Interpretations, and Influences*, University of Washington Press, Seattle.

Smedley, Agnes, 1956, *The Great Road: The Life and Times of Chu Teh*, Monthly Review Press, New York.

Snow, Edgar, 1938, *Red Star Over China*, Random House, New York; Gollancz, London.

Tawney, R. H., 1932, *Land and Labour in China*, George Allen and Unwin, London.

Tayler, J. B., 1928, *Farm and Factory in China: Aspects of the Industrial Revolution*, Student Christian Movement, London.

Wales Nym, 1939, *Inside Red China*, Doubleday, New York.

Wittfogel, Karl A., 1957, *Oriental Despotism*, Yale University Press.

VIET NAM

Arnault, Jacques, 1966, *Du colonialisme au socialisme*, Éditions sociales, Paris.

Benda, Henry J., 1965, "Peasant Movements in Colonial Southeast Asia," *Asian Studies*, Vol. 3, pp. 420–434.

Bodard, Lucien, 1967, *The Quicksand War: Prelude to Vietnam*, Little, Brown and Co., Boston.

Buttinger, Joseph, 1958, *The Smaller Dragon*, Pall Mall Press, London.

———, 1967, *Vietnam: A Dragon Embattled*, Pall Mall Press, London.

Chesneaux, Jean, 1955a, *Contribution à l'Histoire de la Nation Vietnamienne*, Éditions sociales, Paris.

———, 1955b, "Stages in the Development of the Vietnam National Movement 1862–1940," *Past and Present*, No. 7, pp. 63–75.

———, 1968, *Le Vietnam*, Maspero, Paris.

Devillers, Philippe, 1962, "The Struggle for Unification of Vietnam," *China Quarterly*, No. 9, pp. 2–23.

Fall, Bernard B., 1955, "The Political-Religious Sects of Viet-Nam," *Pacific Affairs*, Vol. 28, pp. 235–253.

———, 1960, *Le Viet-Minh. La République Démocratique du Viet-Nam 1945–1960*, Cahiers de la Fondation Nationale des Sciences Politiques, No. 106, Librairie Armand Colin, Paris.

———, 1967, *The Two Viet-Nams: A Political and Military Analysis*, Praeger, New York; Pall Mall Press, London.

Fishel, Wesley R., 1965, "Vietnam's Democratic One-Man Rule," in Marvin E. Gettleman, ed., *Viet Nam*, Fawcett Publications, Greenwich, Conn., pp. 195–204.

Henderson, William, 1968, "South Vietnam Finds Itself," in Wesley Fishel, ed., *Vietnam: Anatomy of a Conflict*, Peacock Publishers, Itasca, Ill., pp. 181–194.

Hendry, James B., 1964, *The Small World of Khanh Hau*, Aldine Publishing Co., Chicago.

Hickey, Gerald C., 1964, *Village in Vietnam*, Yale University Press, New Haven and London.

Hoang Van Chi, 1964, *From Colonialism to Communism: A Case History of North Vietnam*, Praeger, N.Y.; Pall Mall Press, London.

Jumper, Roy, and Nguyen Thi Hue, 1962, *Notes on the Political and Administrative History of Viet Nam 1802–1962*, Michigan State University Viet Nam Advisory Group, Saigon (mimeo.).

Kahin, George McT., and John W. Lewis, 1967, *The United States in Vietnam*, Dial Press, New York.

Lacouture, Jean, 1965, *Le Vietnam entre deux paix*, Éditions du Seuil, Paris.

———, 1968, *Ho Chi Minh, A Political Biography*, Random House, New York.

Le Chau, 1966a, *Le Viet Nam socialiste: une économie de transition*, Maspero, Paris.

———, 1966b, *La révolution paysanne du Sud Viet Nam*, Cahiers Libres No. 88, Maspero, Paris.

Le Thanh Khoi, 1955, *Le Viet-Nam. Histoire et Civilisation*, Les Éditions de Minuit, Paris.

Le Van Ho, 1962, "Introduction a l'ethnologie du Dinh, *Revue du sud-est asiatique*, No. 2, pp. 85–122.

McAlister, John T., 1966, *The Origins of the Vietnamese Revolution*, Ph.D. Thesis, Department of Political Science, Yale University, New Haven (available through University Microfilms, Ann Arbor, Michigan).

———, 1967, "Mountain Minorities and the Viet Minh: A Key to the Indochina War," in Peter Kunstadter, ed., *Southeast Asian Tribes, Minorities, and Nations*, Princeton University Press, Princeton, Vol. 2, pp. 771–844.

Mecklin, John, 1965, *Mission in Torment*, Doubleday and Co., Garden City, N.Y.

Mitchell, Edward J., 1967, *Land Tenure and Rebellion: A Statistical Analysis of Factors Affecting Government Control in South Vietnam*, Memorandum RM-5181-ARPA (Abridged), prepared for the Advanced Research Projects Agency, ARPA Order No. 189–1, June, Rand Corporation, Santa Monica, Calif.

Mus, Paul, 1952, Viet-Nam, *Sociologie d'une Guerre*, Éditions du Seuil, Paris.

Nghiem Dang, 1966, *Viet-Nam, Politics and Public Administration*, East-West Center Press, Honolulu.

Nguyen Duy Trinh, 1962, "A Highlight of the Movement," in *In the Enemy's Net: Memoirs from the Revolution*, Foreign Language Publishing House, Hanoi, pp. 9–42.

Nguyen Huu Khang, 1946, *La Commune Annamite: Etude Historique, Juridique et Economique*, Librairie du Recueil Sirey, Paris.

Pike, Douglas, 1966, *Viet Cong: The Organization and Techniques of the National Liberation Front of South Vietnam*, M.I.T. Press, Cambridge, Mass. and London.

Robequain, Charles, 1944, *The Economic Development of French Indo-China*, Oxford University Press, New York and London.

Sacks, I. Milton, 1959, "Marxism in Viet Nam," in Frank N. Trager, ed., *Marxism in Southeast Asia*, Stanford University Press, Stanford and London. pp. 102–170.

Shaplen, Robert, 1966, *The Lost Revolution: The United States in Vietnam, 1946–1966*, Harper & Row, New York; Deutsch, London.

Special Operations Research Office, 1964, *Case Studies in Insurgency and Revolutionary Warfare: Vietnam 1941–1954*, American University, Washington, D.C.

Tanham, George K., 1961, *Communist Revolutionary Warfare: The Vietminh in Indochina*, Praeger, New York and London.

Thompson, Virginia, 1947, *Labor Problems in Southeast Asia*, Yale University Press, New Haven.

ALGERIA

Aron, Robert, with François Lavagne, Janine Feller, and Yvette Garnier-Rizet, 1962, *Les Origines de la Guerre d'Algérie*, Fayard, Paris.

Bernard, Augustin, 1930, *L'Algérie*, in Gabriel Hanotaux and Alfred Martineau, eds., *Histoire des Colonies Françaises et de L'Expansion de la France dans les Monde*, Vol. 2, Plon, Paris.

Berque, Jacques, 1956, "Vers une étude du comportement en Afrique du Nord, *Révue Africaine*, No. 100, pp. 523–536.

Bourdieu, Pierre, 1960, "Guerre et Mutation Sociale en Algérie," *Etudes Méditerranéennes*, No. 7, pp. 25–37.

Boyer, Pierre, 1960, *L'Evolution de l'Algérie Médiane (Ancien Département d'Alger) de 1830 à 1956*, Librairie d'Amérique et ·d'Orient, Adrien-Maisonneuve, Paris.

Bromberger, Serge, 1958, *Les Rebelles Algériens*, Plon, Paris.

Charnay, Jean-Paul, 1965, *La Vie Musulmane en Algérie d'après la jurisprudence de la première moitié du XX siècle*, Presses Universitaires de France, Paris.

Daniel, Jean, 1962–63, "Echec algérien ou désillusion française," *La Nef*, year 19, Nos. 12–13, n.s., numéro special, pp. 125–138.

Delisle, René, 1962–63, "Les origines du F.L.N.," *La Nef*, year 19, Nos. 12–13, n.s., numéro special, pp. 19–32.

Fall, Bernard B., 1967, *The Two Viet-Nams*, Pall Mall Press, London.

Fanon, Frantz, 1963, *The Damned*, Présence Africaine, Paris.

Favret, Jeanne, 1967, "Le traditionalisme par excès de modernité," *Archives Européennes de Sociologie*, Vol. 8, pp. 71–93.

Favrod, Charles-Henri, 1962, *La F.L.N. et l'Algérie*, Plon, Paris.

Gellner, Ernest, 1963, "Saints of the Atlas," in Julian Pitt-Rivers, ed., *Mediterranean Countrymen*, Mouton, The Hague, pp. 145–157.

Gordon, David C., 1966, *The Passing of French Algeria*, Oxford University Press, New York and London.

Humbaraci, Arslan, 1966, *Algeria: A Revolution That Failed*, Praeger, New York; Pall Mall Press, London.

Julien, Charles-André, 1947, "Bugeaud," in Charles-André Julien, ed., *Les Techniciens de la Colonisation (XIX–XX siécles)*, Presses Universitaires de France, Paris, pp. 55–74.

Lacheraf, Mostafa, 1965, *L'Algérie: nation et société*, Maspero, Paris.

Launay, Michel, 1963, *Paysans Algériens: La Terre, La Vigne et les Hommes*, Éditions du Seuil, Paris.

Luethy, Herbert, 1957, *France Against Herself*, Meridian Books, New York.

Morizot, Jean, 1962, *L'Algérie Kabylisée*, Cahiers de l'Afrique et l'Asie, Vol. 6, Peyronnet, Paris.

Murray, Roger, and Tom Wengraf, 1963, "The Algerian Revolution," *New Left Review*, No. 22, pp. 14–65.

Nouschi, André, 1961, *Enquête sur le niveau de vie des populations rurales Constantinoises de la conquête jusqu'en 1919: Essai d'histoire économique et sociale*, Presses Universitaires de France, Paris.

———, 1962, *La Naissance du Nationalisme Algérien*, Les Éditions de Minuit, Paris.

Ouzegane, Amar, 1962, *Le Meilleur Combat*, René Juillard, Paris.

Soustelle, Jacques, 1956, *Aimée et Souffrante Algérie*, Plon, Paris.

Tillion, Germaine, 1961, *France and Algeria: Complementary Enemies*, Knopf, New York.

Yacono, Xavier, 1955, *La colonisation des Plaines du Chelif (De Lavigerie au confluent de la Mina)*, 2 vols., Université de Paris–Faculté des Lettres, Imprimerie E. Imbert, Alger.

CUBA

Álvarez Díaz, José A., ed., 1965, *A Study on Cuba*, University of Miami Press, Coral Gables.

Arnault, Jacques, 1966, *Du colonialisme au socialisme*, Editions sociales, Paris.

Blackburn, Robin, 1963, "Prologue to the Cuban Revolution," *New Left Review*, No. 21, pp. 52–91.

Blanksten, George I., 1962, "Fidel Castro and Latin America," in Morton A. Kaplan, ed., *The Revolution in World Politics*, Wiley & Sons, New York, pp. 113–136.

Carvajal, Juan F., 1950, "Observaciones sobre la clase media en Cuba," in Theo R. Crevenna, ed., *Materiales para el estudio de la clase media en la América Latina*, Vol. 2, Departamento de Asuntos Culturales, Unión Panamericana, Washington, D.C., pp. 31–44.

Coser, Lewis, 1956, *The Functions of Social Conflict*, Free Press, Glencoe, Ill.; Kegan Paul, London.

Draper, Theodore, 1965, *Castroism: Theory and Practice*, Praeger, New York; Pall Mall Press, London.

Economic and Technical Mission of the International Bank for Reconstruction and Development, 1951, *Report on Cuba*, Johns Hopkins Press, Baltimore.

Gil, Federico G., 1962, "Antecedents of the Cuban Revolution," *The Centennial Review of Arts and Science*, Vol. 6, pp. 373–393.

———, 1966, "Cuban Politics and Political Parties: 1933–1953," in Robert F. Smith, ed., *Background to Revolution: The Development of Modern Cuba*, Knopf, New York, pp. 149–156.

Goldenberg, Boris, 1965, *The Cuban Revolution and Latin America*, Praeger, New York; Allen and Unwin, London.

Guerra y Sánchez, Ramiro, 1964, *Sugar and Society in the Caribbean: An Economic History of Cuban Agriculture*, Yale University Press, New Haven and London.

Guevara, Ernesto "Che," 1968a, *Reminiscences of the Cuban Revolutionary War*, Monthly Review Press, New York and London.

———, 1968b, *Che Guevara Speaks: Selected Speeches and Writings*, Grove Press, New York.

Harbron, John D., 1965, "The Dilemma of an Elite Group: The Industrialist in Latin America," *Inter-American Economic Affairs*, Vol. 19, pp. 43–62.

Hennessy, C. A. M., 1966, "The Roots of Cuban Nationalism," in Robert F. Smith, ed., *Background to Revolution: The Development of Modern Cuba*, Knopf, New York, pp. 19–29.

Klein, Herbert S., 1967, *Slavery in the Americas: A Comparative Study of Virginia and Cuba*, University of Chicago Press, Chicago.

López Valdés, Rafael L., 1966, "La Sociedad Secreta 'Abacuá' en un grupo de obreros portuarios," *Etnología y Folklore* (La Habana), No. 2, pp. 5–26.

MacGaffey, Wyatt, and Clifford R. Barnett, 1962, *Cuba: Its People, Its Society, Its Culture*. Prepared under the auspices of the American University (survey of world cultures, 10).

Mintz, Sidney W., 1964, "Foreword," in Ramiro Guerra y Sánchez, *Sugar and Society in the Caribbean: An Economic History of Cuban Agriculture*, Yale University Press, New Haven and London. pp. xi–xliv.

Nelson, Lowry, 1966, "The Social Class Structure," in Robert F. Smith, ed., *Background to Revolution: The Development of Modern Cuba*, Knopf, New York, pp. 195–200.

O'Connor, James, 1964a, "On Cuban Political Economy," *Political Science Quarterly*, Vol. 79, pp. 233–247.

———, 1964b, "The Foundations of Cuban Socialism," *Studies on the Left*, Vol. 4, pp. 97–117.

Ortiz, Fernando, 1947, *Cuban Counterpoint: Tobacco and Sugar*, Knopf, New York.

Portell Vilá, Herminio, 1966, "The Nationalism of Cuban Intellectuals," in Robert F. Smith, ed., *Background to Revolution: The Development of Modern Cuba*, Knopf, New York, pp. 68–73.

Raggi Ageo, Carlos Manuel, 1950, "Contribución al estudio de las clases medias en Cuba," in Theo R. Crevenna, ed., *Materiales para el estudio de la clase media en la América Latina*, Dept. of Cultural Affairs, Panamerican Union, Washington, D.C., Vol. 2, pp. 73–89.

Seers, Dudley, ed., 1964, *Cuba: the Economic and Social Revolution*, University of North Carolina Press, Chapel Hill.

Smith, Robert F., ed., 1966, *Background to Revolution: The Development of Modern Cuba*, Knopf, New York.

Stokes, William S., 1953, "National and Local Violence in Cuban Politics," *Southwestern Social Science Quarterly*, Vol. 34, pp. 57–63.

Suárez, Andrés, 1967, *Cuba: Castroism and Communism, 1959–1966*, M.I.T. Press, Cambridge and London.

Torres, Simon, and Julio Aronde, 1968, "Debray and the Cuban Experience," *Monthly Review*, Vol. 20, pp. 44–62.

Villarejo, Donald, 1960, "American Investment in Cuba," *New University Thought*, Vol. 1, pp. 79–88.

Wallich, H. C., 1950, *Monetary Problems of an Export Economy*, Harvard University, Cambridge, Mass. and London.

Williams, William A., 1966, "The Influence of the United States on the Development of Modern Cuba," in Robert F. Smith, ed., *Background to Revolution: The Development of Modern Cuba*, Knopf, New York, pp. 187–194.

Zeitlin, Maurice, 1967, *Revolutionary Politics and the Cuban Working Class*, Princeton University Press, N.J.; O.U.P., London.

Zeitlin, Maurice, and Robert Scheer, 1963, *Cuba: Tragedy in Our Hemisphere*, Grove Press, New York.

CONCLUSION

Adams, Richard N., 1966, "Power and Power Domains," *América Latina*, year 9, pp. 3–21.

Alavi, Hamza, 1965, "Peasants and Revolution," in Ralph Miliband and John Saville, eds., *The Socialist Register*, Merlin Press, London, pp. 241–277.

Ayres, C. E., 1944, *The Theory of Economic Progress*, University of North Carolina Press, Chapel Hill and London.

Fei, Hsiao-Tung, 1939, *Peasant Life in China: A Field Study of Country Life in the Yangtze Valley*, Kegan Paul, Trench, Trubner and Co., London.

Fried, Morton H., 1953, *Fabric of Chinese Society: A Study of the Social Life of a Chinese County Seat*, Praeger, New York.

Heilbroner, Robert L., 1962, *The Making of Economic Society*, Prentice-Hall, Englewood Cliffs, N.J. and London.

Hindley, Donald, 1965, "Political Conflict Potential, Politicization, and the Peasantry in Underdeveloped Countries," *Asian Studies*, Vol. 3, pp. 470–489.

Lipton, Michael, 1968, "The Theory of the Optimising Peasant," *Journal of Development Studies*, Vol. 4, pp. 327–351.

Lowenthal, Richard, 1967, "Soviet and Chinese Communist World Views," in Donald W. Treadgold, ed., *Soviet and Chinese Communism*, University of Washington Press, Seattle and London.

Moore, Barrington, Jr., 1966, *Social Origins of Dictatorship and Democracy: Lord and Peasant in the Making of the Modern World*, Beacon Press, Boston; Allen Lane, London.

Polanyi, Karl, 1957, *The Great Transformation: The Political and Economic Origins of Our Time*, Beacon Press, Boston.

Sarkisyanz, Emanuel, 1955, *Russland und der Messianismus des Orients*, J. C. B. Mohr, Tübingen.

Schram, Stuart, 1967, *Mao Tse-tung*, Penguin Books, Baltimore and London.

Shils, Edward, 1962, "The Intellectuals in the Political Development of the New States," in John H. Kautsky, ed., *Political Change in Underdeveloped Countries*, Wiley & Sons, New York and London. pp. 195–234.

Wilson, Godfrey, and Monica Wilson, 1945, *The Analysis of Social Change*, Cambridge University Press, Cambridge and London.

W

Index